Cruising Modernism

Cruising Modernism

Class and Sexuality in American Literature and Social Thought

Michael Trask

CORNELL UNIVERSITY PRESS

Ithaca & London

This book has been published with the assistance of the Frederick W. Hilles Publication Fund of Yale University.

First published 2003 by Cornell University Press

Printed in the United States of America

Library of Congress Cataloging-in-Publication Data

Trask, Michael, 1967–
    Cruising modernism : class and sexuality in American literature and social thought / Michael Trask.
        p. cm.
Includes bibliographical references and index.
    ISBN 0-8014-4170-6 (cloth : alk. paper)
    1. American literature—20th century—History and criticism.
2. Modernism (Literature)—United States.   3. Literature and so-ciety—United States—History—20th century.   4. Social sciences—United States—History—20th century.   5. Social classes—United States—History—20th century.   6. Sex customs—United States—History—20th century.   7. United States—Social conditions—20th century.   8. Social classes in literature.   9. Sex in literature.
I. Title.

    PS228.M63T73 2003
    810.9'112—dc21

                                        2003010030

Contents

Acknowledgments

Henry Abelove, Nancy Armstrong, Sharon Cameron, Christina Crosby, Jonathan Goldberg, Allen Grossman, John Guillory, Walter Michaels, Mary Poovey, and Richard Ohmann are the teachers to whom I owe the largest debt; all taught me valuable lessons that have made their way into this book. I have benefited from the warm friendship and exacting pencils of Jared Gardner, Beth Hewitt, Jonathan Kramnick, Tom Otten, and Tony Scott—each of whom is a close reader in the best sense of that term. My time at Yale, where this book was mostly written, has been enriched by the good company of Nigel Alderman, Leslie Brisman, Jill Campbell, Elizabeth Dillon, Wai Chee Dimock, Kelly Hager, Langdon Hammer, Amy Hungerford, Vera Kutzinski, Joseph Roach, and Sarah Winter. No list of acknowledgments could justifiably omit the intangible blessings provided by those who may not have read my work in its early stages but whose vital imprint I—and, I hope, they—can find in its finished pages: Elijah and Gideon Gardner, Laurel George and Erik Naumann, Sophie Naumann, Justine Henning, Ezra and Carmen Scott-Henning, Lori Schwartz and Colleen Olfert, and Rosalinda Stone. Stephen and Wally Trask, of course, belong in a category all their own.

I thank Yale University's Morse Fellowship Committee, whose largesse provided a much appreciated leave in which to finish the manuscript. I also give a nod to my colleagues in the New York Americanist Group, convened by Maria Farland and Michael Szalay; their intellectual camaraderie made immeasurable improvements, both directly and indirectly, in this book's overall shape. I thank Catherine Rice, my editor at Cornell University Press, for her commitment to the project—as well as Laura Frost, for introducing me to Catherine. I am grateful to the Beinecke Rare Book and Manuscript Library at Yale University, the Mudd Library at Yale University, and the Rare Books Library at Columbia University for their wonderful holdings. I thank the Estate of Gertrude Stein and Calman Levin, executor, for permission to use the unpublished manuscripts, "Pissez Mon Chien" and "Lesson I," in chapter 3. I thank W.W. Norton for permission to cite Hart Crane's poetry and also Four Walls Eight Windows for permission to cite Crane's letters in chapter 4.

A version of chapter 2 appeared in *Novel* (summer 1999); a version of chapter 6 appeared in *differences* (spring 1996). I thank the publishers of both journals for permission to present revised incarnations of those essays here.

I dedicate this book to my two sets of parents, Alfred and Nancy Trask and Bob and Myrna Schwartz, with love and gratitude.

Cruising Modernism

Introduction

Cruising Modernism is about cross-class contact in the early twentieth century and the representational problems such contact raised. I argue that American literary modernism must be defined with reference to the social transformations that brought genteel and upper-class Americans into encounters, either forced or chosen, with their social "inferiors." What marks this contact for particular consideration is that overwhelmingly the elites of modern society chose to couch class difference in the language of sexual illicitness, viewing innovative and unsettling social arrangements as an extension of the irregular or perverse desires that sexology deliberated. I include under a single rubric such distinct groupings as immigrants, vagrants, casual laborers, and the marginal sexual populations of prostitutes and inverts because the epithets pinned on any one class of persons in the first quarter of the century tended to flow into descriptions of the others. This was not exactly a failure of imagination with regard to nomenclature or taxonomy. Because class became widely construed as mobile, slippery, and restless, the period's most serious thinkers adopted sexual science's concept of evasive and unmoored desire to represent what appeared to be a seismic shift in social relations during the Progressive era.

This book thus undertakes a double exploration of class difference. It seeks to describe some of the historical shifts in class relations in the period, including the emergence of a consumer society and a leisure economy as well as a working class characterized by an untraditional makeup of women, foreigners, transients, and casual laborers. It also seeks to describe how traditional social-scientific efforts to measure class relations tried to accommodate these new social facts and, in confronting them, underwent something of an intellectual revolution.[1] What Martin Burke calls the "conundrum of class" in American public discourse was shaped from the late nineteenth century onward by two contradictory perceptions of the social order, which may be summarized as the widely held belief that classes were diverging radically and permanently at the same time as they were blending and dissolving with alarming consequences for customary distinctions.[2] These positions were not as contradictory as they might appear. In arriving at a state of permanence, the working class evolved a set of habits radically at odds with—indeed, that sabotaged—the prerogatives of traditional producer culture.[3] What seemed permanent about workers was repeatedly confirmed as their paradoxical state of *impermanence*, of restless craving and instability, of endless striving and motion.

Just as discussion of social relations becomes stipulated in the idiom of the new psychology of sex, so mobility and desire in this period stipulate each other through the irregular bodies of the underclass. This book examines the implications of that reciprocity for American modernist literature. I am interested in the ways in which social thought alights on the figure of perverse desire to describe the evasive mobility of class others in early twentieth-century life, and I am keen to demonstrate how modernist authors exploit this explanatory circuit when their own writing fixes on the unfixed characters, the underclass floaters, who stray in and out of their texts.

The operative link between the dual material and intellectual histories that *Cruising Modernism* charts is what I call the desire concept. In the broad discourses of social theory after 1900, desire both underpinned the new economy as its basic engine and named the enigmatic and unseemly complex of motives to which the class other was beholden. "Economics, by its very definition of value," Lester Ward writes in *Applied Sociology* (1906), "is based on desires and their satisfaction." Ward's belief that economic life "embodies" "a great mass of desires" was an assumption held by many contemporary social scientists, who together reversed a long tradition of political economy that understood rational and utilitarian motives as the basis of social order.[4] In part this reversal stemmed from a changing economic universe; these thinkers saw bourgeois values like reason and deferred gratification defeated by a consumer culture oriented toward immediate, intense, and transient delights. Born out of working-class morality and attitudes toward sex and amusement, the "pleasure economy" (as the economist Simon Patten dubbed it) became the social style of choice among the middle classes and slowly eroded whatever virtues that elites might have claimed over the lower classes.[5]

The blurring of social levels was a problem that called for urgent address among the period's thinkers—matched only by the complementary crisis of social heterogeneity, of a vertiginous surplus of persons who could not be fit easily into place. In 1915, the sociologist Robert Park wrote of the modern city's capacity for "breaking down . . . local attachments" and producing "new and divergent individual types." "The booming confusion" of city life provided what he called "the moral climate in which [each person's] peculiar nature obtains the stimulations that bring his innate qualities to full and free expression."[6] For Park as for other social thinkers of his generation, the heterogeneity of modern culture with its multitude of "individual types" gravitates sooner or later to the license such proliferation provides for "vagrant and suppressed impulses" to "emancipate themselves from the dominant moral order."[7] By "vagrant . . . impulses," Park has in mind illicit desires; but his choice of adjective demonstrates to what extent these impulses reduced to that great obstacle to sociological classification in the period—the underclass other. The discipline of sociology arose first and foremost as a means to cope with class difference. Men classified things, Marcel Mauss and Emile Durkheim concluded in *Primitive Classification* (1902), because they were themselves divided into classes.[8] Though American social thought took no exception to this measurement and description of entrenched class relations, the recurrent appearance of the vagrant in early twentieth-century sociology indicates that discipline's anxious response to class relations that appeared neither entrenched nor particularly stable.[9]

Thus the "trouble with the hobo," as Park puts it in "The Mind of the Hobo," is that "he has sacrificed the human need of association and organization" in favor of "wanderlust." And for Park the primary victim of this "vice" is normative social order itself. By embracing "locomotion for its own sake," the hobo defies the sureties of place and status, of "locat[ion]" and "permanence," by which society aims to ratify its members.[10] By focusing on the mobile figures of the vagrant, the casual or migrant worker, and the prostitute, sociology and its companion fields located what was perceived as a radical fluctuation in American class relations on the bodies of those persons whose unsettling, disruptive, or defiant status mirrored the unsettling of categories in general. These figures proved to be heuristically valuable because their categorical slipperiness made them endlessly adaptable for analysis. They could stand alone or in any number of combinations—the working-class woman who was a "clandestine prostitute," the immigrant who was a tramp, the vagrant who was a pederast—as the occasion arose among social thinkers for shading or giving nuance to a particular concern.

Just as class others were recombinant and malleable during this period, so social thought itself was a looser and more generous category than we typically construe it. Though vestiges of the original link between the helping professions and the academic disciplines remain in contemporary culture, we may have difficulty recovering the turn-of-the-century intimacy between social work and sociology, or between reform movements and philosophy. Though the human sciences are now fully ensconced in the academy, in the Progressive era they had yet to achieve their disciplinary autonomy from such highly charged moral and social issues as temperance, corporate trusts, immigration, and "white slavery." These were causes on which all the major sociologists of the era took positions by enlisting their expertise in the cause of reform.[11] My concern in the following chapters is less with exploring the interchanges between social work and sociology than with using their proximity to uncover some of the less obvious reciprocities among discourses from the period. Whereas abstract social theory is by definition never far removed from concrete social practices, in the period that this book concerns social theory in the abstract (that is, as a set of conceptual coordinates to be applied as general laws along the lines of natural science) barely existed as a category.

Chapter 1, "Pervert Modernism," presents an overview of social-theoretical discourse in the early twentieth century—a period when social science came to constitute itself around the concept of irregular desire. With this approach in mind I argue for a revised conception of modernist epistemology that de-emphasizes its hyperbolic rationality and identitarian cast—in other words, its pursuit of national, racial, or cultural identity—and instead sheds light on its embrace of the irrational and perverse as constituents of the social world.[12] The first chapter's revisionist account of modern social thought links the next five chapters, each of which explores the relation between literary figures, social theory, and changing class relations after 1900.[13] American writers between 1900 and 1925 both helped to contrive and drew on the reciprocity between motion and eros that formed a staple of the modernity plot I delineate in this book. And as if enlarging on the intimate link that social scientists draw between perverse motion and perverse desire (between "locomotion" and "vice," as Park equates them), the modernists I examine locate moments of polymorphous sexual threat in close proximity to those underclass persons most often imagined to embody it: immigrants, derelicts, prostitutes, unruly servants. For the James of *The Wings of the Dove*, for example, Merton Densher's "alien" attributes (notably his tendency to shuttle back and forth across the Atlantic in pursuit of economic gain in the fashion of the era's Mediterranean migrants) reflect the pivotal, sexually laden encounter between Kate Croy and himself on a London subway train (a public mode of rapid transit that is also defined by its shuttling back and forth).

As the James brothers' example shows in chapter 2, what licenses the excavation of the ties between the immanent concerns of social and material life and the period's most lasting intellectual paradigms is the fact that these discourses share not only a common analytical domain but also basic assumptions about the nature of desire, class difference, and mobility within that domain. Between the radical philosophy of pragmatism and the xenophobic nativism of the early twentieth century stands the new breed of unruly immigrants who, in the words of eugenicist Andre Siegrid, "dislocate the established order of things and sterilize the original superior races."[14] While it is difficult to picture the liberal William James subscribing to the second half of this description of what Siegrid calls "the backward peoples of the world," the first half might be taken as a summary of his philosophy.[15] Yet in fact, as a reading of James from *The Principles of Psychology* to *A Plural-*

istic Universe bears out, James was deeply anxious over the consequences that would follow from the destabilizing effects of pragmatist thought, not least in the arena of social and sexual reproduction. In *The Principles,* for example, desire left unchecked breeds a failure of boundaries; by the same token, in the late essay "The Will To Believe," only brotherhood or membership in "the common soil" moderates the destructive and antisocial tendency to which unbridled desire is prone. In turn-of-the-century culture, this fraternal feeling of common ground and membership was most visibly threatened by the southern European immigrant who, in both pragmatist thought and in Henry James's *The Wings of the Dove,* ignores the dictates of both brotherhood and geopolitical stability in favor of personal interest. Having neither national loyalty nor a sense of racial solidarity even with his own kind, the alien appeared to bend geographic boundaries by shifting back and forth across the Atlantic in the search for employment. No longer conforming to the inherited view of underclass peasants as stationary and subordinate— the "furniture" of the countryside, as Henry James puts it in *The American Scene*—the Italian immigrant emerges in turn-of-the-century life as the dismantler of traditional social hierarchies and the epitome of groundlessness.[16]

The chancy figure of the Mediterranean immigrant stands in for the chanciness that both nativists and pragmatists in different ways understood as dislodging the realm of necessity in turn-of-the-century America. The equally slippery figure of the tramp possesses a similar status in the era's psychology, as William James's thought in this field again bears out. In *The Principles of Psychology,* the tramp crops up repeatedly to caution readers about the high social cost of vagrant consciousness and the perils of too much thinking in the absence of the salubrious balm of "habit." This tension internal to James's book signals the larger dilemma that would divide psychology as a discipline in the United States: the problematic study of "introspection," unexplained motivation, and desires as against the exact and exacting researches into habits, actions, and reflexes. Though behaviorism emerged from a distrust of James's privileging of consciousness, behavioral psychologists maintained a dichotomy at the basis of their experimental science that was central to James as well: the distinction between unruly persons and obedient dogs. The juxtaposition of good dogs and bad people was a staple of a host of turn-of-the-century discourses that promoted the dog's virtues (domestication, loyalty, respect for hierarchy) over human vices. These discourses ranged from antivivisection fiction written by Twain and Kipling (who contrasted loyal pets with uncaring doctors) to canine memoirs written by Jack London and John Galsworthy (who enlisted the dog's fealty to defend the naturalness of hierarchy) to the clinical behaviorism of John Watson, E. L. Thorndike, and other experimental psychologists (who turned to research on animals to avoid the pitfalls they associated with the psychology of consciousness). It is in Stein's writing, the subject of chapter 3, that this convergence of tramps and dogs yields the strangest dividend. The class other in Stein emerges through the complex detour of the animal model of research, which routinely juxtaposed fugitive persons like tramps and loose women with the well-behaved domestic dogs who were prized as research subjects by social and medical scientists alike. Stein's work both early and late exploits the contrast of marginal persons with dutiful dogs. "The Good Anna" places wayward servant girls and transients next to dependent and dependable canines to open the question of what counts as a proper person in *Three Lives.* The repetitive yet inconsequential existence that her contemporaries located in hobo society becomes the model for the serial and interchangeable erotic liaisons favored by Stein protagonists like Melanctha and Ida, who wander away from or out of home and family life.

Sharing Stein's preoccupation with itinerant figures, Hart Crane turns to a crucial subspecies of vagrant during the period—the migratory worker— as a mirror and model for his poetics. In Crane's *The Bridge,* the focus of chapter 4, scenes of cruising are inseparable from the kind of men whose labor is defined through mobility and displacement—either sailors or what Crane's generation called "casual" workers. These often nameless and transient laborers instantiate a kind of erotic transaction anchored in impersonality rather than in narratives of continuity, in casualness rather than causality. Crane's writing displaces the lyric convention of the centered subject with a concept of impersonality that derives as much from the world of industrial labor as from the rich modernist conceit elaborated in Eliot's concept of "tradition." Whereas Eliot sees impersonality—the divorce from bodily attachment and overwrought emotion—as begetting cultural continuity, providing the meaningful and durable link between poetic makers, Crane treats impersonality as the basis for anonymous bodily encounters whose brief intensity, unencumbered by the dictates of personality, defies the relentless cultural campaigns to endow sexuality with meaning or identity.

Cather's books are likewise replete with both transient workers and immigrants, from Carl Lindstrum in *O Pioneers!* (1913) to Tom Outland in *The Professor's House* (1925). That Cather aligns the waywardness of these vagrant souls with irregular passions, desires beyond the decorous settlement of the prairie homestead or the bourgeois nuclear family, might be gleaned from a moment in *O Pioneers!* during which "Crazy Ivar" (both a misfit and a perceived threat to stability) explains his penchant for bare feet by referring to his "rebellious body . . . subject to every kind of temptation." "The feet," Ivar notes, "are free members. I indulge them without harm to any one, even to tramping in filth when my desires are low."[17] The crossing of low desires with "tramping" is a staple of Cather fiction that I trace in chapter 5 through the unlikely stencil of Catholicism—or more accurately, the anti-Catholic ideology of her upbringing, on which Cather based her own highly selective and heretical vision of Catholic experience. Looking in particular at perverse priests in *Death Comes for the Archbishop* and *Shadows on the Rock,* I suggest that these "placid" novels turn out to harbor tumultuous energies when read in light of the common nativist and antipapal equation between Catholicism, erotic excess, and foreign multitudes.

Finally, sexual irregularity and class consciousness assume a privileged place in the leftist modernism of the teens and twenties, a movement preoccupied with the overactive traffic in women against which the era's purity crusaders tirelessly legislated. Figures of prostitution gravitate from the vice committees of the Progressive era to the anti-consumerist protests of 1920s leftist intellectuals like Mike Gold, Max Eastman, and their confreres. Crystallized for these writers in the discourse of prostitution, female sexuality becomes synonymous with the incapacity for political agency engendered by market culture. In the leftist milieu of the twenties, as I argue in chapter 6, the antidote to a promiscuous and debilitating heterosexual desire arises from the peculiar elevation of a virile homosexuality whose icon is Walt Whitman. And nowhere does this reclamation of erotic deviance in the service of political dissidence become more enabling than in John Dos Passos's 1925 novel, *Manhattan Transfer.*

The equation of erotic desire with a failure of agency in twenties leftism focuses the problem of modernity with a coherence that often eluded modernity's observers—for whom the epistemological uncertainty to which modern culture gave rise was so diffuse as to negate any equations or reductions. The question that occupies James's Kate Croy early on in *The Wings of the Dove* might be taken as a version of the problem that flusters contemporary theorists—that of improper or improbable movement, of "strange situations" and "aimless" advance. "Why should a set of people," Kate asks herself with regard to her family's disappointed circumstances, "have been put in motion . . . only to break down without an accident, to stretch themselves in the wayside dust without a reason?"[18] Kate's question resonates beyond the immediate circumstances of the Croys' "failure as a family" (*WD* 1:64) to address the larger matter of "breakdown" in two senses—first of middle-class expectations of comfort and improvement and second of the conventional vehicle for representing those expectations, the novel of manners. Yet at the same time, Kate's question is fundamentally mistaken because she construes the lack of a "profitable journey" for herself and her family as a stalling or stasis rather than what it actually is—a change in direction.

In other words, the velocity of motion (or its sudden absence) is less at issue for the Croys than that motion's vector. Breakdown in James's novel is less a stopping short than a euphemism for the more chilling threat that his protagonists are ill prepared to handle: downward mobility. Whereas Milly Theale is the one who "want[s] abysses" in *The Wings of the Dove* (1:186), Kate Croy and her would-be mate, Merton Densher, are the ones actually staring into the abyss by virtue of her economic dependency and his economic deprivation. The figure of the abyss highlights the downward or oblique glances at work throughout this novel, the feeling of looking into a void that overtakes almost every character at some point in *Wings*—what Milly calls "the grey immensity" (*WD* 1:247). Whether we are dealing with Milly's "view" at the acme of the Brunig, "thrown forward and vertiginous" (*WD* 1:123), or Kate's "eyes aslant no less on her beautiful averted than on her beautiful presented oval" (*WD* 1:5) in the mirror, there are no straightforward views in James's novel because there is no sense of solid ground on which to stand and from which to mount a stable perspective. Yet what looks like an existential problem actually turns out to have an all too social referent. Milly's "grey immensity" is given more acute content by Kate Croy's fear of the dingy and subterranean life that awaits her without money—or, more precisely, without Milly's money. The void is not so much empty as filled with the blurry and ill-assorted bodies of undesirable social types, like Kate's poor and prodigiously fertile sister (with her "four bouncing children" (*WD* 1:9) or, more significantly, the "masses of bewildered people trying," in Lord Mark's telling words, "to 'get' they didn't know what or where" (*WD* 1:150).

As James makes evident in the bewilderment of these "pawing and groping" masses afloat in "the vague billows of some great greasy sea" (*WD* 1:150), his novel raises the specter of a social world broken down so thoroughly that there is no foundation left, no continuation among its parts—a vision that looms large in the awareness of the social theorists and literary practitioners who succeed him.[19] For this reason, *The Wings of the Dove* assumes pride of place among the readings that follow, not only because of its chronological priority in the literary history that my book describes but also because of the priority that *Wings* assigns to the relation between epistemological groundlessness and the problem of class difference. What makes James's book modernist is its sustained narration of the risk relations that modernity entails—and its narration of those relations through the risky figures of the new and overly mobile immigrants who dominated American thought after 1900.[20] That James himself was a virtual alien within the increasingly nationalist contexts of turn-of-the-century culture gives added point to the stresses and tensions, the collapse of class distinctions, that his novel implies between kinds of persons (native-born whites and foreign immigrants) for whom mixture was imagined as improper and indecent at best. In other words, James stood close to the real social instabilities from which *Wings* generates its fictional suspense.

The malaise of social instability and improper motion at the heart of *The Wings of the Dove* found its way into literary texts that treated sexual irregularity, class antagonism, and the collapse of stable movement as different facets of the same plot. Willa Cather's *Alexander's Bridge* (1912) chronicles the midlife crisis of Bartley Alexander, a structural engineer who finds himself tortured by relentless self-divisions that, in the novel's insistent symbolism, he cannot "bridge." Bartley fails to connect his career with his inner life, his outwardly happy marriage with his clandestine affair with an old lover, and—in a breach that Cather develops in her 1925 masterpiece *The Professor's House*—the person he used to be with the person he has become. As if to force the issue of her protagonist as a clinical study in the divided self, Cather lets us see him through the eyes of his former teacher, a psychologist who "could not help feeling that there were unreasoning and unreasonable activities going on in Alexander all the while; that even after dinner, when most men achieve a decent impersonality, Bartley had merely closed the door of the engine-room and come up for an airing."[21] What is remarkable about these "unreasoning and unreasonable activities" is how closely they parallel the "general industrial unrest" (*AB* 27) that Bartley must confront in his line of work: "He had several bridges under way in the United States, and they were always being held up by strikes" (*AB* 27). We hear very little of these threatening workers; like Bartley's own "engine-room," their "unrest" is closed off from view, treated as a clandestine feature of the social world. Yet these workers dwell not so much on the margins of Cather's novel as in its very contours, subtending its plot, serving as its foundation. That the bridges are (in Cather's equivocal phrasing) "always being held up" by industrial unrest points to the inherent ambiguity in this social system. Just as Bartley's outwardly civil demeanor conceals a "machinery . . . still pounding on" (*AB* 11), so the bridges can be seen not as delayed by but rather *erected* on cantilevers of worker discontent.

That the elements of labor unrest, erotic drift, and infrastructural instability make their way into Cather's first novel testifies to the pervasive anxiety that modernity posed to those who would represent it. For Cather, the psychic complications of an adultery plot find their best materialization in "industrial unrest" because both adulterer and laborer are understood as "unreasoning," in that their sense of discontent issues from no discernible grievance. By the same token, the bridge that assumes such symbolic importance in her novel is a not quite graspable or solid entity; its suspended or floating form becomes the model for a culture that does not quite trust in the firmness of its newest technologies, does not quite believe in the sturdiness or durability of its rapidly transforming material culture. As with infrastructure, so with human personality: the psychologist in whose presence *Alexander's Bridge* begins and ends (and thus whose perspective frames the novel) directs the same wonder excited by new means of transportation at the divided self, who appears to him vaguely indecent (in that Bartley lacks "a decent impersonality" and instead conceals a surfeit of hidden "unreasonable activities"). This widespread suspicion turned toward both exterior world and interior life shades readily into a distrust of the durable narrative truths of the past—with plots that, like the coach transporting the unwitting Croy family, find themselves broken down or detoured by the "wayside." It is significant that Hart Crane turns also to the matter of bridges in his long poem of 1929 to work out the logistics of a social world whose material solidity and cultural continuity feel precarious if not absent. Part of the goal of reading Crane in chapter 4 involves restoring a sense of Crane's materialist consciousness to the lopsided picture we have of this poet as a religious visionary or mystic. And one means toward achieving that goal is to argue that the materialism that saturates his poems is frequently missed because Crane imagined material relations, particularly those involving manual labor, as oddly immaterial—that is, as fragile, ephemeral, and liable to implosion or breaking apart.

At the risk of too schematic a homology, I argue that the aversion to traditional plots among writers we customarily group as modernists mirrors the distrust of conventional rationality to be found in the period's social science. Compare the collapsing bridge in Cather's novel to the conclusion of sociologist Edward Ross's *Social Psychology* (1919): "Our culture is like an edifice that, while it is being torn down piecemeal and rebuilt, unites discordant styles of architecture."[22] Social thought between 1900 and 1925 strikes a repeated note of intellectual distress—not unlike the structural fatigue Ross views as threatening to the "architecture" of the modern environment—directed onto positivist and naturalistic paradigms that contemporary thinkers no longer considered suitable for reading the social world. As Ross argues, "[O]ur culture is not allowed to achieve an equilibrium. The steady afflux of new examples, inventions, and discoveries produces confusion" (362).

To grasp the inherent instability and irregularity of persons, social scientists and literary figures consciously or unconsciously turned to the psychology of sex. Perversion becomes both problem and explanation for the period's excesses of mobility and uncertainty. "Sex as a motive-concept is barred from the economic door," Carleton Parker writes in *The Casual Laborer* (1920).[23] Seeking to redress this omission among economists mired in obsolete categories like enlightened self-interest and calculation, Parker argues that when it comes to the "economic motive," economists should attend to the "vagaries of desire" (*CL* 143) rather than to the traditional "middle-class virtues of thrift, justice, and solvency" (*CL* 130). "The motives of economic life," Parker suggests, "are the same as those of the life of art, of vanity and ostentation, of war and crime, of sex" (*CL* 137).

The disobedience and lawlessness that social theorists located in the erotic realm had a close affinity to the disobedience that contemporaries saw as the defining attribute of the class other. "Perversion rather than freely selected habits of instinct expression," Parker writes, "seems broadly a just characterization of modern labor-class life" (*CL* 156). The identification of these different versions of disobedience—a sexual appetite categorically defined as irregular; a working class categorically defined as unruly and discontent—bespeaks a complex social anxiety that traverses any number of sites of turn-of-the-century American culture. This anxiety issued not only from a sense that the social world, broken down and dispersed, could not be reconstituted, but also from a sense that "the very casualness of modern sex life," as one observer saw it, made regulation and regularity impossible to enforce.[24] The "temporary sex relations" indicative of modernity mimic the jerry-built and flimsy social structures that threaten to topple at any moment because, in the logic of Progressive sociology, the persons who enter transitory partnerships and the persons who build the edifice of modern culture allegedly perceive sex and infrastructure alike as casual and trivial. The lack of "equilibrium" and the "confusion" that Ross sees as indicative of modern culture find their best expression in what he calls the "contagion" of "the sex appetite" that can pass from individual to individual without distinction: "Truly appalling is the swiftness with which sensuality and lewdness may infect a people. In a mining camp debauchery is swifter than drink in breaking down steady habits."[25] "Breaking down," whether of the decorous "architecture" of civilization or the "steady habits" on which civilization depends, is a function of perverse desires whose "swiftness" makes them almost impossible to track and to describe.

Cruising Modernism seeks to remind us of what thinkers like Ross (and behind him, Durkheim, Simmel, Tonnies, and Weber) understood all too well: modernity affects its subjects as much through coercive inclusion (incarceration, administration, identification) as through forced exclusion from any number of social contracts, the expulsion from social restraint. Another way to specify this historical moment is to suggest that the cult of management that we associate with modernity arises in conjunction with its dialectical twin, anomie.[26] Alongside the Taylorization of everyday life is the obverse process that the early twentieth-century sociologists viewed as equally characteristic of modernity—the efficiency with which modern life guts and refills the content of traditions, dismantles longstanding moral codes, and produces a world in which no individual can feel guaranteed of a sure place.

To be sure, dislocation has long been a staple of the "modern condition," but at the dawn of the American twentieth century, this logic of displacement inserts itself as an endemic problem calling for timely redress. As historians of American culture have shown, the uncertainty both of the nation's porous borders and of its increasingly congested and confused interior resulted in a number of purity movements around 1900 that sought to recuperate traditional boundaries by resorting to a biological account of national identity in the face of the culture's disturbing array of "centrifugal tendencies." This period in American history witnessed the ratification of Jim Crow laws within the nation (with the *Plessy v. Ferguson* decision of 1896) and ended in the legal barring of undesirable immigrants from the nation (with the Johnson Immigration Act of 1924). The barriers erected during this period by nativists, vice reformers, and others bespeak not simply an upkeep in xenophobia and the moral policing of society but rather a desperate and only partially successful solution to the fact that classes of persons who should keep to themselves had grown too close for comfort.

I consider less how the extralegal conduct of the Klan against black Southerners or the Congressional legislation to curtail Mediterranean and East European immigration contained social difference than how these and other movements relied on a model of licentious erotic threat as a way to compel their followers. The problem of erotic threat always originated as a response to a phobia about social mobility. Though segregation affected many areas of public life in the Southern United States, for example, its enforcement occurred most strikingly around means of transportation—trains, streetcars, and buses—the policing of which implied the struggle to define American mobility, to say who gets to move around. Segregation imposed sanctions on black movement at the same time as it exacerbated that movement by driving a large number of blacks from a region where their opportunities were violently constricted. Translating the undesirable movement of poor blacks and immigrants into overly mobile desire, advocates of racial and national purity bred paranoid fantasies of hyperactive sexual appetites, whether in the form of black men who could not resist white womanhood or of immigrants whose bountiful offspring represented a form of desire gone awry in a maelstrom of promiscuous and unplanned overbreeding.

In addition to its fierce interest in heredity and biological essence, social science after 1900 was committed to a sexological model of perverse or irregular desire that proved less easy to align with physical or racial typologies. In part this is because in its brief but illustrious career, the discipline of sexology had wrested sex from its basis in physiology and encouraged its adherents to understand desire as a function of psychology and environment in tandem with biological predisposition. The erotic became the idiom by which thinkers across the political spectrum and with radically disparate social agendas could speak to each other's concerns. From eugenics to economics, from sociology to literary criticism, excessive erotic desire became synonymous with the risks of dislocation and commingling that imperiled the imagined continuity of the national culture.[27]

With this book I seek to fill a critical gap between two forceful yet incomplete accounts of modernism. Recently critics and cultural historians like Paula Rabinowitz, Cary Nelson, and Michael Denning have uncovered a valuable counter-tradition of twentieth-century literature focused on the varied progressive and class-conscious impulses that energize what Denning aptly names the "laboring of American culture."[28] This work has provided students of modernism with the tools to dismantle once and for all the view that modernism was ever merely a discipline of elites, aloof from the political and social ramifications of aesthetic production. At the same time, critics like Joseph Boone and Colleen Lamos have highlighted the diverse radical erotic energies informing the modernist project, examining what Lamos aptly names a "deviant modernism" attuned to the transformative sexual realities of the modern era.[29] Yet these two important critical interventions rarely acknowledge each other.[30] In class-based readings of modernism, sexuality is trivialized as a "private" or individual concern, a holdover from the high bourgeois epoch of interiority. Likewise, critics with a pronounced interest in the queerness of modernism slight its class provocations in favor of its sexual ones. The specialness of desire in modernist texts eclipses concern with the ways in which sexual desire was a collective phenomenon, a matter not just of distinctive individuals but of groups and classes.

In one sense, the mutual blind spots in these approaches to modernism have everything to do with a persistent way of viewing sexual and class difference in the culture at large. The former is a function of the private self; the latter by definition concerns public or collective solidarity. One is a function of *personal identity,* the other of *social status.* Sexual desire is secretive and mysterious (and hence prone to the "epistemology of the closet"); class identity is immediately visible in numerous codes and markers on the surface of the self. In focusing on the nexus of sexuality and class difference, I show how these two social coordinates articulate each other in modernism and modernity. Sexual desire was a franker subject of public discourse in the early twentieth century, just as class and status seemed to function as a sort of social closet from which our culture still has yet to emerge. Class difference in an officially classless society draws its energies and character from the same wellsprings of shame, embarrassment, and taboo that structure sexual identity.[31] In his history of American cultural refinement, Richard Bushman concludes that the spread of gentility in American life made "refinement and vulgarity . . . the most palpable signs of class, for many the very definition of class."[32] Bushman helps us to see that even as Americans may acknowledge in principle that class difference is a function of socioeconomic levels, they intuit class as a social *style,* a matter of embodied identity akin to the classification of erotic desire less in terms of object choice than according to sexual "types." The assumption that class identity is at once linked to and discrepant from things like occupation and income level accounts for the frequency with which persons were imagined to pass from one social level to another in turn-of-the-century life and so to engage the risky dynamics of "passing" and identity betrayal that figure prominently in American modernist writing on race.[33] Both class and sex are deeply relational, reducible neither to discrete identity nor to sheer essence. I suggest that their relations in modernity are structured according to the same coordinates—irregularity, mobility, and perverse desire—that emerged toward the end of the nineteenth century and which continue to shape our basic conceptions of class and sexual differences.

By invoking the phrase "modernism and modernity," I mean to stress that this book both contributes to a literary history of the twentieth century and attempts to intervene in the assessment of the intellectual and sexual culture of the period more broadly. I argue that for all the perdurable abstractions to which social thought about modern culture lent itself—whether pragmatism, behaviorism, or rational-choice economics—modernity's theorists never lost sight of the underclass figure who epitomized that culture's risk relations, who embodied its epistemological groundlessness in his or her ever-shifting, unsafe person. And students of modernism proceed at their peril when they seek to account for the history of social thought without a similar reckoning with the material culture in which that thought unfolds.

Chapter One

Pervert Modernism
American Social Thought 1900–1930

I

"**S**tudy the philosophers who are busy with problems in all their phases, from eugenic to hygienic, from prenatal to psychic," the economist James Roscoe Day writes in *My Neighbor the Working Man* (1920).

> The man will not stay placed. You are not dealing with natural force or substance or law. There is nothing fixed about him but his restlessness. He is changing oftener than the moon its phases. Like a child, what he sees he wants, and what others have he thinks belongs to him or is held by the possessor in some unjust way. And he becomes the victim of every jealous and dangerous secret purpose. It is that mind, that passion of ambition and desire, appallingly active or equally stupid, which eludes us and which cannot be put into amperes and kilowatts.[1]

This passage offers something like a primer for the concerns that matter to this book. Like many of his contemporaries, Day defines the class other through his "restlessness" and imagines that his inherent mobility, articulated here in the language of erotic irregularity, both defies traditional categorization and compels new modes of apprehension, new cognitive tools. Day sets forth the basic model for classifying class difference in the first quarter of the twentieth century, two features of which are central to the chapters that follow. One is the commutative property of its essential terms. Just as class discontent becomes figured through the language of overactive movement and irregular rhythms, so the changeability of modern life, its syncopation and slipperiness, becomes most acutely visible in the guise of the underclasses. The other is the wide availability of this logic of motile desire outside the programs of the social sciences. As we shall see, it is literary modernism that makes the unstable and restless eros of the class outsider most apprehensible—or more precisely, makes the elusiveness of the class outsider a central problem for modernist representation. The class other's discontent, imagined as a rebuff to knowing one's place, is recast by the experts and elites of modern culture as a transgression of erotic propriety, a kind of polymorphous perversity that equates the working man's "passion of ambition and desire" with the diffuse and "dangerous" eros of "a child" who wants "what he sees." This is the language of sexology and Freud, of Havelock Ellis's *Studies in the Psychology of Sex* or Otto Weininger's *Sex and Character,* the language that Krafft-Ebbing develops in *Psychopathia Sexualis.* For Day and his contemporaries, these are the figures to whom the human sciences must turn to make sense of a culture that, guided by excess and overreaching, no longer obeys the laws of reason.[2] Referring the working man's mobility to the sexual drives, Day simultaneously eroticizes mobility itself.

Day was one among many thinkers committed to treating desire as a problem that social theory was ill-equipped to handle in its current state. The modern human sciences were born in a crisis of description entailed by what turn-of-the-century observers saw as the terminal instability of contemporary culture—an instability they described overwhelmingly in the language of sexual perversion.[3] (Day again: "The destructive socialist . . . may have been a man once, but the perversion has been so prolonged and persistent that all resemblance to God's work has long since ceased.")[4] In *Drift and Mastery* (1914), Walter Lippmann describes virtually the same cultural terrain as Day's when he refers to the "carelessly classified world" in which moderns live: "We are unsettled to the very roots of our being. There isn't a human relation . . . that doesn't move in a strange situation."[5] Like Day, Lippmann sees the modern subject's strange movement and "unrest" as a function of "a revolution in the intimacies of his life. He has lost his place in an eternal scheme, he is losing the ancient sanctions of love, and his sexual nature is chaotic" (*DM* 100). Though Lippmann differs from Day in viewing "unrest" and the disruption of "sexual nature" as dilemmas integral to the social life of all moderns, he agrees with Day that the menace such dilemmas pose is aggravated by the underclass in its various guises, whether "the threat that recent immigration brings with it" or "the threat of an alien and defenseless class of servile labor" (*DM* 100).

It was underclass persons whose provocative movements, seemingly ungoverned by reason and certitude, invited the most scrutiny from thinkers like Day and Lippmann, who tended to focus issues of class and status—issues of economic relations—through the lens of sexuality and erotic relations more generally. For Day, perversion went hand in hand with the rise of consumer economics; he attributes the "disturbed operations of supply and demand" found in early twentieth-century culture to the fact that "millions of men and women, turned aside from their normal pursuits, are made consumers."[6] Here perversion appears in something like its etymological purity—a turning away or deflection from "normal pursuits" or expectations—as the name for the displacement of producer culture by monopoly capitalism. Spurred by the advances of sexology and Darwinism, social-scientific thought around 1900 underwent an intellectual revolution of its own, marked by the expansion of its traditional objects of scrutiny to include such previously unanalyzed domains as sexual passion. Thus Lippmann argues: "Men's desires are not something barbaric which the intellect must shun. Their desires are what make their lives, they are what move and govern" (*DM* 123). One of the earliest professional sociologists, Lester Ward, pioneered the study of desire as a category of social analysis. In *The Psychic Factors of Civilization* (1893), Ward conceives of desire as an all-encompassing "faculty" that "helps to swell the vast tide of surging passion that propels the ship of life."[7] Like Lippmann after him, Ward construes desire primarily in terms of motion—a "vast tide" whose groundlessness is a function of desire's "widely varying, complex, and recondite" copiousness.[8] Such beliefs paved the way for later thinkers like the economist Carleton Parker, who identified "one of the most important generalizations about human life which can be phrased" in *The Casual Laborer* (1920)—"that human life is dynamic, that change, movement, evolution, are its basic characteristics."[9]

Parker's discovery of life's essential dynamism occurred at the convergence of two intellectual paths in his own scholarly career: his study of a 1914 hop pickers' strike in California and his introduction to Freud's writings, which led him to "a scientific approach" based on "abnormal psychology" into the "important fundamentals" of labor "unrest and violence" (*CL* 30). For Parker, the merger of modern economics and theories of "abnormal" sexuality made eminent sense by virtue of their basic shared term— the element of "change" or "movement" integral to both class relations and the order of desire. Parker's move was less eccentric than precocious. It predicted a long struggle to dislodge "orthodox economics" (*CL* 29) from its study of "static states," "market price," or "exchange value" and to recast it in terms of "tendencies," including "sex" (*CL* 31) and "perverted habits" (*CL* 33). And Parker felt compelled to mount this paradigm shift by the rise of an unconventional class of workers—that of the "casual laborer" who gives his book its title.

It is not news that the intellectual revolution at the start of the twentieth century replaced static principles with dynamic ones, monistic accounts with pluralistic ones—a shift codified nowhere so clearly as in James's 1906 lectures on pragmatism. The innovation of this book is to trace this alteration in the domain of thought—whereby figures of motility and contingency, drift and discord, overtook figures of synthesis, stability, and coherence—to some of its material conditions in the world of social relations, and to explore to what degree the new habit of mind in the theoretical realm was a response to unsettling transformations in the realm of class structure and sexual norms. My explicit aim here is to set in motion the metaphorical deposits of class and sexuality that inflect early twentieth-century culture and energized some of its most important authors. My implicit aim in uncovering these deposits is to suggest that they have never become quite fossilized, that our current assumptions about class and sexuality owe a great deal to the paradigm that evolved around the turn of the century. If sexuality is the great American taboo, class difference is a very close second. Both erotic irregularity and class difference were officially nonexistent in the homogenizing ideology of nineteenth-century America. What emerges in the early twentieth century is a crusade to open up both taboos, a drive precipitated in part by the increasing salience of sexual minorities and class others on the American scene. Often these minorities and class others emerged to visibility in the same sordid person—the immigrant armed with socialist propaganda and free-love pamphlets. Emma Goldman is the iconic figure here, fusing radical politics with radical sex in the uneasy national imagination. Yet the effort to confront these once-taboo subjects gave rise to new means of evasion.[10] However dedicated to exposing and apprehending the sexual problem or the class problem, reformers and social theorists everywhere converted these problems into what could not be exposed and apprehended—the discontent that defied categorization, the desire that baffled fulfillment. In the cognitive geography of the new century, there was no solid ground.

The commutative relation between eros and motion, between desire and dynamism, spans every plane of society in the first quarter of the twentieth century—from academic treatise to infrastructure. As discussion of the inner self in social theory and philosophy becomes oriented around desire and movement, so the physical sites of mobility, the locales where actual movement takes place (train depots and hotels, subways and city streets), come to be understood as conducive to desires and attractions once reserved for the stations of courtship and married life. "The principal effect of the gridiron plan," Lewis Mumford writes in "The City" (1922), "is that every street becomes a thoroughfare" in which "the tendency towards movement . . . vastly outweighs the tendency towards settlement."[11] In a turn of thought that predicts a familiar pattern in the era's social analysis, Mumford suggests that the rationality of the "gridiron" begets the unsettlement and *irrationality* that city planning aims to mitigate. The standardization of the urban plan paradoxically lays the conditions for the dissolution of moral standards. For Mumford further interprets "movement" on the "thoroughfare" in terms of the transient erotic "commerce" to which it inclines persons. "Up and down these second-hand Broadways, from one in the afternoon until past ten at night," Mumford explains, "drifts a more or less aimless mass of human beings, bent upon extracting such joy as is possible from the sights in the windows, the contact with other human beings, the occasional or systematic flirtations." Turning streets into "thoroughfares" transforms them from places where persons might reside to places where persons come and go at their whim, with all the "risks and adventures" such peripatetic motion implies.[12]

The aimless, casual traffic in desire that Mumford denounces as "a sort of spiritual masturbation" is given a different valence in a poem by Edith Wharton that also glosses sex in terms of transportation.[13] The speaker in the 1909 poem "Terminus," written the morning after Wharton's sordid weekend rendezvous with her lover, Morton Fullerton, describes a "long secret night" of sex in an "inn" as though it were the occasion for a Whitmanesque assembly of all lovers past and present who have done the same thing in the same "common-place room." "The hurried, the restless, the aimless," the speaker intones of the other guests that the room's bed has hosted, "perchance it has also thrilled / With the pressure of bodies ecstatic, like ours." This perverse poem understands a night of passionate sex not just in terms of bodies in motion but also in terms of motion itself. Hence the "low wide bed" is figured as "a high-road" that various lovers have traversed; and erotic encounter is likened to "the whirlwind of travel, / The shaking and shrieking of trains, the night-long shudder of traffic." The kind of desire the poem espouses—transient and unsanctioned, "hurried, aimless, restless"—is unthinkable without trains and inns to facilitate this clandestine yet strangely public, virtually collective pleasure.[14]

II

In their different ways Mumford and Wharton illuminate a feature of the new century that we are accustomed to overlook. This is the fact that the period's various technologies of standardization and mechanization—whether of consumption or train schedules, of hotel rooms or street layouts—scarcely conduce to the cultivation of routine or standardized *subjects*. The logic of equivalence that underwrites the world of hotels, trains, and department stores—where each consumer is substitutable for any other—has the effect not of generating social equilibrium but of voiding it. In a world where persons are viewed as fundamentally substitutable, as Mumford and Wharton imply, the whole notion of social placement becomes compromised by the ease with which modern culture allows persons to move in and out of spaces. It is this phenomenon that we find social theory and literary culture confronting in the first quarter of the twentieth century, and it is their acknowledgment of this phenomenon that accounts for the restlessness with which both social theory and literary culture responded to intellectual paradigms and cultural models they viewed as obsolete.

The skepticism shared by social theory and literary culture toward their respective inheritances is worth considering more fully—the better to draw out the wider implications of the current project. Though critics have paid careful attention to the intensification of modes of social control during the early twentieth century, to the ascent of managerial science and the triumph of Weber's "iron cage," they have been far less attuned to the conditions that gave rise to these diverse bureaucratic and disciplinary impulses. Hence students of modernism and modernity have arrived at an account of early twentieth-century culture that takes the ideological reactions of the day— the calls for standardization, administrative leadership, and efficiency—as equivalent to social reality. Largely omitted from this account is the background against which such intensive arguments made sense: a world that was widely diagnosed as irregular and restless, changeable, and, most important, not to be trusted. The idealization of managerial control that forms a staple of Progressive-era discourses belies the violent struggles its advocates had to wage on its behalf. By inscribing the discourse of social control in a wider historical dynamic, I aim to redress the critical tendency toward linguistic or textual determinism. In order to map a more accurate social totality, I read the literary texts of modernist culture alongside its social-theoretical works in terms that emphasize that culture's ambiguity and evasiveness as much as its bureaucratic management. This wider historical vantage would benefit most readily from moving our view of the period beyond the perspective of the managerial elite and directing our attention to the underclass persons who compelled theirs.

Emile Durkheim's name for modernity's "dissolving" aspect is "anomie." Far from abstract, anomie for Durkheim had a particular locale—the modern workplace—and entailed a concrete dilemma—that workplace's inability to regulate boundaries for human desire. In Durkheim's view, the proper role of social theory is not only to bring about efficiency in the economic system but also to restore the constraints on individual desire that the managerial system has inadvertently dissolved with its minute parsing of roles on the factory floor. Because the latter situation destroys traditional means of solidarity among workers, it breeds an atomistic population of men and women for whom self-interest runs unchecked by the moral brakes of collective conscience and practice. If, as Durkheim avers in the preface to the second edition of *The Division of Labor*, "men's passions are only stayed by a moral presence they respect," those passions in the modern world "tend to grow beyond all bounds, each clashing with the other, each warding off and weakening the other" in the absence of a common purpose.[15] This riot of "passions" finds its direct analogy in the excesses to which modern industrial capitalism has given rise. By "concentrating resources" in "large-scale industry," according to Durkheim, the "corporation" "ha[s] stirred people's minds to wish to satisfy new wants" and threatens to produce "a so-ciety made up of an extremely large mass of unorganized individuals, which an overgrown state attempts to limit and restrain."[16]

As if confirming Durkheim's theory of anomie, Lippmann's *Drift and Mastery,* which sought to calm the volatility of personal whims by advancing the case of a disinterested professional class, begins with an acknowledgment that such melioration is an acute desideratum of "the current unrest" (*DM* 54). For Lippmann, the middleman becomes a creature not to be condemned for his dissociation from the institution he manages but rather to be commended for his distance from the base self-interests that a too-close attachment to the corporation implies. Yet singling out Lippmann's creed of managerial disinterest and dynamism only highlights how tenuous were the period's efforts to maintain social control at the level of status distinctions. The detachment from corporate loyalty that Lippmann valorized in the salaried manager was just as likely to invite censure when viewed as a characteristic of those lowest on the social ladder. For members of the professional-managerial class, mobility connoted their capacity to remove themselves from the entanglements of unreasonable attachments in the divisive battles between labor and capital; for the lower classes, mobility connoted removal from social order itself—in the form of a willingness to walk off the job, or in the form of the general insolence that appeared to mark the new wage-earning classes. In the managerial mind, there was little difference between concerted strikes and slowdowns on the one hand and rapid employee turnover on the other, since both pointed to a crisis in motion that the worker embodied.

Distinguishing between orderly and disorderly movement, managerial rationality sought to negotiate disobedience among the working classes by seizing most directly, as Frederick Taylor's motion studies aimed to do, on how workers ought to move. In a bid to improve worker "competence," Taylor's *Principles of Scientific Management* (1911) directly equates "wastes of human effort" with the "awkward, inefficient, or ill-directed movements of men."[17] But the primary boon of scientific management's regulation of worker movement turns out to be less a matter of improved efficiency than "the elimination of almost all causes of dispute and disagreement" between "the manufacturer and the workman," "the friction and discontent," or the "open warfare" that such class relations typically entail.[18] Eliding the bodily motion of the worker with the idea of a workers' movement, Taylor conjures a managerial fantasy in which controlling the first type of movement dispels or obviates the second. As Taylor's emphasis on the link between "ill-directed movements" and "discontent" suggests, the underclass laborers had acquired a startling feature that appeared by turns both cause and effect of modernity's dislocations and displacements. The working poor comprised a floating population whose most obvious members—immigrants, tramps, Northern-bound blacks—revealed a widespread habit of unrest among all lower-class persons. "The tendency is for the place-roots of the working class to be somewhat more shallow than are those of the business class," Robert and Helen Merrell Lind write in *Midddletown* (1929). "The working class group of today appear to exhibit more mobility than the families of their mothers."[19] I argue throughout the remainder of this chapter that sexology, with its concept of indefinite and aimless desire, provided the idiom of choice among the period's thinkers to canvass this new social order.

Lothrop Stoddard's racist polemics from the early twenties demonstrate the extent to which even essentialist and identitarian accounts of society relied on a language of irregular desire and its consequences. This language was in crucial respects at odds with the rigidly hierarchical scheme of racial difference such accounts also favored, insofar as what defined inferior or degenerate races was precisely their tendency to overstep their categorical fastness. In Stoddard's *The Rising Tide of Color* (1920), the "inferior" races are routinely associated with "unbalanced" and destructive movement, most notably in the tide of the title.[20] The "swarming, prolific aliens" who in Stoddard's account "adapted" (*RT* 144) to the work of the industrial revolution are notable for the proficiency with which they adjust to change. Stoddard suggests that "aliens' " mutability precipitates an "ebb" among the superior Nordics, whose admirable devotion to "agricultural" (*RT* 164) civilization, and the "healthful living conditions" such a culture brings, turns out to be a liability in the deracinated world of "urban, industrialized" (*RT* 164) Europe. With his penchant for tidal metaphors, Stoddard shares Day's sense that the lunar cycle provides the proper analogy for understanding modernity's social relations. The moon's fluctuations most closely reflect the instability that characterizes contemporary life. "Nothing is more *unstable* than the ethnic make-up of a people," Stoddard writes. "Matings between whites, Negroes, and Amerindians" result not in "amalgamation" but in "a walking chaos" (*RT* 166). Erotic disorder begets disorderly movement, a slipping of the self from its proper moorings.

Yet though Stoddard attributes to the Nordics a high-minded sense of place that keeps them rooted in native soil even as their constancy appears to compromise their fit into "industrial" life, elsewhere in *The Rising Tide of Color* he equates the low birthrate among Nordics with their overactive motion, and particularly with the "handicaps of war and migration" (*RT* 167). In Stoddard's view, the former disrupts the love that should flower among pure whites, replacing sexual attraction with hostility; the latter draws Nordics away from their stationary bulwarks in the countryside and into the erratic movement that is scarcely distinguishable from the "walking chaos" he attributes to the cross-racial bastard. "The era of discovery and colonization which began with the sixteenth century further depleted the Nordic ranks in Europe," he writes, "since it was adventurous Nordics who formed the overwhelming majority of explorers and pioneers to new lands" (*RT* 163). The migratory spirit of the Nordic man leads inexorably to a drift away from marital ties and the racial benefits such ties augur for the reproduction of the white race. Embedded in Stoddard's assumption about the extinction of the Nordic race is the intuition that the turn toward the expanses of modern culture triggers a veering away from the traditional alignment of sexual conduct with social injunction—in other words, from marriage and family life.[21]

Even as Stoddard argues for the inviolability of racial solidarity, then, in which "the white nations . . . may be regarded as so many planets gravitating about the sun of a common civilization," this "constant" solar orbiting, or what Stoddard calls "the sustained and intimate race-solidarity," is sabotaged by the tendency of whites—and white men in particular—to disregard this closeness in favor of the lunar patterns that influence their uprooted and adaptable inferiors. Modern Nordics have developed the habit of "avoiding marriage altogether," he says in *The Revolt against Civilization* (1922).[22] Men don't marry and hence don't breed. As Stoddard was well aware, this tendency differentiated native-born white Americans from their European counterparts. In northern Europe low birthrate was a function of small families, whereas in the United States it was correlated with a disincentive to marriage *itself*. The anti-immigrant writer Prescott Hall thus attributes low birthrate among American whites to the fact that "natives did not marry" in the late nineteenth century—a fact he in turn refers to "the movement toward cities, in which the young men played the leading part, leaving girls at home upon the farms, and diminishing their opportunity for marriage."[23] Stoddard holds the white bachelor responsible for his own "racial displacements" (*RT* 165) from the American nation by virtue of his tendency to replace the virtues of "domestic life" (*RC* 121) with the pleasures of ranging and dissemination.

However his own work might flirt with "the exploded doctrines of environmentalism" (at least to the extent that he traces the problem of low birthrate to "the stressful complexity of high civilizations" [*RC* 132]), Stoddard is in the final analysis a staunch adherent of hereditary theory. Thus is it all the more surprising that he ultimately casts the problem of racial reproduction less in the diction of biology and heredity than in the psychological language of stray and errant desire that his contemporaries favored. Claiming that "race solidarity" necessitates "sustained and intimate" commitment, Stoddard makes racial identity look like marriage. And while biology can explain the transmission of racial identity across generations, it has more difficulty explaining the loss of interest among Nordics in the proper sexual congress that facilitates such transmission. In other words, biology can prescribe why racial equals should marry, but cannot describe why they no longer want to.

Ousting the causal primacy of biology, thinkers in the period increasingly turn to what they see as the socioeconomic determinants of physical or sexual attitudes. "It is in the age of the Individual that the revolt against marriage has risen to its present irresistible tide," Will Durant writes in an essay aptly titled "The Breakdown of Marriage."[24] For Durant, modernity's atomization of society into a series of disconnected individuals awakens "the natural varietism" in all matters sexual: "man is secretly and ravenously polygamous," and it is this desire for multiplicity that modern life has reinvigorated. The breakdown of community in turn produces the woman who "wanders about aimless and dissatisfied, moving from one place, one man, or one amusement to another" (*SP* 167) or the "unstable and superficial" man who "flits from mate to mate" (*SP* 166). Durant shares not only Stoddard's (and Ross's) privileged metaphor for describing the new sexual irregularity but also the sense that breakdown and tidal tumult are synonyms for the general commotion that he associates with the "experimental perversions that stigmatize our contemporary life" (*SP* 162).

"The general belief is that Americans are destined not to renounce, but to enjoy," Herbert Croly writes in *The Promise of American Life* (1909).[25] By the time Stoddard and Durant are publishing their work in the next generation, Croly's "general belief" has become a widespread paranoia focused on those perverse desires that misdirect or thwart the dutiful perpetuation of the American race. Even so staunch a propagandist for a hereditarian doctrine as Stoddard cannot avoid this complex of perversions. "Wanderlust" is the unspoken disease infecting Stoddard's cherished Nordics. This particular perversion was widespread in the early twentieth century, often used to trace the etiology of hobo life. "In its pure form," as Robert Park and Herbert Miller put it in *Old World Traits Transplanted*, "the desire for new experience results in motion, change, danger, instability, social irresponsibility."[26] And economist Rexford Tugwell claims, "Even those of us who seem to have settled down quite comfortably are sometimes intolerably stirred by the wanderlust. It comes upon us unaware; and often we cut away and go."[27] In keeping with this undoing of the self by what Tugwell calls "the moral side doors" of the "wander tendencies,"[28] Stoddard diagnoses the white man's own "wander tendencies" thus: "His virtual abolition of distance has destroyed the protection which nature once conferred" (*RT* 302). Here the quest to break down space omits the natural prophylactic against sexual "intermingling" that "isolation" brought with it. Stoddard conflates breaking down with overly mobile persons, and further conflates both of these with erotic excess.

III

The concept of sexual perversion regulated the discourse of social thought in the first decades of the twentieth century, permeating knowledge systems well beyond the domain of sexology as the explanation of a host of social effects and behaviors (as in Durant's "experimental perversions"). Durant's "The Breakdown of Marriage" appeared in a Modern Library anthology called *The Sex Problem in Modern Society* (1930), one of many volumes that essentially equated modern society and the "sex problem." As John Francis McDermott explains in the book's introduction, "[S]ex and its functioning are now looked upon as a basic study toward the understanding of human nature, which is, after all, our most immediate problem" (*SP* viii). Yet even as sex increasingly became an object of what McDermott calls "curiosity," the authors represented in his anthology had difficulty sorting out where to fit sex into explanatory schemes. However "basic" sex might have been among "the principal functions of the body" (*SP* vii), the problem with sex was that, perpetually mobile, it never stayed put at the level of function or physique. And if naming its function proved difficult, assessing whether sex was a cause or effect appeared insuperably challenging. "The interconnections of economics and sex do not appear to me to show any clear primacy of the one over the other," Bertrand Russell writes in the anthology's opening essay, "Why a Sexual Ethic Is Necessary." "I am not prepared to assign primacy to either the economic or sexual factor, nor in fact can they be separated with any clearness" (*SP* 3). The proneness of sex to indeterminacy turns out to be its most enabling heuristic feature for the period's observers. In eluding a referential harness as either cause or effect, sex mimics the dislocation, uncertainty, and general unmooring to which modernity itself is prone. The social psychologist Charles Ellwood, for example, argues in *Cultural Evolution* (1927): "Many things in human life can be studied only as tendencies. We can observe facts here and there . . . and thus we can get the direction of a movement even though we cannot observe its beginning or end."[29] The most "pronounced tendency" on which Ellwood bases his reorientation toward "movement" rather than origins or conclusions is what he calls "unstable sex relations."[30]

Ellwood reveals a habit of intellection that repeats itself during this era in a variety of thinkers: the aspiration to methodological renovation coupled with a barely submerged dread of the social ramifications from which such renovation ensues. A forward-looking theoretical perspective, in other words, is routinely wed to a conservative social morality. Thus "the increase of divorce and of shifting sex relations seems to have characterized every period of decadence in culture," Ellwood writes, "and appears to be a phenomenon of social disintegration and dissolution rather than a phenomenon of normal social development. In other words, it is pathological."[31] And Russell, who regards with dispassion the unfixed role of the sexual "factor" as a philosophical puzzle, speaks in different tones when he traces the "complete breakdown of traditional morality" to the changing economic habits of "the wage-earning class" (*SP* 6). Just as Ellwood's belief in the progressive improvement of social science is twinned with his belief in the regressive or "pathological" nature of a sexually dissolute culture, so Russell's somewhat nonchalant philosophical response to the indeterminate nature of sex becomes the source of much more anxiety elsewhere in McDermott's volume. The failure to attach primacy to sexual or social factors, to get the cognitive map in order, becomes synonymous with the disarray and promiscuity implied by sexual license itself.

"A realistic view of actual sex opinion and sex behavior leads to the feeling that on every hand," Edward Sapir writes in "The Discipline of Sex," "life is being immeasurably cheapened by an emotional uncertainty in matters of sex, matters that no healthy society can long brook uncertainty of" (*SP* 9). Sapir sees the cultivation of "abstract freedom" in "matters of sex" as "but the homelessness of the outlaw" (*SP* 10). For early twentieth-century culture, sex becomes most visible at the moment of its "breakdown"—which is to say, at the moment it ceases to be a normative and tends to become a perverse feature of an increasingly perverse world. "Sex irregularities" (*SP* 18) form the exclusive basis of "curiosity" for observers like Sapir. Rather than cultivating an interest in what McDermott calls sex as a "function," contemporary thinkers are overwhelmingly preoccupied with sex at its most dysfunctional—and with the social world such dysfunction discloses. Just as discussions of sex inevitably conjure the specter of wage earners, outlaws, or homeless men and women, so perversion encroaches on the most venerable of traditional institutions. "It is no longer permissible for an enlightened person to be horrified by perversion," Samuel Schmalhausen writes in *Why We Misbehave* (1928), because "what used to be called sex perversion has become the new normality."[32]

These various instances demonstrate that even as early twentieth-century social sciences made recourse to "sex perversion" to mediate the complexities embodied by the persons who made up their opaque and unreliable object of analysis, the explanatory dividend these disciplines anticipated from sexology was itself scarcely a given. This is because sex appeared increasingly unhinged from any exact referential station, physical or otherwise. Hence we find sociologist Charles Josey arguing emphatically against the idea that the sex impulse can be reduced to innate instinct or "original nature." Refusing the idea that sex has an essence residing in the body, Josey claims instead that the sex impulse, "like all other interests and impulses, arises as the result of the experiences of the individual, and is to be regarded as such rather than the experiences regarded as the result of the impulse."[33] In a reversal characteristic of his contemporaries, Josey denies sexual desire any biological basis in order to exploit it as a social factor, a matter of environment: "With changes in our environment there come into existence a world of new desires and impulses, which begin to show their influence in social and cultural phenomena."[34] In Josey's view, any effort to infer erotic perversion from biological essence fails to account for the constitutive randomness of sex. "Deviation in the sex behavior from the normal," he writes, "is the result of certain accidental experiences of the individual."[35] Similarly, sociologist Ernest Groves treats "perversions" as "accidental variations in the expression of sex," "resulting from the breaking down of the mental stability of the person."[36] Seeing perverse sexual impulses as divorced from bodily necessity turns perversion to advantage for social scientists. This vantage makes sex a logarithm for the reckoning of a contingent or broken world.

Even among writers deeply opposed to any sexual irregularity, sex inexorably gravitates from the concrete precincts of the physical body to the more nebulous recesses of mentality and feeling, of "accidental experiences." "The influence of sex is not only limited to the physical sphere," the reform crusader Dr. Moses Schotz writes in *Sex Problems of Man in Health and Disease* (1916). "In fact its influence on the psychology and mentality of the individual is equally powerful."[37] Sex not only roams across the mental landscape of the self but, in doing so, defies categorization. "People are so different as to their sexual capacity and preferences that no hard or fast rules can be enjoined on the average man or woman," Schotz writes, "and not even approximate limits can be given in an individual case." Schotz's depiction of the sexual "temperament" as infinitely variable paradoxically licenses social order because the indeterminacy of sex makes it less an urgent necessity of the body than a matter of personal choice: "Surely an instinct that is so changeable and so widely differs with different people is not a physical necessity of our body, and can be held in abeyance for a long period of time."[38]

Yet the variance that Schotz views as making "the sexual impulse" a matter of personal decision-making and thus redeeming sex from social disruption turns out by and large to be the thing that for his contemporaries makes sex dangerous to social order. The opacity that contemporaries increasingly imputed to sex closely approximated the failure of communicative transparency in the social order at large. Acting on a similar logic to Schotz's with regard to the essential inconsistency of sex, Jacques Fisher reaches the opposite conclusion in the McDermott anthology: "Lost in the midst of a mass of individuals, not of his own age," he argues, "man will not be very favorably circumstanced for the accomplishment of his sexual evolution together with those individuals of his generation, in physical, physiological, and rhythmical harmony with whom he ought logically to make love" (*SP* 43). The lack of "rhythmical harmony" that Schotz sees as keeping the sexual instinct from having free rein—because no two people will approach sex in the same frame of mind, thus minimizing the chances of getting together in bed—turns out for Fisher to be the wellspring not of abstinence but of wanton promiscuity. The failure of the modern self to find proper (coeval) objects for his sexual attraction gives rise to a vicious circle in which there is no hope for sex or society to function "logically." The irregular movement of modern eros cedes to a failure of categorical stability because persons are not in sexual synchronization; they lack the "homogeneous" erotic drives of other animals, with their "autonomous generations" (*SP* 38) all breeding at once. Because what Fisher calls "the sexual ground swell" (*SP* 35) of modern life is "apt to be set in motion at any moment," "there will be, on the contrary, an almost infinite series of individuals" (*SP* 42).

"The rhythm of the jazz age has infected our sex life," Franklin Woodland writes in echo of Fisher's tectonic eros. "Pathology is woven into the very texture of contemporary civilization." Making explicit the connection between sociological paradigm shift and "unstable sex relations" that his contemporaries embed in their accounts, Woodland sees the "mad quest for stimulation . . . driving men and women into the arms of abnormality" as inseparable from modernity's "pluralistic tendency"—its "differentiation of unity into variety, the dismemberment of reality into a number of realities." In other words, he understands the "stimulation" of science not as a corrective to but as a symptom of the "pathology" of "sex life" in general. Thus the instruments of secular science are conceived as analogous to the "pleasure-seeking" associated with "novel sensations" (*SP* 64).

I want to summarize two ramifications of the sexological turn in early twentieth-century social science. The first is the interchangeability of sexual drive and any number of human motives and the epistemological vexations this reciprocity poses. Whereas thinkers in the realm of social theory lean on sex as a sort of explanatory default, more traditional students of sexuality in medical and life sciences depart from their nineteenth-century predecessors in viewing sex as lacking referential solidity or biological necessity. And just as sex becomes hard to pin down on or in bodies, so a kind of isomorphism comes to define economic and political motives and sexual drives—which were used, almost tautologically, to explain each other. The second is the effort to grasp the differentiation among classes of persons, or rather the virtual impossibility of such classification, in terms of sexual "varietism." "The infinite series of individuals" that Fisher sees in modern social life finds its proper analogue in the "pathology" of what Schotz calls an indefinitely "changeable" sexual "temperament." Thus Olive Schreiner in her treatise *Woman and Labor* (1911) avers that "sex relationships may assume almost any form on earth as the conditions of life vary."[39]

The speciation of the social body into a multitude of diverse sexual agents has received much attention in the work of Michel Foucault. In volume 1 of *The History of Sexuality,* Foucault writes of the "multiplication and intensification of the pleasures connected to the production of truth about sex."[40] Often lacking in Foucauldian analyses, however, is the fierce anxiety, the disturbing uncertainty, that speciation (and its likely failure) entailed for its practitioners. Modern analysis of sexual desire not only has a frequent class referent but also conceals the expert's anxiety of not being able to classify classes, to overcome the sublime numbers of modern persons or their equally sublime movement. We can glimpse both the class referent and the expert anxiety at work in the frequency with which "casualness" emerges within expert discourses after 1900 to describe both working-class life and sexual desire. "The old stability has given way to the new instability as the normal pattern of life," Frankwood Williams writes. "Casualness"—as in "the very casualness of modern sex life"—"best expresses the nature of this transvaluation of values" (*SP* 66).[41]

Casualness takes the place of causality in this historical moment, as if the inability to make sense of the social problems of workers—to attribute them to a cause—were a function of the workers themselves. "It is very difficult," Edmond Kelly writes in *The Elimination of the Tramp* (1908), "to determine at what moment the able-bodied working man can be blamed for lapsing into the army of casual laborers and acquiring the evil habits that result from casual employment."[42] For Kelly, the indeterminacy of analysis mirrors the indeterminacy of casual employment itself. As his vaguely invoked "evil habits" suggest (elsewhere Kelly explains that these include "seduc[ing] the young into sharing his fortunes" and "spread[ing] disease, physical and moral"),[43] the casual laborer, like sexual desire that "obey[s] no fixed law," is as disobedient and restless as the modern market that no longer has a use for him. In *What's on the Worker's Mind* (1920), Whiting Williams refers to the "degenerating irregularity" of "the migratory worker," who thrives because of the unreliability structured into the division of labor. Schreiner's work is useful for teasing out the analogy between what Williams calls "the town's jobs," which are overwhelmingly informal and impermanent, and "the town's morals—or immorals."[44] "There has arisen, the world over," she writes, "a large body of males who find that their ancient fields of labor have slipped or are slipping away from them, and who discover that the modern world has no place or need for them" (*WL* 44). What Schreiner calls "the problem of the unemployed male" (*WL* 42) is for her never far from another problematic person, "the curled darling, scented and languid," "the product of decay" (*WL* 108), who like the unemployed male has been rendered socially useless as a result of his failure to abide by the norms of producer culture—norms that Schreiner explicitly equates with a strenuous but no longer attainable masculine ideal. In their superfluity and parasitism, the laid-off laborer and the decadent "darling" are the twin figures of perversion in Schreiner's book.

"Varietism" as a concept of difference is never far removed from erotic intemperance in early twentieth-century social thought. And by the same token, the study of "varietism" is haunted by the very element of perversion that writers like Schreiner, Woodland, and others view as motivating modern life. As Woodland's reference to "the mad quest for stimulation" implies, social theorists were anxiously aware of the scandalous facility with which sex as an object of inquiry could exceed the distance between observer and observed to shape the experience of cognition as itself a sexually charged one. One of the revolutionary moves in psychoanalysis was the theorization of this possibility as a therapeutic benefit—the dynamic of the transference, as Freud called it in an essay of 1915. "Sexual love is undoubtedly one of the chief things in life," Freud writes in "Observations on Transference-Love." "All the world knows this and conducts its life accordingly; science alone is too delicate to admit it."[45] One problem with such an admission, I would argue, had to do with the nebulous status of sex. When it came to talking about sex, science was scarcely equipped to specify what it was admitting to, just as scientists were always haunted by the suspicion that their own pronouncements identified them as guilty of the very perversion they had set up for detached clinical analysis. Both the inability to agree on what sex means and the inescapable salaciousness that studying sex invited defined the paradigm shift in social thought more than any other features.

Yet this only confirms that social theorists who borrowed sexology's ideas also borrowed its complications and confusions. Despite its practitioners' abiding interest in unity or coherence, that field produced no monolithic or normative ideology of sexuality. In *The Sexual Life of Our Time in Its Relations to Modern Civilization* (1908), Iwan Bloch claims that "the human sexual impulse has undergone a progressive individualization" that makes apprehending its significance virtually impossible—and thus all the more imperative.[46] Despite his confidence that it stands as "the inalienable gain of civilization," the "sexual impulse" remains altogether alienable and even alien to Bloch's best efforts to grasp it. "The nature of sexual tension is still entirely unknown," he concludes, owing in large part to the absence of "really exact investigations regarding the different phenomena occurring during the sexual act."[47] In particular Bloch singles out "the demeanor of the woman during [the] act" as "extremely obscure," thus obliquely calling attention to a dilemma familiar to theorists of sexuality from Freud to Krafft-Ebing to Havelock Ellis.[48] For all these authors, the case study remained the predominant instrument of analysis, and the problem with case studies was that they invariably involved persons who might or might not be telling the truth. In *Sexual Inversion,* Ellis protests the obviously widespread belief that case histories amounted to "falsehood" or "empty fiction": "I am assured that many of the inverts I have met not only possess a rare power of intellectual self-analysis . . . but an unsparing sincerity in that self-analysis."[49]

Pinning down sexual desires or agents with any clarity remained a theoretical impasse for sexology. Like the woman in Bloch's example, sex remained an "obscure" object of both desire and analysis. August Forel begins his widely read book *The Sexual Question* (translated into English in 1906) by claiming that when it comes to "the sexual appetite,"

> The desire to procreate dominates everything. A single pleasure, a single desire, a single passion lays hold of the organism and urges it toward the individual of the opposite sex, and to become united with it in intimate contact and penetration. It is as if the nervous system or the whole organism felt as if it had for the moment become a germinal cell, so powerful is the desire to unite with the other sex.[50]

No sooner does Forel generate this vision of singular and determinate erotic desire, however, than his book departs from its harmonious unity. *The Sexual Question* in fact may be read as a continual tug-of-war between sexual desire as a "single pleasure" rooted in the normative and natural aim of procreation ("if we look at nature we see everywhere the same desire and the same attractions of the sexes for each other" [*SQ* 74]) and sexual desire as complex and differentiated, "var[ying] from individual to individual" (*SQ* 77). Despite his insistence on the naturalness or typicality of sexual desire, Forel finds it impossible to keep "sexual appetite" in analytical focus. It is at once singular and "variant," coherent and unstable, concentrated and diffuse. Thus "in man," Forel writes, the "desire for change" supplants the natural urge for "reproduction" with "the stronger excitation produced by all that is new" (*SQ* 83). Forel has difficulty not only asserting the primacy of single sexual aim over the "multiplicity of pleasures" (*SQ* 154) that civilization fosters but also drawing a cordon around the domain of "sexual pathology," which he defines as "capable of so much extension that no definite limit can be fixed between the normal state and morbid states, which are themselves connected by numerous transitions" (*SQ* 208). Even as he favors "hereditary dispositions" as the root of "pathological aberrations" (*SQ* 208), then, Forel ultimately fails to bracket sexual abnormality as belonging solely to a discrete group of "defectives." "Sexual power varies so much in individuals," he writes, "that it is hardly possible to fix a limit between the normal and the pathological" (*SQ* 81). In fact the biological basis of sexual disorder cohabits with that disorder's near-universality and its continuous or transitional nature.

The same compatibility between organic and situational models of sexual perversion finds its way into Havelock Ellis's *Sexual Inversion,* resulting in the same equivocation between sexual perverts as discrete persons and sexual perversion as an endemic condition that transcends any given individual. The equivocation manifests itself most readily in Ellis's admission that "classification of the varieties of homosexuality is a matter of difficulty and no classification is very fundamental" (*SI* 82). Rather than following the "no longer acceptable" distinctions made by "Krafft-Ebing and others," Ellis acknowledges what he calls "a general undefined homosexuality—a relationship of unspecified nature to persons of the same sex—in addition to the more specific sexual inversion" (*SI* 83). This "general undefined homosexuality" takes up so much space in Ellis's volume that it pushes "the more specific sexual inversion" to the margins of the text. Like Forel, Ellis construes sexual pathology as different in degree rather than in kind. "True inverts" are not qualitatively but quantitatively different from their heterosexual counterparts—not another species, as Foucault would have it, but simply possessed of a "homosexual impulse" of a higher order of magnitude. In a remarkable passage, Ellis lays out this quantum theory of inversion:

> The real distinction would seem, therefore, to be between a homosexual impulse so strong that it subsists even in the presence of the heterosexual object, and a homosexual impulse so weak that it is eclipsed by the presence of the heterosexual object. We could not, however, properly speak of the latter as any more "spurious" or "pseudo" than the former. (*SI* 87)

From this Ellis concludes that "while therefore the division into heterosexual, bisexual, and homosexual is a useful superficial division, it is scarcely a scientific classification" (*SI* 88). And what looked like a heuristic advantage—the development of a concept of "general undefined homosexuality"—results finally in Ellis's lack of interest in speciation as explanation: "it has seemed best to me to attempt no classification at all" (*SI* 89).

Taking the place of the species model of sexual inversion is an environmental narrative in which persons who document their case histories for Ellis typically populate them with lower-class men—"a man-servant who had long been with the family" (*SI* 116); "the dormitory servant, who showed me his penis when he woke me in the morning" (*SI* 121); "a youth, some years younger than himself and of lower social class" (*SI* 125); "a very good-looking groom" (*SI* 130); "young soldiers . . . invariably of a lower social rank than his own" (*SI* 143); "farm laborers" (*SI* 148); "a common workman" (*SI* 154). In Ellis's volume the scene of seduction for the invert is almost always a scene of class difference. If classical sexology tacitly construed homosexuality as a category of bourgeois identity, as some historians have argued, it bears noting how for Ellis that customary mapping of the homosexual self appears implicated in something of a class betrayal. Sexologists frequently represent nonnormative sexual desires in terms of a trespassing of class boundaries in which the lower-class other becomes the dangerous catalyst of, for example, the "homosexual impulse."[51] If Ellis sees homosexuality as an "unspecified" condition, this is because the lines between customary categories of persons have blurred, adulterating pure divisions between homosexual and heterosexual types just as persons from different domains are all too liable to mix with one another. Echoing Ellis's theme of licentious cross-class combinations as the source of perverse desire, Forel claims that "the promiscuity of their life" impels "the sexual appetite" of "the lower classes" to be "artificially increased and often directed into unnatural channels" (*SQ* 89). The ambiguous nature of sexual perversion uncannily parallels the ambiguity of a culture in which persons of different social ranks mingle indiscriminately.

Ellis's book makes a careful distinction between the invert as a type of person and homosexuality as a type of practice. Whereas the invert is a figure securely bounded by congenital circumstance and relatively easy to classify according to a stable (if specious) ontology of gender and physiognomy, homosexual practice by contrast is widespread, casual, accidental, and, as *Sexual Inversion* makes clear, almost always associated with lower-class men—soldiers, criminals, tramps, and so on—who prostitute themselves with alarming frequency in both Europe and the United States. According to turn-of-the-century students of sex, the desire that animates homosexual practice exceeds the body of the invert and encroaches on virtually everyone.

Contrasting sexual identities and sexual behaviors, then, sexology views the former (the invert) as more or less transparent and stable and the latter (inversion) as "latent," obscure, mobile, and diffuse—a "kind of sexual appetite," as William James suggests in *The Principles of Psychology* (1890), "of which very likely most men possess the germinal possibility."[52] The strangeness of this ambiguity is worth savoring, for there is something profoundly paradoxical about an object of knowledge at once disproportionately influential in the formation of the social fabric and utterly incapable of being identified with clarity or certainty. Early twentieth-century culture's privileged object of knowledge, perverse desire, presents a peculiar epistemic conundrum: the "sexual impulse" is so slippery and evasive, so restive and obscure, that it appears to defy categorization. In constructing sexuality as infinitely displaceable, theorists of modern society acknowledge its breakdown and groundlessness, its unmooring of identity, even as they remain reluctantly committed to a traditional morality of self and social life. The frequent recurrence of perversion in social-scientific texts as the name for any number of irregular social relations suggests that perversity, rather than perverts per se, is the topic of most enthusiastic interest to both sexology and the social theorists who have adopted its precepts. Perversion turns out to be epidemic in such a way and to such a degree that anyone might be infected by it regardless of sexual identity or essence. "Human sexuality has been unfortunately perverted and in part grossly altered by civilization," Forel claims. "Forgetful of the natural aim of the sexual appetite, civilization has transformed it into artificial enjoyment, and has invented all possible means to increase and diversify it" (*SQ* 85). Modernity's diversifying function, its habit of breaking things down into ever more discrete components, is what induces the culture-wide amnesia of sex's "natural aim" in favor of "artificial enjoyment." The diffusiveness of modern society morphs into the indeterminate licentiousness of excessive and ill-placed desire. "The sexual passion," sexologist Conolly Norman claims, "is always indefinite, and is very easily turned in the wrong direction" (cited in *SI* 80). Rather than an essential or predetermined component of the self, perversion is situational and environmental, a function of what Schreiner calls the "maladjustment" of "modern economic life" to which a "vast and increasing" number of persons are prone. For Schreiner, this "maladjustment"—the fact that "man has not been modified" at the same rate "the material conditions of life have been" (*WL* 39)—results in the "most terrible social disease that afflicts us" (*WL* 17): prostitution.

The slippage from modernity's signature "maladjustment" to the oldest of vices is not an eccentric or even a particularly original one on Schreiner's part. (I analyze the period's widespread interest in—and borrowing of—the figure of the prostitute in chapter 6.) Everywhere in turn-of-the-century American life, modern conditions were described in terms of irregular erotic relations. I want to emphasize the environmentalism, the constructivism even, of this discourse of sexualized social theory, as well as to play down the overemphasis that recent sexuality studies have accorded to Progressive-era and modernist social theory's identitarian and essentialist cast. However sexologists might have promoted ideal or regular sexual identities, those identities always remained ideal. Like Forel with his "numerous transitions" among "normal" and "morbid" mental states, sexologists self-consciously construed identities not as normative but as fluid, as plotted along a spectrum the ideal centers of which few persons approached. "The fact is," Otto Weininger alleges in *Sex and Character,*

> that every human being varies or oscillates between the maleness and fe-
> maleness of his constitution. In some cases these oscillations are abnor-
> mally large, in other cases so small as to escape observation, but they are
> always present, and when they are great they may even reveal themselves
> in the outward aspect of the body. Like the variations in the magnetism
> of the earth, these sexual oscillations are either regular or irregular.[53]

Although he maintains an opposition between "regular and irregular" types, Weininger represents a host of sexologists who replaced a static model of sexual identity with a dynamic model of "variations." Typology in this discourse yields to the "oscillations" among categories "of which any individual is capable."[54] Just as "modern economic conditions" inevitably engendered "maladjustment," so normative sexual identity was a frustrated category to which only the rare individual could stake a genuine claim.[55]

Highlighting these features of the sexological literature restores the discussion of modernity and desire to the referents that mattered most to thinkers at the start of the twentieth century—the class and sex relations that were seen as American culture's most acute social problems. The crisis of modernity concerned the terminal evasiveness of status fixity—as notable in the tendency of the affluent to lose caste as in the ability of the lowborn to pass for affluent. That caginess encompassed not only the slipperiness of the working-class unemployed or partially employed who could not be settled down but also the sexual subjects whose desires were likewise unsettled and roaming, divorced from conventions and typical traits even as they outwardly appeared to conform to them. For Iwan Bloch, sexuality represented not only an intensifying "individuation" on the part of modern subjects but also an ever widening "freedom." As we have seen when looking at writers like Edward Ross and the essayists writing in the McDermott anthology, both individuation and freedom were understood as profoundly ambiguous dividends of modernity. Whereas intensive individuation makes it difficult to come up with categorical wholes or homogeneous groupings, at the same time the freedom Bloch describes looks distressingly like the alienation or detachment that sociologists like Simmel, Durkheim, and Tonnies were exploring at the beginning of the modernist period. Durkheim's "anomie" echoes the desire that "obeys no fixed law" to be found in writing on sexuality from roughly the same moment. Writing in 1924, the psychologist Beatrice Hinkle asserts, "Natural, long-restrained desire is being substituted for collective moral values, and individuals are largely becoming a law unto themselves."[56]

Continental sociology arose in tandem with what it understood as a vastly dispersed (or, to use Durkheim's term, "centrifugal") social order—what Ferdinand Tonnies dubbed the *Gesellschaft* (usually translated as "association"). As Niklas Luhmann points out, the nascent field of sociology sought to corral the profuse differentiation of the modern world through its own increasingly diversified methodologies and theories. Far from a synthesis, this plurality of concepts and specializations ultimately contributed to the fragmentation it had hoped to overcome.[57] Likewise sexology exploded as a discourse, falling out in ever more unusual fields of study outside its strict domain, insofar as its own mania for categorization issued from the belief that sexual subjects must be studied not as a totality but rather as a discontinuous and heterogeneous series of "cases" (whose equivocal testimony formed the uneasy evidence of the discipline). This "constant creation of otherness" (Luhmann's phrase) disconcerted the rule of reason, making disorientation itself central to social thought in the first decades of the 1900s. Even as sexology and its social-scientific offspring combine analysis of breakdown, individuation, and social groundlessness with a traditional belief in a natural or regular sexual identity, the latter commitment finally yields pride of place to the restless and irregular desires, the perverse relations and the prolific instances of "maladjustment," on which its practitioners are fixated.

IV

Cast in these terms, the sexological bent of early twentieth-century social science might appear to substantiate Foucault's claim that "modern society is . . . in actual fact, and directly, perverse."[58] And as much as the present book is indebted to Foucault's genealogy of modern sexuality, I also elaborate features of the modern period that have not received their due under the aegis of Foucauldian method. Just as this method tends to devote more attention to discipline than to anomie, so Foucault's attitude toward sexuality (as outlined in his important studies of "bio-power" from *The Birth of the Clinic* on) has focused on the coherence rather than on the contingency or fragmentariness of power/knowledge systems. As a form of taxonomy, a function of categories and nomenclature, sexuality in the Foucauldian scheme emerges as the means to singularize and to place each individual with a specific identity. It provides a safe ontological harbor for an ever more efficacious epistemological governance. Yet for social theorists around 1900, neither ontology nor epistemology was particularly stable, and the focus on sexual desire rather than on sexual identity was indicative of the conceptual crisis these thinkers faced. Foucault refers to "the frozen countenance of the perversions" as "a fixture of th[e] game" of power through sexuality.[59] Yet far from fixed or "frozen," perversion was not a categorical niche populated by distinct species of sexual deviants so much as synonymous with the breakdown, the vexing precariousness, of categorization itself.[60] "In modern society," the sociologist Elsie Clews Parsons writes in *Social Freedom* (1915), "there is much shifting within each category and much friction."[61] For Parsons, moreover, such categorical slippages were most visible in what she calls the ascent of "sex mobility" (*SF* 28)—in which, among other changes, "the principle of permanence will cease to be the final criterion of virtue in mating" (*SF* 34).

In this study of modernism and sexuality I have thus supplemented Foucault's "will to knowledge" with the work of social theorists who trace a different genealogy of post-Enlightenment thought from the Foucauldian account that has set the general terms of recent inquiry. These authors describe a modernity that both complements and diverges in crucial ways from the disciplinary model. Foucault has characterized "modern society" as "a closely linked grid of disciplinary coercions whose purpose is in fact to assure the cohesion of [the] social body."[62] Embracing the modernist tradition of social thought that Foucault disclaims, the sociologist Anthony Giddens denies the possibility of such "cohesion" on the very grounds that Foucault premises it: the proliferation of knowledge systems. Rather than integrating the individual with the social world, according to Giddens, modern knowledge "actually subverts reason, at any rate where reason is understood as the gaining of certain knowledge."[63] And Niklas Luhmann argues that while modern expert systems may hope to make the social world transparent, their simultaneous aims to refine their techniques, "to improve them, to render them more complex, and to make them more easily comprehensible" undo one another in practice. The contradictory drive to intricacy and simplicity in expert systems "raises the levels of complexity and opaqueness in the shared universe and certainly does not lead to consensus."[64]

Giddens and Luhmann together resituate the terms for grasping how knowledge is experienced by those on whom it is exercised. Since I am concerned here with those figures whom modern knowledge has been most ambivalent about defining or classifying—the largely underclass others whose deviance from social norms became articulated simultaneously as an erotic deviation—I have felt drawn to the sociological account of sexuality and knowledge less as a replacement than as a foil for testing the Foucauldian description of modern socialization. Even in the most abstract accounts of social life (as in Luhmann's systems theory) the sociological tradition retains, if uneasily and confusedly, a connection between epistemological dislocation and the material conditions of that dislocation. This is only to say that whereas Foucault privileges discourses, sociology by definition privileges social relations. The failure of consensus that Luhmann and Giddens find in expert knowledges parallels the dislocation that Luhmann attributes to the modern self in particular and to modernity in general.

Given this commitment to social relations as "ultimately determining," we might not be surprised that in a study called *Love as Passion,* Luhmann closely ties the functional differentiation of modern society to the development of a structure of intimate sexual desire alleged to stand outside general laws and categories. It is a short distance from the dissolution of uniform knowledge systems to the legitimation of an erotic life that exceeds the protocols of familialism and social reproduction. Both Luhmann and Giddens locate modernity's decentering and dislocating features at the heart of modern sexual relations, and offer forceful speculations on how sex, instead of

merely being "socially constructed," helps in fact to determine or to produce the modern social order. In contrast to Foucault's identitarian model
of sexuality, Luhmann's "love as passion" and Giddens's "transformation of
intimacy" both gesture toward conceiving of sexuality as a form of social relation in modernity—rather than the self's exit strategy from the displacements modern society trails in its wake.[65]

In bringing into view the perspective of critics who draw their energy
mainly from the sociological tradition (whose heyday happens to coincide
with the period under discussion in this book), I want to make the case for
a more precise periodization of modernity than those to which we are accustomed. The geographer Peter Taylor has spoken of "the modernization
of modernity" to refer to the beginning of the twentieth century as inaugu-
rating a sea change in what was meant by the appellation "modern."[66] Taylor distinguishes three "modernities," each roughly coincident with a
particular national hegemony: the era of Dutch mercantilism; the era of
British industrialism; and the ascendancy of American mass consumerism.
Taylor's pluralization of modernity is useful for introducing a concept of period that studies of modernity typically omit. We might suggest that whereas
Foucault's modernity concerns the liberal industrial culture of the nineteenth century, the modernity that preoccupies the thinkers of the early
twentieth century concerns the shift away from the confident positivism of
that earlier epoch. The "intellectual concerns" of this generation, Stuart
Hughes has written, "displaced the axis of social thought from the apparent
and objectively verifiable to the only partially conscious area of unexplained
motivation."[67] In the more recent words of James Livingston, who writes
specifically in the context of American modernity, "What distinguishes and
characterizes the intellectual (and political) innovation of the period is its
refusal to be bound by the categories of necessity, production, or class relations."[68]

Livingston's bracing account of this transitional period focuses on "the
confusion of spheres" precipitated by "the transformation of capitalism" between 1890 and 1930.[69] Yet perhaps most distinctive about his book is the
privileged place it accords to the deconstruction of customary class relations
and the correlative principles of production and necessity that served to naturalize those relations for the three centuries we customarily define as "modern." For Livingston, the renovation of social thought in America around
1900 is a response to the breakdown of the fundamental class relations of
the industrial era. "We are suffering today in America from what is called
the labor-question," William James writes in a lecture called "Talks to Students" (1900). "When you go out into the world, you will each and all of you
be caught up in its perplexities."[70] Aside from the "anarchistic discontents
and socialist projects" it encompassed, the labor-question's most vexing di-

mension for James concerned the recession of the foundational moral and economic distinction of the industrial era: the difference between productive and unproductive labor, between work and idleness.[71] This distinction had collapsed paradoxically under the weight of industrial expansion itself. Weber recognized that this paradox—in which thrift and hard work produce the wealth that inevitably erodes asceticism—had been intrinsic to the Protestant ethic dominant in the West since Taylor's "first phase" of modernity.[72]

If the class relations of the industrial era were organized around keeping persons productive at all costs, the custodians of industrial society achieved this objective through what Livingston calls "the extraordinary *cultural* significance accorded the realm of necessity." "It was here, under the sign of necessary labor," Livingston claims, "that the citizens of bourgeois society found the condition of salvation and the groundwork for the production of values in every sense."[73] The rise of monopoly capitalism with its virtually infinite capacity for generating products in effect robbed necessity of its ideological force. "What distinguishes the development of industrial capitalism," Livingston notes, "is surely the expansion of socially necessary labor beyond every inherited limit, to the point where it seemed as if commodity production had become an end in itself."[74] According to Livingston, this transition to the distinctly American modernity of the twentieth century entailed a shift in mentality whereby thinkers like James, Dewey, and their followers sought to dismantle necessity and productivity as fundamental determinants of the material world. By 1900 the causal primacy of production and the enshrinement of necessity as the basis for social meaning were giving way to what Simon Patten called "the new basis of civilization" in a 1907 book of that title. This "new basis," according to Patten, was a society founded on surplus and abundant wealth, on the evolution of a "pleasure economy" based on desire out of the archaic remnants of a "pain economy" rooted in subsistence.[75] And hence it was a society in which, according to Elsie Clews Parsons, class was vanishing as a social factor in the "solvent" of a money economy. "Money undermines the customary foundations of caste," Parsons claims; "it introduces confusion into those matters caste once claimed for its own . . . not least into caste endogamy" (*SF* 59).

Surplus of the sort that Patten and Parsons view as an unqualified social boon in the form of breaking down "distinctions of dress or diet, or housing, of consumption in general" (*SF* 59) was of course only the obverse of the less agreeable abundance that took the form of an excessive population of unemployed and underemployed workers. Crucial to the undermining of the inherited antinomy between productive and unproductive labor that James and his contemporaries puzzled over was the development of an economic order that, in the words of William Miller Collier, "rendered labor useless."[76] "Displacement of labor is the inevitable incident of labor-saving machinery and labor-saving organizations," Collier argues in *The Trusts* (1900). "It is the absolutely necessary accompaniment of industrial progress."[77] While Collier treats the displacement of labor as more or less a function of mechanization, he skirts the fact that displacement bolstered the new corporate-managerial economy in the form of "seasonal" unemployment—whereby masses of workers were regularly put off jobs to protect profits from wages. This period spawned what Livingston calls American thought's "discovery of contingency"[78] as a radical alternative to the principle of necessity that had previously ordered philosophical discourse. Yet the jubilant exploitation of this philosophical potential among pragmatists like James was always pursued in the darker shadow of a very different form of exploitation—that of a social world that incorporated what economist Don Lescohier called "persistent labor surpluses" directly into the economic engine of modernity.[79] The dislocation of the self that James advocated as a way of liberating consciousness from the tyranny of necessity and nature was never far removed from the dislocation of those laborers whom market capitalism understood as a fetter on the expansion of profit. "The employing part of society long ago adjusted itself to an excess of workers over positions for them," Patten writes (*NB* 99).

We might surmise that the goal of the new century's social thought, which was obsessed with perversion and unexplained desire, arose from a crisis rooted in an economy that, prizing portability and chance, made displacement a fundamental condition of a whole class of persons. Parsons alludes to the "compact host" of "restless, ambitious spirits who cross the boundaries of class, passing from class to class for varying lures" (*SF* 52). Because they were essentially dispensable and mobile, such persons became difficult to classify according to conventional rules. Patten refers to "the hundreds of thousands of workers" whose "advance has been so swift and urgent that social restraints have fallen from them" (*NB* 80). For Patten, this "new class" of laborers was by definition restive and unruly, and their actions appeared unguided by any principle except that of sheer desire. "They have been changed," he writes, "from drilled and dutiful beings to raw recruits of an economic freedom, which to them is complete because in the exercise of it they for the first time gratify their wants and keep pace with their material desires" (*NB* 80).

Given the susceptibility of this workforce to the pull of desire, to what Parsons calls "varying lures," it is no surprise that Patten would define these "peripatetics of industry" through their embrace of "a mobility which is without thoughtful far-seeing purpose" (*NB* 81). Yet Patten views the working class not only as victims of the displacements of a surplus society (with its "excess of workers over positions") but also as its paradoxical beneficiaries.

The ability to move from job to job with a "line of discarded employers trailing behind him" indicates the worker's own canny exploitation of the modern division of labor, whose expansive variety of positions "swings his mind into wider arcs and gives the spur to his imagination" (*NB* 99). As Lescohier claims, the new economy has generated a class of persons "who are continually passing through jobs rather than into them."[80]

Neither Patten nor Lescohier is pleased by this turn of events where the working classes are concerned. The downside to such freedom from "restraint" among the new class of workers is that, or so Patten argues, "they have broken old habits of fealty to bonds; they have forgotten the sympathies that made good service to employers a virtue to be sought" (*NB* 80). In other words, they have traded in the questionable virtues of a static, stratified society (faithfulness, common cause, a shared sense of purpose) for the "dynamism" of a free market in labor that brings both risks and pleasures. Thus for Patten "the environment of the respectable poor has become identical with that of the underworld" because both attend to the same "glittering unwholesome pleasures" (*NB* 52) fostered by urban life. In embracing the pleasure economy as a way to fend off the "unbroken round of monotonous work" that "disintegrates" the proprieties of "family life" (*NB* 52), among other "bonds of fealty," the poor have given up on respectability as a social aspiration. In this surrender, according to Patten, "the careless, insolent workmen" are indistinguishable from "the domineering, self-centered capitalists" who exploit them, "in that they have broken the social bonds that curbed their ancestors" (*NB* 84). And this mutual resemblance leads Patten to conclude, as Parsons does, that capitalists and laborers have ceased to be "distinct classes" and instead appear as "fluid groups of men hastily passing through the temporary economic stages that replace the older social stratification" (*NB* 85).

Patten explicitly voices the widespread suspicion that the customary "distinct classes" were undergoing radical erosion by dynamic and "fluid" processes by turns locatable in industrial transformation, in the development of a leisure economy, and in individual desires. As Patten's example also implies, this suspicion could take either progressive or reactionary form—or more typically a dense blend of the two. Yet if Patten's analysis remains divorced from real persons, circulating in the referentially fuzzy domain of an undifferentiated multitude of "workmen," then it may be useful to attend to a contemporary type who crystallized the fluidity, the dissolute sexuality, and the class-mixing brought on by the waning of what historians call "producer culture." I have in mind a social type that Lewis Erenberg analyzes in his study of New York nightlife around 1900—the "tango pirate" who embodied the middle-class nightmare of collapsed moral sensibility, caste boundaries, and the ethos of productive society. His "employment" consisted of giving pleasure for money to the single and married women who attended the afternoon dances, the "tango teas," that New York cafes began organizing around 1912. As Erenberg describes these occasions, "the management hired dancing partners, or gigolos, to take the unescorted women through their paces." These "swarthy, lower-class" men tended overwhelmingly to be "marked as disreputable by their sensuality and ethnicity" and to embody an ambiguous gender performance—both "willfully aggressive" and "effeminate, will-less, and dependent on women for money."[81] As one of the "parasites" of the pleasure economy, the lower-class café gigolo made his living, as Ethel Mumford put it in a *Harper's* column in 1912, off the "careless forming of undesirable acquaintances, the breaking down of barriers of necessary caution."[82] To the question that Patten, William James, and others posed—what becomes of people in the absence of a producer culture?—the tango pirate was the disturbing answer where the working classes were concerned. Confusing gender roles and confounding caste lines, collapsing work into play, the tango pirate combined the idleness of the loafer or "parasite" with the improper motion of a turbulent dancing body. He not only made all the wrong moves but seduced others into making them too.

Like many lurid figures in the period, the tango pirate stood at the intersection of rhetorical excess and material reality. The actual number of tango pirates bore no legitimate relation to their perceived social impact. Yet while the hysteria incited by such figures (including immigrants, tramps, and "clandestine prostitutes") may have overestimated any genuine threat they posed, our realization of this panic does not moot either the causes or the consequences of the Progressive-era discourse of class and sexuality. Whereas the sociological reality of racial suicide, white slavery, or the tramp invasion may have been negligible, the real social changes to which these outbreaks of erotic and class instability referred were not. Just because it distorts real social crises, the hysterical mode that informs much of the class conflict and erotic difference of the early twentieth century has significant allegorical value in parsing that society. Few women may have actually been prostitutes, for instance, but many women professed to work to gratify their desire for independence; and many women, especially among the working class, did not draw a fine line between dating for the sake of affection and dating for the sake of a paid night out. Likewise, few immigrants were as bloodthirsty, degenerate, or antisocial as the nativists made them out to be. But a great number of immigrants eschewed American culture and treated the nation (as did its capitalist overlords) in sheerly instrumental terms, having no interest in the country's value system apart from those of its relatively high wages and easy economic opportunities. Women workers, immigrants, tramps, and casual workers all enacted a social mobility whose lack of inherited direction or aim inverted the dictates of social mobility as producer culture understood it—as a gradual and orderly elevation of the self-controlled and strong-willed individual. It is the subject in transit, the migrant worker without a sense of place or the fast woman without a sense of restraint, who dominates the modernization of modernity. It is to such figures I now turn.

Chapter Two

Chance, Choice, and *The Wings of the Dove*

"I t is assuredly true," Henry James writes in "The Question of the Opportunities" (1898),

> that literature for the billion will not be literature as we have hitherto
> known it at its best. But if the billion give the pitch of production and
> circulation, they do something else besides; they hang before us a wide
> picture of opportunities—opportunities that would be opportunities
> still even if, reduced to the *minimum,* they should be only those offered
> by the vastness of the implied history. It is impossible not to entertain
> with patience and curiosity the presumption that life so colossal must
> break into expression at points of proportionate frequency. These
> places, these moments will be the chances.[1]

"Chance," the operative term in this passage, unites the sense of fate or accident with the more modern and positive connotation of opportunity. The new public invites James to speculate on the coming of an innovative kind of social possibility composed of equal parts risk and choice. To James observing "the billion," opportunity becomes inseparable from questioning (hence the title of his essay). Every instance of it requires interrogation of its conditions, just as the recording of "history" (the novelist's prerogative) becomes bound by the need to explore the implicit or hidden "places" within the seemingly unbreachable carapace of the mass public. Further scrutiny reveals this casing as honeycombed with intimate, strange, and chance encounters, both chosen and risked. In this chapter, I examine the difference that masses make in James's thinking about what counts as a proper story. If the "billion" herald the obsolescence of the traditional forms that literature has taken, what they put in their place is not yet knowable. Rather than reproving the "colossal" scale these masses represent, James is far less sure of how to take them, largely because their "break[ing]" the forms of traditional society makes it difficult to see where he stands. As this citation implies and as this chapter makes explicit, "places" in late James are less the means of determining where one belongs (as in knowing one's place) than footholds from which one might gain only "moment[ary]" purchase on an increasingly tractionless world.

Multitudes cannot help giving rise to "expressions" like these. The sheer volume of persons that modern culture mobilizes seems to James coincident with randomness and so coincident with the displacement of proper conduct by unseemly chance. Take the case of Densher and Kate's relationship in *The Wings of the Dove,* which James traces to a series of accidental "moments" and "places" of encounter. Though the affair begins typically enough under the auspices of a party at a gallery, during which Kate and Densher "had taken each other in with interest," James is intent on assigning this romance not to the careful precincts of courtship and elite party-going but to the eddies of sheer fluke.[2] "Without a happy hazard six months later," he writes,

> the incident [their meeting at a garden party] would have closed in that account of it. The accident meanwhile had been as natural as anything in London ever is: Kate had one afternoon found herself opposite Mr. Densher on the Underground Railway. The day and the hour were darkness, there were six other persons and she had been busy seating herself; but her consciousness had gone to him as straight as if they had come together in some bright stretch of a desert. They had on neither part a second's hesitation; they looked across the choked compartment exactly as if she had known he would be there and he had expected her to come in; so that, though in the conditions they could only exchange the greeting of movements, smiles, abstentions, it would have been quite in the key of these passages that they should have alighted at the very next station. (*WD* 1:54)

It is only through the "choked compartment" that Kate and Densher can apprehend each other: the "all but full[ness]" of the subway car reveals the "angle" by which Kate views Densher. The "busy" public surrounding them becomes the unwitting audience for the tense sexual game of "abstentions" they play together. It is taken for granted that an unchaperoned woman cannot acknowledge the advances of a strange man on a crowded train; Kate's awareness and clandestine flouting of this social rule give this exchange its erotically loaded and cruisy "key."

Not only the crowded train but also the fullness of time has vanished in Kate's vision of Densher: "her consciousness had gone to him as straight as if they had come together in some bright stretch of a desert." In an important sense, the train car is exactly such a desert, since the standard culture of "the billion" paradoxically abolishes the culture of standards as James has known it by burying traditional modes and norms of conduct in the shifting sands—the "Underground"—of anonymity and mobility. The subway shifts people around, puts them together in new configurations, and, as the "chance" meeting between Kate and Densher proves, alters the relation between public and private, giving rise to an unorthodox domain of connec-

tion founded on "happy hazard" rather than on rituals of courtship and social connection.[3] Rumors of Kate's romantic attachments, after all, come to
Kate's sister not through channels of licit discourse but rather because that
woman's sisters-in-law, the Misses Condrip, have kept "their ear to the
ground" and "spent their days in prowling" (*WD* 1:43).

In calling attention to their subterranean character, James doesn't give
Densher and Kate a proper ground to stand on as they navigate their
charged erotic exchanges; he withholds from his characters (and his readers) confidence in where they are coming from or going. Nor is this withholding of a trustworthy frame of reference limited to the subway. The
beginning of *The Wings of the Dove* reveals Kate Croy alone in her father's
apartment, "changing her place, moving from shabby sofa to the armchair
upholstered in a glazed cloth that gave at once—she had tried it—the sense
of the slippery and of the sticky" (*WD* 1:3). This "sense" pervades Kate's relation both to the apartment and to what the apartment represents: a di-
minished expectation of what the world can give those who have thwarted
its norms, as Lionel Croy has. Lionel's "crime" is never named, though Eve
Kosofsky Sedgwick makes the compelling case that he has been compromised by a homosexual "scandal."[4] All that Kate knows for certain is that "he
has done some particular thing. It's known—only, thank God, not known to
us" (*WD* 1:68).

Part of the reason is that it simply cannot be known—not only because it
is unspeakable but also, and more interestingly, because what it means to
defy the norms of decency has become uncertain. Like the hideously upholstered chair, those norms are "slippery" as well as "sticky," requiring one
to adhere to them as much as they are prone to shift their meaning. Kate instead experiences her father's room as a place that will not admit of proper
positions. As she notes on the balcony: "the narrow black house-fronts . . .
constituted quite the publicity implied by such privacies. One felt them in
the room exactly as one felt the room—the hundred like it or worse—in the
street" (*WD* 1:3). In the simplest terms what Kate feels she is doing in her
father's apartment is wrong, a trespass James likens to prying into someone's
private life. In the more complex light by which we are meant to interpret
this scene, Kate's restless shuttling indicates that the homely sphere of private life has ceased to provide a guarantee to self-containment or certitude.
Divided between publicity and privacy, slippery and sticky, Lionel's home
leaves Kate with the uncanny feeling of not knowing exactly where she
stands. Thus when Lionel arrives, "it was as if the place were her own and he
the visitor with susceptibilities" (*WD* 1:8)—a hypothetical situation that
makes Kate sound more like a prostitute than a dutiful daughter.

This inversion of the order of things is built into the material world that
James's novel renders, making the stabilization of norms a task both futile

and interminable. Thus Densher considers it his job as a journalist to "keep setting up 'codes' " for the "public" (*WD* 1:91) because those codes are continually under duress; the role of the newspaper is to tell people insecure about their conduct how they should or should not behave. And he reaches a similar impasse to Kate's when confronted by Mrs. Lowder's "massive florid furniture," the "immense" "expanse" (*WD* 1:76) of which he sees as a "desert" (*WD* 1:77). "These things," James writes, "finally represented for him a portentous negation of his own world of thought" (*WD* 1:79). Why furniture should have this affinity for disorienting the self in *The Wings of the Dove* is a question that can be answered only by referring to the sheer abundance of it—a plenitude that paradoxically, as with the subway interlude between Kate and Densher, transforms traditional claims of propriety and place into a "desert" of uncertainty. In Aunt Maud's case, the furniture estranges "thought" not only because it is "vulgar" but also because it fails to be "rangeable under one rubric" (*WD* 1:78). While "conclusively British," for example, Maud's things "abounded in rare material—precious woods, metals, stuffs, stones . . . rosewood and marble and malachite" (*WD* 1:79). In short these things are only *barely* British, having been delivered from the far reaches of a global market of which the British empire is the undisputed master. Their multiplicity bespeaks a varied world at odds with "the good conscience" and "big balance" with which the British drawing room endows these objects. Just as Maud's furniture cannot finally disguise its multiple origins, so the abundance of matter in James's novel mirrors a social world in which no decision or choice can be "conclusive."

James forges a strong link between a global culture of consumption and the epistemological problem of a recognizable "rubric," of legible "codes" by which to navigate that material culture. Returning to Lionel Croy's own drawing room, we can see how this relation between disheveled matter and unstable judgment ramifies into the novel from the beginning. Having arrived at her father's "sordid lodgings" with the noble aim of throwing her lot in with his, Kate quickly confesses that this choice (like the layout of the drawing room itself) originates in no discernible design: "I don't at all . . . make out your life," she tells her father, "but whatever it is I hereby offer to accept it" (*WD* 1:15). From its opening scene, the novel explores what it means to imagine desire as a function of choosing, and more important, as a choosing whose determination remains inevitably "slippery," beyond one's reference or control.

This pervasive sense of slippery referents should give us serious pause. It indicates that our own efforts to gain real interpretive control over *The Wings of the Dove* through historical analysis inevitably risks a mistaken vantage, since the novel explicitly makes problematic such ideas as vantage, context, and frame of reference. I advance a reading of late James somewhat different from the critical model that has sought to expose the real historical referents—consumerism, class privilege—just barely contained within his novels.[5] The problem with such accounts is that in exposing, say, "the consuming vision of Henry James" (as Jean-Christophe Agnew does in a classic essay of that name) these analyses assume that consumption is a static or monolithic as opposed to an endlessly malleable category, which is how James understood it. Though my reading owes a great deal to approaches like Agnew's, I mean less to uncover a shadow plot hidden under and stalking the surface drama of the Jamesian novel than to articulate the structure of feeling that led James to see categories as referentially chancy, as unsettled and mobile. My argument is that James's late fiction responds to a cultural context imagined at every level to be in danger of groundlessness. I suggest that even as it attempts to suspend the diffuse social anxieties over improper movement from one class (of persons or things) to another, the Jamesian novel inevitably reconfigures groundlessness, referential slipperiness, and categorical confusion as subjects of suspense. The drama of chancy mobility becomes for James the very means for moving his novel along.[6] I also argue that the proper historical vantage for witnessing these formally and thematically embedded aspects of James's fiction is not a single static cultural referent—consumerism, for example—but a confluence of developments in the late nineteenth century, from the ascent of risk culture and the rise of incorporation to the emergence of a transient population of immigrant workers and the questions of placement they raised.

One of the most evasive terms hovering over *The Wings of the Dove*, a novel that relentlessly joins chance and mobility, is the word "choice." If we try to focus this term for a moment by grounding it in historical context, we discover that choice derives from an ideology that, if not necessarily new, was forcefully *renewed* at the turn of the century: opportunism. James's novel rehearses the implications such an ideology might have for a society undergoing unprecedented transformations in both technology and demography, from the rise of mass transport and communications to the immense redistribution of persons that immigration entailed at the turn of the century. Around 1900 opportunism, like choice, was a referentially fitful term. Though inscribed in the national imaginary from as early as the Declaration of Independence, opportunism underwent a conceptual renovation around 1900. An earlier moment in American culture understood the lariat of opportunism to extend no farther than a modest rise in social class or the attainment of self-sufficient employment or enterprise. The Hawthorne who emerges from James's 1879 book might illustrate the exemplary opportunistic American at mid-century. "His six volumes of notebooks," James writes,

are a sort of monument to an unagitated fortune. Hawthorne's career
. . . was passed, for the most part, in a small and homogeneous society, in
a provincial, rural community; it had few perceptible points of contact
with what is called the world, with public events, with the manners of his
time, even with the life of his neighbors.[7]

What licenses this distorted view of Hawthorne's "unagitated fortune" is less
James's failure to recall Hawthorne's early incarnation of literary celebrity
or the numerous government posts he held than James's not incorrect perception that American life in Hawthorne's day placed a premium on the
miniature, the "provincial" (*H* 17), the "picturesque" (*H* 12). In Hawthorne's America, "fortune" is fortunate when it resists agitation. "A village,"
James writes, summing up this antebellum attitude, "thinks extremely well
of itself, and is absolute in its own regard" (*H* 15).

James's exile from American soil has long been seen as a flight from the
"absolute" self-regard of a society whose horizons of opportunity were un-
equal to his worldly aspirations. If claustrophobia describes James's tone in
Hawthorne, a kind of agoraphobic fit aimed at the disorienting groundlessness of American life would overtake the James of *The American Scene* decades
later. James's sense of the chances awaiting him was thwarted in the American context, where opportunity knocked but seldom. In the twenty-year in-
terval of his visits to the United States, however, opportunism acquired far
grander pretensions than the reflexive self-sufficiency of the New England
town. If the "pursuit of happiness" in antebellum society tended to perceive
striving in terms of an eventual settlement of the self within the normative world of domesticity, the late nineteenth century witnessed a shift in
opportunism that, reversing the coordinates of the earlier dispensation,
sought happiness in pursuit itself. Mobility became key to amending the social calculus of opportunism in American life. The dissolution of traditional
social ties and the rise of the urban society made it clear that where one
was—the "self-regarding" rural village, the "provincial" town, the city neighborhood encroached upon by undesirable arrivistes—was not so alluring as
the place one ultimately wanted to be. The horizon of opportunism receded
incessantly by unsettling the narrow range of things customarily subsumed
under the rubric of the chosen, the contingent, the conditional.

The desire to move onward and upward was informed above all by the
company one wanted to keep. Though anti-immigrant sentiment was hardly
new in American society, by 1900 a fresh concern dominated nativist consciousness with regard to the great wave of eastern and southern European
migrants who arrived in the decades on each side of the turn of the century.
The discourse of immigration at 1900 was characterized by equivocal desires
both to embrace the immigrant as a convert to American life and to distance

the alien as racially and linguistically unassimilable. This ambivalence reflected the fact that many arrivals, especially Italian and Sicilian, saw the United States as a place of sheer opportunism and as a culture they would never assimilate. "They pay allegiance to some other country while they live upon the substance of our own," Representative James Thomas Heflin told Congress in 1921.[8] As historians of Atlantic immigration have argued, an important pattern of migration from southern Europe to urban enclaves in the United States was that of short-term, intense labor and accumulation to facilitate a return to a Mediterranean village with enough capital to marry, settle, and acquire property.[9] Such "birds of passage" raised fears not only about the infiltration of U.S. society but also about a more disturbing threat: the idea that the borders of that society were not fixed gateways with clearly marked entrances but porous apertures through which persons and things could flow easily in and out. Nativism in the United States was as much a protest against foreign invasion as a way to deflect the more troubling idea of a nation without a certifiable sense of place.[10]

If this brief digression on immigration patterns seems far afield of *The Wings of the Dove*, we might recall that Merton Densher's excursion to America on behalf of a London magazine is undertaken as a necessary labor and a prelude, however precarious, to his being sufficiently capitalized to settle the question of marriage to Kate Croy. Like communities of immigrants who flocked to the United States for the industrial labor, Densher also exiles himself temporarily to the "land of opportunity" in order to reap its rewards. But Densher's fate is not simply analogous to the immigrant's; James explicitly likens him, along with his "migratory parents" (*WD* 1:91), to an immigrant who, "brave enough though his descent to English earth," "had passed through zones of air that had left their ruffle on his wings—he had been exposed to initiations indelible" (*WD* 1:93). Like the immigrant, the winged Densher is eternally a bird of passage, a stranger in the land, and this is what draws Kate to him: "It was revealed to her how many more foreign things were in Merton Densher than he had hitherto taken the trouble to catalogue" (*WD* 1:92). Densher's life consists in "his want of the right marks, his foreign accidents, his queer antecedents" (*WD* 1:90). Just as he cannot "refuse" the offer of the trip to America, "not being in a position to refuse anything," what determines Densher is a haphazard or volatile existence which, like Kate's "restless" one, he has not so much elected as been forced to navigate at his own peril: "his being chosen for such an errand confounded his sense of proportion" (*WD* 1:85).

As James's novel suggests, the question of choice at the turn of the century was affiliated with risk more than it was aligned with the certitude of a progressively more satisfying middle-class life. Densher's "confounded" "sense of proportion" hints at the lack of compass or scale implied by the expanding horizon of opportunism. In a conversation with Kate, Densher alludes to his mother's "scale of opportunity" as a copyist of "famous pictures in great museums." This recollection gives a measure of the distance between her successful labor and her son's more precarious career. Because her copies "had a perfection that persuaded," the "'placing' of her work" was "blissfully usual" (*WD* 1:93). As a portraitist who not only frames the world but also copies other images of it exactly, Mrs. Densher shares with the Hawthorne of James's 1879 biography a sense of place and scale that eludes her son's generation, for whom opportunism becomes detached from "placing," from business as "usual."

Densher's inability to refuse the trip to America, or even to figure out whether he is permitted to refuse (since not he but someone else has "chosen" this trip for him), indicates a great deal about the dilemma of choice in James's time. For James, choosing assumes a complexity that cannot be quite mastered or domesticated by the precepts of consumer culture. One way to phrase this complexity would be to note the paradox that, however we might resist it, we cannot live without the belief that we "choose ourselves." "Choice and its passive form, consent," legal theorist Lawrence Friedman writes, "remain part of the inner definition of freedom. In the West, moreover, there is no cultural alternative to choice, that is, to the notion of the rational, independent human being who chooses her life."[11] We might accord to "choice" in modernity the status of what Cornelius Castoriadus calls a "metacategory," under which are ranged, subsumed, and equated social forms as distinct as desire, preference, expression, individualism, volition, and autonomy.[12] Prying apart this metacategory and its expectations is one thing James's novel allows us to begin doing.

Choice is arguably the master narrative of twentieth-century subjectivity. In the guise of "rational choice," for example, it is the narrative at the center of the most influential analytical model in contemporary social science. The rational-choice economist Gary Becker characterizes the "economic approach to human interaction" as the study of how persons—what Becker calls "decision units"—enter human exchanges with the goal of "maximizing benefits." "All human behavior can be viewed as involving participants who maximize their utility from a stable set of preferences."[13] Choices, in other words, are necessarily transparent to the agents—"decision units"—who act on them, and this transparency extends as well to the clarity and predictability of their actions. If choosing is a cultural narrative, then its fictional analogue would be realism, with its emphasis on probability and its sense of events unfolding in an orderly fashion in time and space. Realism, Elizabeth Ermath suggests in her study of the genre, provides the "fullest expression" of the "revelations of sequence": "In realism, identity becomes series-dependent."[14] It makes sense that James—who whetted his career on a

realist enterprise he would by the turn of the century come to distrust—
would be inclined to take the narrative of choosing to task as well, given that
both realism and choice devolve on an irreducible sense of probability.

To see that James was attuned to the problem of choice and made its complexities a topic of his fiction throughout his career, we need only recall the
harsh lesson Isabel Archer learns in *Portrait of a Lady* (1881). Whereas early
in the novel Isabel can tell Caspar Goodwood, "I can do what I choose—I
belong quite to the independent class," thus equating choice with autonomy, by the end of the novel she thinks very differently of this freedom.[15]
"The world in truth had never seemed so large," James writes. "[I]t seemed
to open out all round, to take the form of a mighty sea, where she floated
in fathomless waters" (*PL* 2:435). The story that *Portrait of a Lady* tells is not
so much the disenchantment of Isabel's romance of choice as its transformation into a reality of "fathomless" risks, where to judge means less to seize
the world's possibilities than to struggle for survival among its sublime "train
of images" (*PL* 2:436). Far from clarifying matters for Isabel, the freedom
to choose is inseparable from opacity: "When darkness returned, she was
free" (*PL* 2:436). Choice, which begins as the promise of freedom for the
self, ends as a set of compromises that the self experiences as inescapable.
Isabel's understanding of her judgment as a compensation for her lack of
money and conventionality is transformed over the course of the novel into
a sense that judgment is both fated—one cannot help judging—and unreliable—while one cannot help judging, one can never be certain of the propriety of one's decisions. *Portrait of a Lady* ends by treating choice as a
compulsion, a matter of survival—in other words, something her life depends on rather than the sign of her independence.

And in fact what Isabel chooses at the end of the novel is exactly a life in
which questions of choice, of independence, no longer apply. In *Portrait's*
penultimate scene she does not choose what she most desires—a physical
connection with Caspar Goodwood, a man not her husband whose "hard
manhood" (*PL* 2:436) blinds her and makes her feel as if she is drowning.
If the liaison with Goodwood represents a kind of "fathomless" plummet
into a form of desire that allows for no purchase on the world, the "very
straight path" that "she knew now" (*PL* 2:436) to take—the path back to
Rome and to Gilbert, to what Goodwood calls the "ghastly form" (*PL* 2:433)
of a sham marriage—at least has the advantage of appearing right and
proper. Here Isabel trades in the opacity of an open-ended desire for the
certitude of a social "form"—marital life—whose sanctity neither she nor
anyone around her quite believes in. Yet the very artificiality of that form
becomes the grounds for sanctifying it. In other words, *The Portrait of a Lady*
produces the renunciation of desire through the belief in a social form
that makes choice feel like fate, like destiny. In this novel belief and choos-

ing are at odds, and the former state ultimately redeems the excesses of the latter.

Early and late, James was interested in the problem of belief, and particularly in whether and to what degree belief in the "ghastly form" of marriage might subdue the amorphousness of sexual desire. But whereas *The Portrait of a Lady* generates a narrative of renunciation through the metaphor of a "straight path," *The Wings of the Dove* is a book in which straight paths are all but impossible to come by—and thus a book in which any advantage to believing in such paths is radically attenuated. In general in *Wings,* belief is a category under duress, as we can glean from a moment involving Kate and her patronymic. Early on in *The Wings of the Dove* Kate wonders what she would do about her family's shame "had she only been a man."

> It was the name, above all, she would take in hand—the precious name she so liked and that, in spite of the harm her wretched father had done it, wasn't yet past praying for. She loved it in fact the more tenderly for that bleeding wound. But what could a penniless girl do with it but let it go? (*WD* 1:6)

This name, of course, is Croy. It is a name we hear early on in the novel, but it is not the first word; from the beginning of the novel, Kate's name is pleonastic: "She waited, Kate Croy, for her father" (*WD* 1:3). What this name does for James, as for Kate, is to deflect uncertainty, pronominal or otherwise, by stabilizing the figure to whom the name belongs. But as Kate herself suggests, the name does not really belong to her; it is a displaced classifier, and moreover is split or disintegrated, suffering from a "bleeding wound." Not just a surname, Croy has an allegorical connotation this passage makes plain in its reference to "praying": it derives from the French for "belief." If this brief passage stages Kate's relation to the name of the father as a Christian passion play replete with stigmata, it is only because the status of belief here has acquired the agon of a testing of faith.

The assault on belief in revealed truth would have been quite recognizable to James. It was the interrogation of this category, after all, that provided the catalyst for the development of pragmatism at the turn of the century. Why do people believe? According to William James in "The Will to Believe" (1896), people believe because other people believe: "Our faith is faith in someone else's faith, and in the greatest matters this is most the case."[16] For James, belief is contingent on "the *prestige*" of opinions, a term that evokes the crucial basis of faith: "*[o]ur passional nature*" (*WB* 20). "Faith based on desire is certainly a lawful and possibly an indispensable thing" (*WB* 29). Understanding belief as an expression of desire, James further defines the process of believing as a form of choosing among "options," "living, forced, and momentous" (*WB* 14). The assimilation of belief to desire and choice is pragmatism's legacy to American philosophical thought. This particular transfer has far-reaching consequences for James's conceptualization of pragmatism, leading him to conclude in his 1906 lectures on the topic that "our obligation to acknowledge truth, so far from being unconditional, is tremendously conditioned."[17] And what turns out to condition belief in James is something like the vicissitudes of the material body. In *Pragmatism* he claims, "Temperament gives man a stronger bias than any of his more strictly objective premises" (*PMT* 12), by virtue of the fact that "no one escapes subjection" to "self" or to "body in the substantial or metaphysical sense" (*PMT* 88). Thus when James shifts belief from the realm of the absolute to the realm of the possible, he does so by supplanting a theological calculus with a calculus of pleasure and gratification. "A new opinion counts as true," then, "just as it gratifies an individual's desire to assimilate the novel in his experience to his beliefs in stock" (*PMT* 36).

Yet the ambiguous or chancy space opened up here by a retreat from the absolute is one into which James oddly refused his own invitation to enter. This demurral issues, I argue, from James's awareness that a world in which each person desires according to his own "temperament" would be a world of intolerable dissensus and uncertainty. I take this awareness to be what is at stake in *Pragmatism*'s last lecture, in which James says: "In our world, the wishes of the individual are only one condition. Other individuals are there with other wishes and they must be propitiated first" (*PMT* 139). Here something like desire as a potentially coercive or disruptive form of power comes into play. James cites F. H. Bradley's claim that humanism "demands that we "hold any end however perverted to be rational if I insist on it personally" both to acknowledge the common misperception of pragmatic thinking as "a doctrine of caprice" (*PMT* 124) and to distance himself from the threat of perversion that pragmatism always entails. That James casts this potential state of affairs in an idiom of virtue corrupted is striking. In "The Dilemma of Determinism," James writes: "Future human volitions are as a matter of fact the only ambiguous things we are tempted to believe in" (*WB* 121). This temptation feels like a betrayal of social order by the randomness of desire, and that is in fact how "The Dilemma of Determinism" treats such belief. Appearing in the same volume as "The Will to Believe," this essay resolves the problem of arbitrariness and conditionality hovering over the former by leaving nothing to chance:

> Do not all the motives that assail us, all the futures that offer themselves
> to our choice, spring equally from the soil of the past; and would not ei-
> ther one of them, whether realized through chance or through neces-
> sity, the moment it was realized, seem to us to fit that past, and in the
> completest and most continuous manner to interdigitate with the phe-
> nomena already there? (*WB* 122)

If in "The Will to Believe" James defines belief as something willed or voluntary, in "The Dilemma of Determinism" he redefines belief as valuable because it grants a predictability to the uncertain future by making that future "continuous" with the past:

> A social organism of any sort whatever, large or small, is what it is because each member proceeds to his own duty with a trust that the other members will simultaneously do theirs. Wherever a desired result is achieved by the co-operation of many independent persons, its existence as a fact is a pure consequence of the precursive faith in one another of those immediately concerned. (*WB* 29)

Belief turns out to be the name for a game of mirrors in which the pluralist's tendency toward an irreducible multiplicity of diverse interests cedes to a discourse of resemblance that James justifies by appealing to a metaphor of premodern life—the agrarian "soil of the past," which buries disagreeable or volatile differences of belief, Eumenides-like, in the garden (or grave) of consensus. "Common men find themselves inheriting their beliefs," James writes in *A Pluralistic Universe* (1909). "They jump into them with both feet, and stand there."[18] In drawing out this view of belief in James's work, I suggest that its status is much more vexed and tense than we are accustomed to noting. In an important sense, the idea of inherited belief solves the problem of an endless array of choices and interests by appealing to a notion that we might as well call *chthonic*. By "common men," James means both average and like-minded; the double meaning reinforces the sense that shared beliefs are normative, amounting to something like a mean. Like the autochthons who arise from the soil of Athens, these "common men" are spared the excesses of pluralism by virtue of a propensity to "stand there" on the ground of belief—a propensity both natural and native. "Each would feel an essential consanguinity in the other" (*PU* 12). Such ties rectify the problem of individual choice or desire that James routinely associates in this same essay with the concept of "foreignness" (*PU* 19).

Why such an appeal is necessary has everything to do with the problem that foreignness poses to the stability and order of thought. "The philosophic attempt to define nature so that no one's business is left out, so that no one lies outside the door saying 'Where do *I* come in?' is sure in advance to fail" (*PU* 19). That James chooses a "door" to defend philosophy's necessary and inevitable exclusivity is telling in light of the frequency with which immigrants in U.S. culture were understood to be knocking at the gates— or more precisely battering down those gates with a dizzying array of unsavory philosophical ideas, as in an image by the anti-immigrant illustrator Frank Beard. The unpleasant baggage this cartoon alien shoulders includes "anarchy," "superstition," and "Sabbath desecration." With its implication of

THE STRANGER AT OUR GATE.

EMIGRANT. Can I come in?   UNCLE SAM. I 'spose you can; there's no law to keep you out.

Frank Beard, *The Stranger at Our Gate,* from *The Ram's Horn,* 1896. Courtesy of the Cartoon Center, Ohio State University.

unbelief, the last of these qualities is perhaps most germane to a discussion of James's "will to believe." James's sense that the portal of philosophy can open only so wide gestures toward a tension in the ambivalence with which his culture greeted the "foreign element"—who brought along not only dirty bodies but also dirty minds littered with the detritus of radical Europe.

But this is only to draw out of James's account of pluralism and pragmatism what seems all too frequently overlooked there: the sense that for James the "pluralistic universe" is "a world of finite multifariousness" (*PU* 28), where the accent falls more strongly than we usually note on the "finite." Throughout his late essays on pluralism James betrays the fear that if left unchecked—if allowed to drift out of "finite multifariousness" and into some unspecified infinite—individual choice will lead the self from community into a state of radical anomie. The emphasis these essays place on finiteness, proximity, consanguinity, and belief is meant to put a brake on this ubiquitous threat. Thus, James claims in "A World of Pure Experience" (1904), though it would seem that "the whole system of experiences as they are immediately given presents itself as a quasi-chaos," this disorder is only a mirage, since "out of an initial term in many directions," persons "yet end in the same terminus."[19]

Pragmatism and pluralism emerge in James's thought as complementary answers to a single problem—the radical pluralization of desire that was spurred in large part by strong-willed, mobile, and unassimilable immigrant laborers flooding into and out of the United States around 1900. Above all, James's work introduces and deflects tensions that remain at the heart of modern ideas of how to negotiate cultural otherness. Even as he introduces a compelling account of random and plural choosing—of "alternative paths" for the self to take—James finally draws back from the chasm toward which such paths lead by reverting to the steadfastness, the foundational necessity, of "common" belief.

Such an account of pragmatism may strike us as counterintuitive, given what we know about pragmatism's brash disregard for foundational truth. Yet joining belief to contingency where before it had been inscribed with necessity, pragmatism rewrites belief as a target of opportunity rather than as a symptom of foundational thinking. Richard Rorty argues that "pragmatists drop the appearance-reality distinction in favor of a distinction between beliefs which serve some purposes and beliefs which serve other purposes—for example, the purposes of one group and those of another group."[20] Rorty's winsome account of belief, like James's, is just shy of admitting that belief is fakery, that one believes not out of any spontaneous sense of revealed truth but out of a different kind of necessity. In short, the appearance of belief is necessary because the alternative—a radical absence of consensus—is liable to paralyze the self.

If the will to believe looks on the surface like the apotheosis of radical individualism, minimal burrowing below the discourse of pragmatism reveals its more fitting orientation around the trans-individual collective embodied during pragmatism's emergence by the corporate trust, belief in whose fictive personhood comprised the exemplary article of faith for the "age of surplus." The corporation arises, after all, as a means of dealing with what the late nineteenth century called the problem of "overproduction," the disparity between supply and demand for consumer goods exacerbated by the relentless competition of manufacturers. The aim of the managerial revolution was to foreground planning as the corrective to the randomness of consumer desire. To trust in the trust is to assume that desire can be regulated if not controlled. As James Livingston notes in his important study of the "cultural revolution" of early twentieth-century America, corporate mergers, increased mechanization, and the ascendance of management were different responses to eliminating "the human element"—the factor of interested persons and competing desires, whether of skilled laborers, uncooperative employees, middlemen, or even fickle customers—from the economic equation.[21] Pragmatism was to philosophy what trust-building was to the economy. Both sought to balance a fundamentally contradictory set of values: to embrace desire and the contingency it allowed and to delimit or to channel that desire in ways that maintained social, civil, and economic order.

If on the one hand pragmatism appears to endorse desire as a philosophical "good," on the other hand it clearly prefers desire to be referentially precise, to be shareable and even, in the abstract, identical across persons. And such an understanding of desire ultimately mandates the omission of the very persons—the "human element"—in whom desires are rooted and who are thus inevitably, irreducibly in conflict. The rise of the artificial person implies the eclipse of the real one because in the final analysis, according to corporate mentality, real persons cannot be trusted. Pragmatism's tactical belief in the artificial and conditional operates on similar principles, for pragmatism is the first sustained codification in modern U.S. society of what Niklas Luhmann calls "system trust." He defines such trust as "the ability of the systems" comprising modernity (which range from governments and markets to professional services and communications media) "to maintain conditions or performances which are, within certain limits, identical." Within modern social structures, Luhmann writes, "each trusts on the assumption that others trust."[22] In its emphasis on the circularity of modern trust, Luhmann's definition is close to the anti-foundational structure of belief embedded in William James's claim that "our faith is faith in someone else's faith." The paradox of trust that emerges from the cultural revolution of the turn of the century should be understood as an inverse ratio whereby trust in individuals and in tangible relations decreases the more trust in abstract systems increases. In mass society, with its radical atomization of the self, persons don't—can't—trust one another; they can trust only the impersonal and anonymous structures that other people trust.

Returning to James's novel allows us to see what happens when the eclipse of individual trust by no means bespeaks the triumph of system trust.

This is one of the crucial interventions that James's novel makes. Though James assumes that face-to-face relations between individuals can no longer be relied on to provide even minimal communicative transparency or mutuality (here we might remind ourselves of what Leo Bersani has dubbed "The Jamesian Lie"), he is unconvinced that system trust provides the ground of group consensus that pragmatism requires.[23] Just as Densher disbelieves that the eclectic objects in Maud Lowder's drawing room add up to any "conclusively British" "balance," so James seems less persuaded than his pragmatist contemporaries and successors that belief can be wrested from epistemological doubt and yoked to positive knowledge. For the characters who populate James's novel, belief is not, as it is for pragmatism, equivalent to trust. If "what she believes is the principal thing for us" (*WD* 2:228), as Kate says of Maud Lowder, the very difference that exists between Kate and Densher's belief (on the one hand) and Aunt Maud's (on the other) names this "principal thing" not trust but deception. Like William James, who argued that "the true is the name of whatever proves itself to be good in the way of belief, and good, too, for definite, assignable reasons" (*PMT* 63), Rorty's commitment to the contingency of belief stops short of a referential free fall that would make the "purposes" a belief serves interpretatively inaccessible. Whatever else a belief may refer to, it must refer to a "definite, assignable" purpose clearly discernible to its canny possessor.

One of the odder aspects of *The Wings of the Dove*, by contrast, is a neglect toward referential firmness that is extreme even for late James. Not only are we kept from learning the nature of Lionel Croy's "awful thing," or of Milly Theale's illness, but, more important, we are also prevented from ever realizing the endless "values" in which almost all the novel's characters "believe." Lionel describes Kate as a "tangible value," and she later tells Densher: "My position's a value, a great value, to them" (*WD* 1:95), meaning her father and sister. But Kate's value consists in its instrumentality; it is only through her, as Kate explains to Densher, that Aunt Maud can be reached: "[I]t's through her and through her only that I may help him [Lionel]; just as Marian insists that it's through her, and through her only, that I can help *her*. That's what I mean . . . by their turning me back" (*WD* 1:71). As James suggests by drawing attention to "her eyes aslant on her beautiful averted no less than on her beautiful presented oval" (*WD* 1:5) in the mirror in her father's house, Kate's value is elliptical, "turning back" on itself, never available to straightforward views. Densher refers to her as "a woman whose value would be her differences" (*WD* 1:50). Kate is not the only figure of deflected value in the novel; the value of Aunt Maud also turns out to inhere in her instrumentality. Similarly, Susan Stringham prides herself on Luke Strett's "interest" in her, which amounts to "what he can do with me" (*WD* 2:110) on behalf of Milly.

"The best thing about" Lord Mark, Kate tells Milly, "was that Aunt Maud believed in him" and so "his value was his future" (*WD* 1:178). Like the elliptical belief that understands its object not as a value in itself but as a mediation of another value elsewhere, belief here assumes that the content and certitude of present values must be deferred to an unnamed futurity. Such deferral of value informs the believed no less than the believer, "since," as Kate tells us, "by the same principle she believed in herself."

> "You may ask," Kate said, "what in the world I have to give; and that indeed is just what I'm trying to learn. There must be something, for her [Aunt Maud] to think she can get it out of me. She *will* get it—trust her; and then I shall see what it is; which I beg you to believe I should never have found out for myself." (*WD* 1:180)

Whereas "The Will to Believe" assesses belief as the trust that makes the volitional self continuous and confident in its presence, *The Wings of the Dove* treats belief as an endless deferral and withholding of confidence about the self. Rather than providing Kate with the ground for action, for example, belief in this passage tends to mobilize the believer in states of anticipation. If "The Will to Believe" offers the promise of belief as an option that one seizes irrespective of alternatives, *The Wings of the Dove* understands belief as the name for the thing that one never possesses and is, more important, never sure that one wants. In James's novel, characters never quite apprehend what they're believing in. That is, while the novel's characters believe in choice, they are never certain what their choices are, by virtue of a deferral of value that fails to make any object present for their ready discernment.[24]

What *The Wings of the Dove* produces is not a community of "precursive faith" but a "community of collapse" (*WD* 1:290) wherein different persons with different desires vie for position in the absence of unanimity. This phrase occurs in Milly's reverie at the National Gallery, as she "count[s] the Americans" "whose relation to her failed to act—they somehow did nothing for her" (*WD* 1:290). The novel introduces the problem of perspective or vision as a distinctively *American* failure of connection even if it dwells on a more general, phenomenological opacity that seems to defy national lines. Chastising Densher for his lack of vision, Kate tells him, "I marvel at your seeing your way so little" (*WD* 2:222). Yet despite his acknowledgment of Kate's own "multiplied lights" (*WD* 2:223), which allow her to see "deeply" (*WD* 2:224), Densher articulates the problem that multiple views pose for stable reference in the novel: "[H]er view of the right thing," he says of Susan Shepherd, "may not be the same as yours" (*WD* 2:227). As Densher's retort to Kate implies, the more perspectives one is able to accommodate in the elaboration of alternative scenarios the less likely is one's chance to predict a probable or reliable outcome.

Densher's clearest, least contingent vision in the novel, "in view as noth-ing of the moment, nothing begotten of time or of chance could be, or ever would" (*WD* 2:236), occurs unsurprisingly in the afterglow of Kate's visit to his quarters—during which they have had sex. If this "view" appears to con-tradict the idea that contingency and indeterminacy structure how one sees one's chances in the novel, we need only note the cost Densher must pay in order to preserve this clarity. Maintaining the sanctity of this experience of erotic fulfillment (as well as its necessity or predictability) requires Densher to withdraw entirely from the world at large into the private confines of his Venetian flat, as if the pleasure taken there were so precarious that the slight-est intrusion would dissipate its "value":

> He remained thus, in his own theater, in his single person, perpetual or-chestra to the ordered drama, the confirmed "run"; playing low and slow, in the regular way, for the situations of most importance. No other visitor was to come to him; he met, he bumped occasionally, in the Pi-azza or in his walks, against claimants to his acquaintance . . . but he gave no address and encouraged no approach; he couldn't for his life, he felt, open his door for a third person. Such a person would have in-terrupted him, would have profaned his secret or perhaps have guessed it. . . . He was giving himself up—that was quite enough—to the re-newed engagement to fidelity. (*WD* 2:237)

Densher's renewal of faith ("fidelity") in Kate ("only believe in me," we recall her saying) depends on his removal from the contingent world at large, any encounter with which inevitably "profane[s]" the vision of a "con-firmed 'run'" he has made of their relation. With its virtually carceral con-finement in the private world of monogamous "fidelity," this is a very different scenario from the cruisy impromptu on the Underground that brought Densher and Kate together in the first place. Just as James implies that multiple views undermine the effort to bank on necessary outcomes, so he suggests that the plausibility of Densher's "ordered drama" of hetero-sexual performance is so fragile that it is easily compromised by the inter-ruption of another spectator. In normalizing his relation to Kate according to a sexual dominant of conjugality, Densher must will away third parties, must forget that the presence of such spectators provided the initial impe-tus to their renewed attraction on the London subway. While betrothal may still the restless, ambiguous desires that circulate in the subway car, the price for such quiet and clarity is a kind of agoraphobic cessation of movement. To be settled in married life, in other words, requires a form of "faith" that feels like interment—a connection James makes even more strongly with re-gard to the proposed affiancing of Milly and Densher.

Yet Densher cannot sustain a state of companionate resolve with Kate any more than he can remain confined within the hermitage of his Venetian hotel room. This is because locomotion in the novel is no more amenable than vision to stability or composure; the way characters move, like the way they see, is up for grabs. James frequently describes the way his characters move about in terms of their being swept away. As he writes of Milly and Susan in London: "Their immediate lesson accordingly was that they just had been caught up by the incalculable strength of a wave that was actually holding them aloft and that would naturally dash them wherever it liked" (WD 1:167). The movement implied in this sentence is neither self-propelled nor calculable; the wave both holds them "aloft" and moves them along, here as elsewhere confusing motion and stasis. "Kate at least had the perched feeling," James writes in another context, "it was as if she were there aloft without a retreat." And in the preface, James claims of Densher and Kate's relation: "[I]t is into the young woman's 'ken' that Merton Densher is represented as swimming" (WD 1:xvi). Milly is likewise awash "in a current determined by others" in which "not she but the current acted" (WD 1:274), while Densher considers Milly the source of the "current" that moves him along with a "swiftness" "beyond . . . control" (WD 2:80). In these and numerous other instances, The Wings of the Dove divorces motion from agency and self-possession.

The novel maps Kate and its other characters within a stark antinomy of spatial options that appear incompatible: a "gilded cage," like Maud's house, from which there is no "retreat" and the mobility and "extension really inordinate" (WD 1:55) inscribed in the patterns of travel and migration at work in the novel. What joins the void of anticipation "without a retreat" and the "extension really inordinate," however, is the sense that both spatial configurations are oriented around an anxious groundlessness. They connote a *mise-en-abyme* either of paralytic doubt or of equally disabling because indeterminate possibilities. If "being perched aloft . . . without a retreat" leaves Kate without a sense of origin, as she feels in having lost her name, then the "extension really inordinate" leaves Kate, Densher, and Milly in the opposite dilemma: it voids them of purpose or expectation. This groundless feeling—the sense of belonging, "in a world of rushing about, to one of the common orders of chance" (WD 1:188)— encroaches on the geography of the interior self, whose anticipatory status discharges it of both presence and self-possession. Whether she is Kate Croy from "nowhere" or "a nobody from Bayswater"(WD 1:174), the relation between Kate and her identity results in "a sort of failure of common terms" (WD 1:190). The two concepts—place and self—do not align so much as they cancel each other out.

"Everyone was everywhere," Lord Mark explains to Milly over dinner at Maud Lowder's; furthermore, nobody was anywhere. He should be put to it—yes, frankly—to give a name of any sort or kind to their hostess's set. Was it a set at all, or wasn't it, and were there really no such things as sets in the place any more?—was there anything but groping and pawing, that of the vague billows of some great greasy sea in mid-Channel, of masses of bewildered people trying to "get" they didn't know what or where? (*WD* 1:150)

If James's novel is dominated by an anxiety of groundlessness, Lord Mark provides a spectacular rationale for this sense of displacement of the self from its bearings. As Lord Mark sees it, everyone wants in, and this craving and its satisfaction have evacuated the privileged interior of society of any "set" name, value, or "kind." Indeed, the "groping and pawing" of the "bewildered masses" on the "great greasy sea" is a palpable reference to an immigrant population that contaminates the proper bounds of society with its own slippery yearnings.

The problem with masses, according to the turn-of-the-century anti-immigrant discourse with which James was acquainted, is that they want too much and don't know exactly what they want. In *The American Scene* (1905), James, as if echoing Lord Mark, names the groundlessness of an America infiltrated by the immigrant thus: "The fusion, as of elements in solution in a vast hot pot, is always going on, and one stage of the process is as typical or as vivid as another."[25] The "hot pot" transforms the New York street with its interminable activity into a place that fails to preserve discrete divisions. On the other hand, as the following passage makes clear, the alien presence, which represents a collapse of distinction, threatens James with an equally troubling gap between the immigrant and the citizen, a too-wide fissure based on an irreducible social misrecognition. James relates the occasion of a visit to an estate in New Jersey during which the failure of "the element of communication" with the grounds workers there evokes the following explanation:

> The men, in the case I speak of, were Italians, of superlatively southern type, and any impalpable exchange struck me as absent from the air to positive intensity, to mere unthinkability. It was as if contact were out of the question and the sterility of the passage between us recorded, with due dryness, in our staring silence. This impression was for one of the party a shock—a member of the party for whom, on the other side of the world, the imagination of the main furniture, as it might be called, of any rural excursion, of *the* rural in particular, had been, during years, the easy sense for the excursionist, of a social relation with any encountered type, from whichever end of the scale proceeding. Had that not ever been, exactly, a part of the vague warmth, the intrinsic color, of any honest man's rural walk in his England or his Italy, . . . and was not the effect of its so suddenly dropping out, in the land of universal brother-

hood . . . rather a chill, straightway, for the heart, and a puzzle, not less, for the head? (*AS* 119)

These aliens have tipped the "scale" of common measurement which serves as the tourist's level for gauging where he is and with whom. The alien in New Jersey obdurately refuses to be plotted on the continuum of the "scale proceeding" and so throws its careful class calibrations out of balance. The immigrant's inversion of the natural order, whereby laborers are meant to serve as scenic "furniture" for the rural "excursionist" yet somehow have failed to keep their stationary and decorative place, is converted into a failure of the immigrant to embrace the natural order of "universal brotherhood" that James locates in America. Barring "brotherhood," the immigrant's "expectation" remains opaque to James. Avoiding the question of what such expectation might be, James translates the immigrant's lack of interest in him into a failure to observe the basis of society, now reconstructed around fraternity and shared expectations.

Based on his virtually lifelong indifference to his native soil, we could reasonably argue that James's profession of "universal brotherhood" in this instance is at best shaky, a matter of convenience; yet this would simply confirm the pragmatist account of opportunistic belief in appearance for appearance's sake—and not least in the appearance of a coherent social unit, "universal brotherhood," in which James (perhaps for the first and last time) chooses to include himself. Henry shares William's sense that "consanguinity" "provides the only really organic social relations," as he puts it in distinguishing Philadelphia as "the most rounded and complete" (*AS* 279) of American cities. The city of brotherly love provides the basis of a genuinely American society modeled on "the Happy Family" (*AS* 284). James evokes the sentimental obverse of the violent xenophobia with which Italians were greeted in U.S. culture at the turn of the century. "The knife with which he cuts his bread he also uses to lop off another 'dago's' finger or ear," a turn-of-the-century penologist observed of the Italian immigrant. "He is as familiar with the sight of human blood as with the food he eats" (cited in Higham 60). The "dago" abolishes consanguinity as a collective value by dismembering his compatriots and spilling their blood; he refuses brotherhood to both James and his own countrymen. Committed to self-transformation through class mobility and opportunism, the American "alien" proves paradoxically incapable of domestication either through the bonds of fraternity or through assimilation.

This immigrant is of a different species from what observers and editors referred to as the "agricultural classes" whose influx from northern European nations dominated U.S. immigration until 1890. These earlier arrivals made good citizens and were easily assimilated primarily because, springing from and working the soil, they "shared" a commitment to the land with the native population. Anti-immigrant sentiment was occasioned by those immigrants who would not assume their right place: "No one can travel much in the East without seeing that with no small proportion of our vast foreign element," Francis Walker wrote in *The Advance* (1874), "occupation is determined by a location that is accidental, or practically beyond the control of individuals; that these people are doing what they are doing, because they are where they are."[26] In the same year, E. L. Godkin expatiated in the *Nation* on the necessity of "settling" the question of immigration—no less than of settling immigrants—and traced the failure to resolve the issue of settlement to the eclipse of agricultural labor by unskilled labor. "The increasingly minute divisions of labor," argues Godkin,

> are making it every year more and more dangerous for the emigrants to attempt this old-fashioned role [of asserting a claim to citizenship through homesteading]. Therefore, the question is not so much, Is there not plenty of land in the United States, and a welcome for all? as it is, Can a particular individual find in the United States the particular work for which he is trained? And where, and when?[27]

The link between aliens and unsettlement informs much of the discourse on immigration, whether negative or positive. Edward Steiner, the most sympathetic commentator one might expect to find writing on immigrants at the turn of the century, singles Italians out for their peculiar aptitude for the disorientation and displacement that Walker and Godkin lament. "They regard their quarters as purely temporary," Steiner writes of Italian laborers in the United States, "and treat them as one might a camping-ground, which tomorrow is to be abandoned for a better site."[28]

"We shall get . . . from the Italian his mobility," Steiner claims.[29] His view suggests how we might interpret James's choice to set the last third of *The Wings of the Dove* in Venice, a locale that throws into question the very idea of a setting. "Nowhere else," James says of Venice in *Italian Hours,* "is the present so alien, so discontinuous."[30] In the Jamesian imagination, Venice is a city populated entirely by noncitizens—either the "polyglot pilgrims" of the tourist industry or the cosmopolitan hustlers like "the great Eugenio" (*WD* 2:132), whose sympathetic ministrations to Milly Theale in *Wings* are indistinguishable from the machinations of a confidence man. "The poorest Venetian," James writes, "is a natural man of the world" (*IH* 36). Venetians conflate the stationary poverty of the Italian peasant with the mobility of the wealthy tourist in a general habit of "misconduct" (*IH* 36). Moreover, with its floating avenues and mercantile past, Venice is the birthplace of risk in modernity. James clearly has this connotation in mind when he shelters Densher from a storm by placing him at the pillars of St. Theodore and the

Lion—the ancient area, as Ruskin's *The Stones of Venice* informs us, of gaming and execution, fortune and death. We might also refer to the game of the caskets in *The Merchant of Venice,* a play to which James gave much thought. The play is obsessed with the impasse between what Portia calls "the lottery of my destiny" and the "right of voluntary choosing" as much as with the relentless association between risk, death, accident, and choice. "Who chooseth me," the first casket tells Aragon as he tries his hand at winning Portia's, "must give and hazard all he hath."[31]

As James understands them, immigrants are persons for whom choice is inseparable from risk, and for whom risk exists without trust. This generalized social insecurity is an essential feature of industrial society and the labor relations that underwrite it. In the early twentieth century, these risk relations get rewritten on the one hand as the discourse of opportunism and on the other as a xenophobic exclusion that posits the alien as inassimilable to the settlement that opportunism entails. The new immigrant is not upwardly mobile; he is simply mobile. The relation of the immigrant to his future is abstracted from the kind of connection to the past which would make that future a matter of necessity. This understanding of the alien is distinctive not because it is original to James but rather because it is the customary description voiced by foreign observers of American life throughout the nineteenth century. If the James of *The American Scene* regards the alien as the figure whose self is forever doomed to be unfinished, this account merely shifts the paradigm embodied by the American self from the nation's founding onto its latest avatars.

The alien's inconstancy would thus appear to confirm the native citizen's constancy. Gaining mobility, the immigrant surrenders security. The immigrant has, like Milly at the acme of the Brunig, "a view" of the future "pure and simple, a view of great extent and beauty, but thrown forward and vertiginous" (*WD* 1:123). And though for this reason—her tendency toward a sort of spiritual vertigo—Kate thinks of Milly as "a person [not] to change places, even to change chances with" (*WD* 1:176), the remainder of *Wings* from the moment of their discovery of each other might be read as the story of Kate's predatory desire to substitute herself with Milly in the form of swindling her fortune. The novel has in fact invited this reading for as long as critics have been interpreting it: Milly is the dove-like prey, Kate and Densher the opportunistic predators. In faith with this neat opposition, it would be entirely possible to treat the novel as an allegory of what happens to the "constant" American after the "poor bewildered and newly landed alien" (*WD* 2:40), as Densher refers to himself regarding Milly's reception of him in New York, has got his hands on her innocent and generous bounty.

But such a reading would have to ignore the way Milly herself figures into the novel's deployment of alien attributes. Milly is, we learn through Kate's perspective, the beneficiary of a fortune that descends to her precisely from the dissolution of "brotherhood":

> Her visitor's American references, with their bewildering immensities, their record of used-up relatives, parents, clever eager fair slim brothers—these the most loved—all engaged, as well as successive superseded guardians, in a high extravagance of speculation and dissipation that had left this exquisite being her black dress, her white face and her vivid hair as the mere last broken link. (*WD* 1:174)

James compounds "speculation and dissipation" as the obverse and reverse of Milly's wealth to demonstrate how Milly's fortune derives from a kind of risk-taking that, while it leaves her with the rewards of "speculation," appears to deprive her of the advantage of a secure bond of trust or frame of reference. She has made her fortune at the expense of any sustaining "connection"—particularly to the "most loved" "brothers." If brotherhood is the supreme sign of national and cultural unity, Milly turns out to be the most alien of all the protagonists in the novel.

At one point Milly says, "I want abysses" (*WD* 1:186). In *The American Scene*, James refers to the "upper social organism" of New York as "floundering there all helplessly" "in the "splendor" of an "environment" "betrayed by its paucity of real resource" (*AS* 162). He is describing a new form of "aristocracy" that has embraced the "interesting struggle in the void" (*AS* 162) instead of the solid grounding in "civilization" (*AS* 163) that earlier generations prized. While James's sense of despair at this turn of events clearly feels like the condescension (and barely submerged class resentment) of an older patrician caste, it is much more than that. The mobility that characterizes these nouveaux riches is the distinctive factor in the lives of their exact counterparts at the bottom of the social ladder. "The extreme examples" of what one contemporary calls "the nomadic habit" "are found among the families of the very poor and the very rich, who have regular seasonal migrations."[32] *The American Scene* makes frequent reference to the nomadic habits of the new rich, who leave a trail of empty houses and opulent hotel rooms in their wake as they pursue, like Milly, "abysses."[33] To "want abysses" is to imagine desire as an incessant series of contingencies for which fulfillment becomes irrelevant and in which substitution, change of scenery, displacement become central. It is this situation that James in *The American Scene* defines as the "last revelation of modernity" (*AS* 183): "We have everything, don't you see?" James mimics the "vocal note" of Milly's class, "so that all we now desire is . . . the great 'going' chance of a time to come" (*AS* 184). And as if to reinforce even more emphatically the link between the extremes of the social scale, James provides his "vision" of the new rich with a "kind of analogy: for what were the Venetians after all, but the children of a Republic and of trade?" (*AS* 164) In *The American Scene* and *The Wings of the Dove,* James sees the "intensely modern" (*AS* 183) structure of desire as an endless negotiation between choice and chance, and in turn finds the basic "analogy" for that negotiation in the migratory Italian who crops up repeatedly in the vicinity of these crucial terms.

For all her wealth, of course, Milly is the extreme "case" (*WD* 2:109) of a figure defined through "the paucity of real resources" in *Wings,* the figure defined in terms of her floating figure, her "Venetian" disposition. Her "matter" is almost wholly defined in terms of her possibilities; what is the matter with her, we might say along with everyone else, is that she has no permanent matter. As Kate puts it with regard to her illness, in one of the novel's most equivocal lines: "she has nothing" (*WD* 2:52). Even Milly's fortune turns out to be less a guarantor of her person than the source of her possibilities. Nothing constrains her ("I can do exactly what I like—anything in all the wide world" [*WD* 1:243], she tells Luke Strett), but at the same time nothing anchors her. "Milly's range was thus immense," we are told. "[S]he had to ask nobody for anything, to refer nothing to any one" (*WD* 1:175). It is through Milly's incarnation of possibility that James works out the contradictory agency of choice he unearths in the groundlessness of alien experience. In the preface, James directly links Milly's "blooming alone, for the fullest attestation of her freedom" to "a strong and special implication of liberty, liberty of action, of choice" (*WD* 1:ix). It is as if the soil that breeds Milly is, like the free-floating immigrant's, a desolate place, as if liberty of this sort necessitated an antisocial solitude.

In pressing on the analogies that *Wings* makes between persons of different fortunes—the American heiress, the migratory Italian laborer—I draw attention to a sense felt throughout James's culture that fortune, in the sense of chance or randomness, had acquired a very different status in shaping attitudes toward opportunities and desires for persons of all classes. Chanciness and choosing collapse into each other in the mental world that James imagines; this is one way of glossing the "liberty of action, of choice," with which he endows Milly, and with which he and his contemporaries endowed the immigrant. It is by no means a freedom that James or his culture embraced. Rather, this "intensely modern" and hence intensely ambiguous freedom was associated with the anomie and discontent routinely embodied in what nativist thinkers like Texas Congressman Lucian Parrish called the "uncertain element."[34] Members of this element "have stirred discontent in our midst," according to Parrish's fellow representative Mitchell Palmer, primarily because they have "caused irritating strikes" and "have infected our social ideas with the disease of their own minds and their unclean morals."[35] The lack of constraint or solidarity that Milly's "liberty of action, of choice" poses was primarily an infection that arose from the ranks of the alien population, even if its worst effects were reserved for the better sort.

In the turning point of *The Wings of the Dove* the confusion between chance and choice, contingency and constraint, works up to a fever pitch. Of course, that turning point is the moment in her doctor's office when Milly is forced to confront the "great rare chance" (*WD* 1:245) Luke Strett has "put to her": "the question of living . . . living by option, by volition" (*WD* 1:247). James was heavily invested in this scene as a turning point in the novel; he chose the door to the doctor's office as the frontispiece portrait for volume 2 of *The Wings of the Dove,* as if to draw graphic attention to the scene's status as a portal. In giving her a "great rare chance" that is also an "option," James makes Milly undergo the drama of risk without trust that his culture understood as the special experience of the alien. Thus when Kate tells Densher that Milly "must take her risks, and she surely understands them" (*WD* 1:96) she is either mistaken or lying, since Milly has recourse neither to the transparency of her choice (a "grey immensity" [*WD* 1:247]) nor to a "precursive faith" that would make any choice she arrived at a function of necessity in retrospect. All Milly can do when faced with this "great rare chance" is to move forward without stopping: "she found herself moving at times in regions visibly not haunted by odd-looking girls from New York" (*WD* 1:249). Transforming "the question of living" into a choice for Milly, Sir Luke converts life from a matter of trust, whereby one pursues one's existence in the belief that it will continue regardless of one's actions or decisions, into a game of risk, in which living becomes a function of the right moves or the willed effort to undertake what has previously come "naturally." If living is what we do without even thinking about it, Milly arrives at an inversion of this definition that makes thought a matter of life and death.

Insofar as death might be defined as a form without a content—indeed, a formal category organized around the absence of content (as Sharon Cameron has noted)—for Milly to face death as an option is for her to merge choice with risk absolutely.[36] James expresses this merger in spatial terms when he has his protagonist (in keeping with her name) *milling* around the city in the aftermath of her visit to Sir Luke. She has become a figure of aimless and pointless motion, and in this guise has also trespassed class lines into "regions visibly not haunted by odd-looking girls from New York." Like the lower-class immigrant on the streets of America, she is an outsider, a transgressor of social boundaries by virtue of both her sudden mobility and her isolation.

It is both strange and strangely fitting that the "remedy" (*WD* 2:112) that will broker Milly's path back to vitality will be her falling in love with Densher. Though this cure does not in fact take, it is not for lack of trying (nor for lack of precedent; the love of a good man, we are routinely informed by the nineteenth-century novel, has healed many a flagging woman). Just as living or dying becomes a function of choice, so desire in the novel becomes a matter of prescription—what Aunt Maud calls falling in love "by the doctor's direction" (*WD* 2:112). Directing someone to choose to fall in love is like directing someone to choose to live: a confusion of agency that imposes on the self's involuntary workings a set of imperatives the self must treat as if they were a matter of consent. The proliferation of these consent games in *The Wings of the Dove* mirrors, in a condensed and displaced fashion, the technologies of citizenship and national community whose rejection by the alien so frustrates James in *The American Scene*. Pledging allegiance to the flag is structurally equivalent here to the marriage vow: a naturalization of one's desire to choose, a settlement of the self's variable desire in the most necessary of institutional grounds. In this light the machinations surrounding Densher and Milly's relationship look not devious or perverse so much as utterly conventional. Insofar as Maud, Susan, and Kate "arrange" for Milly to fall in love with Densher, "put[ting] him in her way" (*WD* 2:114), as Susan says, this is business as usual in the marriage market. Falling in love is a prophylactic that will cut Milly off from the abysses she thinks she wants. Yet James is clearly uninterested in treating marital bliss as the necessary ground for rescuing Milly from the uncertainties of her all too mobile matter. When Lord Mark tells her, "[W]e're all in love with you. . . . You were born to make us happy," Milly answers that listening to him "simply kills me" (*WD* 2:160), as though aware of the ambush that awaits the bride who walks the path of least resistance.

If *The American Scene* finds James disturbed by the alien's failure to settle, *The Wings of the Dove* finds him committed to Milly's refusal to do the same. The grafting of alien attributes onto that novel's characters suggests an awareness that the problem of consent involved in the immigrant's experience—the compulsion to naturalize or to assimilate even when endowed with desires for economic gain irrelevant or antagonistic to citizenship—can be translated into traditionally more private registers like erotic choice. If settlement and membership are continually frustrated by the alien's desire to make his own way, James's novel transforms this liability into a virtue where individual desire is concerned. The immigrant who thwarts expectations by exercising the wrong choices—namely in his withdrawal from the American "community of consent"—allows James to imagine a different expectation for erotic desire from its regulation within the members-only private sphere of marriage.

I conclude by suggesting that Milly's refusal to see Densher in the penultimate book of James's novel is a choice of death not over life but over the kind of love he by now fully represents to her—a relation that, even if it might cease to be deceptive, never leaves her in anything but the cheated position, the victim of a confidence game in which what she gains will always be the short end of the stick. If Milly gives up on life and love by taking her chances with death, James seems to suggest, she is nonetheless still managing to keep her options open. Death promises the negation of expectation in the service of "desire." This is the word James uses to specify why life must continue beyond death in the strange essay of 1910, "Is There a Life after Death?" "It isn't really a question of belief," James writes. "[I]t is on the other hand a question of desire, but of desire so confirmed, so thoroughly established and nourished, as to leave belief a comparatively irrelevant affair."[37]

Conceived as "sprouting in that eminently and infinitely diggable soil" of what William James would call "precursive faith," life "dishonors the greater part of the beauty and the opportunity even of this world," James writes.[38] Understanding death as the beginning of new opportunities, his equation of death with desire overturns a long-standing tradition of thought which comprehends death as the cessation of desire, in the form of worldly striving. This is of course how everyone thinks of Milly's death—the end to her suffering. Everyone, that is, except for James, for whom Milly's death marks her flight into abysses of desire that leave behind her grounding in (and being ground down by) the inevitable disappointments of the love she's been bargaining for. Milly's "options" do not die with her so much as they are released into the world upon her death. Even if her dying seems to resolve the conundrum of the choice Sir Luke presented to her by making this choice appear to have been no choice all along, such an outcome does not resolve or conclude the vertiginous effects of choosing unleashed in the Jamesian text.

Milly's dying is understood by *Wings* less as the end of her nebulous "matter" than as the liberation of that matter—in the form a generalized and infectious incertitude—across the novel's other central characters. The content of Milly's bequest to Densher and Kate is finally less important than the form she continues to take for them. Milly's posthumous presence in their lives revokes the shaky stability of their relation, as Kate exclaims in the novel's last line: "We shall never be again as we were" (*WD* 2:405). More than money or redemption, what Milly leaves them—"she did it *for* us" (*WD* 2:403), Kate claims—is the dilemma of coercive choice on and against which her own life was grounded. Kate understands this all too well when Densher confronts her with the choice between him and the money he assumes he has inherited from Milly. Though Kate correctly infers from his demands on her, "I must choose"—choose, that is, between the security of wealth without Densher and Densher without the security of wealth—she places him in an identical fix, asking him to choose between her and Milly's "memory" (*WD* 2:404). For both Densher and Kate, choosing is closely associated in this final exchange with the word "surrender" (*WD* 2:404), as if to choose means to participate in a game in which the stakes are nothing less than self-possession and self-mastery. This is how we are finally meant to take James's understanding of the romance of choice. At least as Densher and Kate come to view it after Milly's "surrender," the choice of one thing entails the refusal of another; likewise, one person's choice necessarily entails another person's sacrifice.

Trading in the transparency of rational choice for the radical opacity of crooked motives in *Wings,* James ultimately dislodges the assumptions that lie behind the romance of choice that encroached on the mental geography of his time. If choosing motivates the self and structures the way the self desires, the problem with this cheery vision of accumulation "by option, by volition" is elemental: what to do when the things to which our choices refer —like other persons—not only make choices themselves but don't, referentially speaking, stay in place. I have been arguing that in his understanding of the alien in turn-of-the-century Atlantic culture, James reaches an impasse in how properly to frame persons in place or to sort persons into categories. When the Italian laborer ceases to be imaginable as an element in the tableau vivant of a leisure-class tourist and begins to assume the very characteristics of that tourist in his mobility and opportunism, James ceases to be able to divide bourgeois from proletariat, native from foreigner, on the axes to which habit has accustomed him to draw the line. Yet James's anxiety about the right way to sort persons, and immigrant persons in particular, translates into a recognition of the irreducible "human element" which contemporary theories of choice or desire seek to elide by their tacit assumption of homogeneity among members of a group. In its fierce insistence that persons are "different and different—and then . . . different again," as Densher says of Kate (*WD* 2:61), *Wings of the Dove* spells out a feature of the pluralistic culture of choice that continually threatens to rupture that culture and hence requires continual recuperation and denial, continual appeals to a common soil, a common past, a common faith.

We are used to seeing William James's pluralistic universe as a progressive answer to the breakup of social consensus associated overwhelmingly with the arrival of immigrants around 1900, and we are equally used to viewing Henry James's defense of "the consecrated English tradition" as a reactionary distaste for these same aliens. I argue that because Henry takes the mobility and fragmentation of those immigrants to their logical extreme in *The Wings of the Dove* by drawing out their deep affiliation with the logic of choice in general, he produces the more radical account of desire. This is an account that pragmatism, with its assumption of a "precursive faith" among a bounded community of fellow believers, cannot quite withstand. Whereas pragmatism fosters the will to believe as the antidote to social fragmentation which can only be resolved through trust in systems, the obverse of the same historical development of mass society—the unchecked and seemingly random migration of working-class laborers—raises the suspicion that chance rather than choice sounds the dominant note of the American century. If James's culture rewrites chance as choice, and rewrites risk as opportunity, James undoes this rewriting in *Wings*. Hence the position of the chooser in the novel tends toward the anticipatory state of becoming without alighting on a distinct or transparent identity, without a particular investment in one set of beliefs over another. James's society located this permanently contingent state in the body of the antisocial alien—a figure both continually on the go and continually thwarted in his movement toward any viable end. Even though James distrusted the immigrant Italian's marginal and itinerant status, his novel leans heavily on this social type when working through the intricacies and contradictions of the ideology of choice. Just as his protagonists remain permanently indecisive, so James in *The American Scene* cannot finally separate the alien from the native, the Italian bootblack from the New York heiress, long enough to make any clear distinction between the two. James exploits the Italian's indeterminacy as the basis of his protagonists' ambiguous potential in the face of too many options—characterized by their continually floating along without settling into place.

James often recurs to a particular phrase to designate this state of continual arrest: "to hang fire." If we imagine this act—the delay in shooting a pistol—as the prevailing stance of the protagonists in *The Wings of the Dove*, several assumptions fall into place. Withholding a bullet from its target absolves the shooter of both the inevitability of misfiring and the fatalism accompanying a dead-on mark. It is the potential to fire, not the fatal discharge itself, that confers agency on the shooter, for whom power is imagined as the ability to reserve ammunition for something more worthy of its impact. Perhaps this is why for James "belief" becomes comparatively irrelevant when the question of opportunities arises. If belief presupposes a world that makes sense of one's actions by asserting their necessity, then desire opens the door through which one can still look upon the options one hasn't selected as if they were still possibilities. In other words, one might choose one thing and still risk wanting another.

Chapter Three

Making Do with Gertrude Stein

I

Piss my dog.
Piss my dog.
Piss along the houses
If I were a concierge I would give you a kick with my foot.
Piss my dog.

Piss my dog.
Piss my dog.
If I pissed on the wall of your house you'd shoot me to death.
Piss my dog.

Piss my dog.
Piss on the streetlight
A poor tramp would be forced to clean it.
Piss my dog.
Piss my dog.[1]

This unpublished and undated Gertrude Stein poem serves as an entrée into her work's peculiar fixation on dogs, who appear there so frequently that their absence from Stein criticism is almost scandalous. Presented as fixtures in households who somehow fit in without taking center stage, dogs in Stein function like servants in traditional novels—the domestic players who keep the home running smoothly as a steady backdrop for the real drama that takes place between maiden and suitor. In Stein's plays from the teens, for example, the dog Polybe assumes a frequent role somewhere between prop and character, centering vertiginously diffuse dramas by virtue of his habit of being "seated." What defines dogs in Stein's work—their supporting role, their likeness to servants or subordinates in a human domain—is exactly what Stein means to draw to our attention. In *Ida* (1940), Stein's nomadic heroine anchors herself by way of her pets: "She always had a dog, at every address she had a dog." Subject to remarkable turnover, these dogs are nonetheless strictly associated with places even though Ida herself cannot be pinned down. "She did not even have a dog, she did not have a town," Stein writes, in parallel clauses that make dogs and towns appear synonymous.[2]

As dogs are both always there and not quite there in Stein's work, bolstering social structures to which they do not seem immediately relevant, so they are nearly ubiquitous in the scientific and medical writings of her age, where dogs play a similarly passive yet influential role in the development of twentieth-century behavioral science. This chapter pursues two arguments that parallel and shape each other. On the one hand I uncover the privileged position of dogs in modern psychology; on the other, I place Stein within and against this milieu. I wish to keep in focus here a crucial topic that absorbed both Stein and her behaviorist contemporaries—the "making" of persons, to use a favorite Stein term—while also maintaining that such making usually occurs with the unlikely assistance of dogs. Beginning with William James, I argue, consciousness comes to signify a concept of peripatetic desire that, inimical to traditional modes of prediction and regulation, incites psychology to develop a science of control founded on the erasure of consciousness itself. Stein shares this discipline's intuition that consciousness presents problems for orderly subjectivity even if she does not quite share the implications that behaviorism draws from this intuition. We can begin to see their shared interest in the unruliness of consciousness by noting that in both Stein's writing and that of modernist psychologists, dogs are always attached to overly mobile persons, like Stein's Ida, in danger of sliding out of place and so in dire need of the categorical fastness that dogs strangely exemplify.

"Pissez Mon Chien" may seem an inauspicious place from which to launch an inquiry into Stein's work. First, it is written in poor French, a language Stein rarely used. This poem is unrepresentative of Stein in a second and more telling sense, for in its simple reiteration of the command *pissez mon chien,* the poem's syntax lacks the subtle dynamism Stein worked into her repetitive style in other texts. Likewise, its conditional clauses—"if this, then that"—are too balanced for the woman whose "A Completed Profile of Picasso" begins with the open-ended and redundant predication "if I told him."[3] In the latter phrase, Stein's speaker calls attention to the indefinite conditionality of conversation, the issues of trust and skepticism that inhere in any dialogue: will the person to whom I address myself, asks the speaker, respond to me? "Would Napoleon would he?" (*SR* 464) But in "Pissez Mon Chien," the nature and outcome of the speech act are never in question. The address to the dog, *pissez,* takes the form of a short, terminal imperative. In this poem, there is no inferred dialogue; there is only the command, the rule, to be obeyed.

Yet in its subject matter, its use of the imperative, its simple repetition, and its finely balanced conditional syntax, "Pissez Mon Chien" illustrates

Stein's awareness that dogs stood close to the disciplinary grammar of modernity elaborated in the behavioral psychology of her time. The conditional tense in the poem recalls Ivan Pavlov's theory of the "conditioned reflex," which he derived from canine research, and echoes the dictum of John Watson, the father of American behaviorism, that "Order in the universe is merely a matter of conditioning."[4] By "conditioning," Watson and Pavlov mean the exercise of proper behavior through a rigorous application of cause and effect, or what behaviorism translates into the idiom of stimulus and response. The achievement of Stein's work resides partly in her interrogation of this conditionality and of the sociality it implies—a world in which things follow logically or necessarily one from another. The linguistic ideal for behavioral psychology is the command, and its communicative ideal is obedience compelled through the repetition of a command. In behaviorism, repetition does the work of causality.

The francophone language of Stein's poem gestures toward her first fully sustained literary work, *Three Lives* (1909), a book that not only emerged from her efforts to learn French (she began the project as a translation of Flaubert's *Trois Contes*) but also dealt with the implications of the new psychology. In her struggle to adapt to the language of France, her new home, Stein learned to associate French with the dynamics of obedience that behaviorists sought to develop. This association factors into what readers have long experienced as the jarring stylistic inelegance of *Three Lives*. Meaning both to make and to do, for example, the French verb *faire* points to the desirability among behavioral psychologists of a constructionist theory that is simultaneously a theory of control, of *making do*. I argue that the verb "to make" shapes the basic idiom of *Three Lives* by forcing our attention to the grammar of artificial control underwriting the revisionist psychology of the new century.

Because dogs were defined in terms of obedience both inside and outside the expert discourses of modern culture, they find their way into the Stein texts that rehearse her preoccupation with the misbehavior characteristic of modernity's inhabitants. As I argued in chapter 1, one of modernity's founding contradictions is the imperative for obedience within a social system subject at every level to dispersal and fragmentation. The domestic dog, at once obedient and misbehaving, faithful and straying, becomes one of the most compelling figures for this contradiction. The persons most in need of the fastness that dogs instinctively modeled, according to the earliest behaviorists, were those predecessor psychologists (James most prominently) who were given over to the slippages and distortions to which the belief in consciousness committed them.[5] Behaviorism sought to break with that parent discipline's murky "introspection" by means of animal experimentation, as E. L. Thorndike's *Animal Intelligence*

(1911) affirms.[6] "It is so useful, in understanding the animal," Thorndike argues, "to see what it does in different circumstances . . . that one is led to an intrinsic interest in varieties of behavior" (*AI* 4). Reversing the parent discipline's privileging of consciousness over behavior, Thorndike asserts that "behavior includes consciousness" (*AI* 15).

Thorndike arrived at this assertion through his own "box experiments" on chicks, cats, and dogs, which led him to "den[y] the existence in animal consciousness of any important stock of free ideas or impulses" (*AI* 153). The general "stupidity" of animals (*AI* 22) makes what look like intelligent acts—a hungry cat's or dog's escape from a box "by pulling the proper loop" to get to food outside—"represent the wearing smooth of a path in the brain, not the decisions of a rational consciousness" (*AI* 74). Because they don't think too much, Thorndike implies, animal subjects pose few problems to the measurement of behavior according to external and hence shareable criteria.[7] Their actions turn the brain inside out, making its routines discernible to the clinical eye. "We have known for a long time that we cannot get our animal to introspect and tell us about its consciousness," John Watson writes in *The Battle of Behaviorism* (1928). Yet "without asking it anything, we can with . . . systematic, controlled observation, tell volumes about what each animal does" (*BB* 17). For Thorndike and Watson, animals save psychology for science by saving it from consciousness.

This disciplinary sea change was intimately recognizable to Stein, whose writing borrows freely from the accounts of canine consciousness she first came across in the nascent realm of cognitive science—in the psychology laboratories at Harvard and the medical laboratories at Johns Hopkins. Both environments familiarized Stein with animal models; she was a third-year medical student when Harvey Cushing introduced his students to canine vivisection in his Hopkins physiology classroom in 1901.[8] And like Thorndike's effort to see past the dog's escape from the box to the plain workings of its cortex, Stein's own laboratory work consisted of mapping cross sections of human brains, turning them inside out to look for evidence of intellection. During the period Stein spent in medical school, the use of dogs to test claims about physiology and pathology was moving beyond the study of nerves and brain tissue into the more nebulous realm of social science. Long an important resource for medical research because of their anatomical resemblance to persons, dogs around 1900 become a litmus test for understanding the anatomy of human behavior as well.

Pavlov began his stimulus-response experiments with canine subjects in 1898 and published his findings over the next two decades, culminating in the translation of *Conditioned Reflexes* in 1926. Pavlov's isolation of the reflexes made possible the reduction of a vast array of behavioral responses to "machine-like" certainty; the study of canine cortices in particular allowed

Pavlov to conclude that "under natural conditions" an animal would react identically to the same set of stimuli. If certain behaviors failed to submit to sure apprehension, this was no mystery—only a deficit in the ledger of reflexes that science had not yet filled. "If the animal were not in exact correspondence with its environment," Pavlov writes, "it would, sooner or later, cease to exist."[9] Its penchant for regularity and correction made the dog a sort of default in the modernist milieu, the standard against which to measure persons who simply failed to correct themselves or to correspond to their environment. Because dogs could be trained from their grosser instincts, they became a prototype for a host of disciplines made anxious by persons whose behavior was too erratic to submit to conventional description and planning.[10]

We can begin to draw out the relation between Stein's literary experiments and the canine analogy by revisiting "Pissez Mon Chien." That poem gives us a snapshot of the ideal relation between social prescription and embodiment that modern institutions curry, in that Stein depicts the exercise of bodily function as simultaneously a form of social obligation, a duty or law. Commanding a dog to urinate, as the poem suggests, burdens the dog with a sort of higher intellectual faculty—almost a moral sense—since the command requires the dog not only to regulate his bladder but also to make mental distinctions, to draw boundaries, to classify his world. ("Piss along the houses, the speaker says. "If I were a concierge, I would give you a kick with my foot"; the lesson here is that the houses are not to be trifled with or trespassed.) The poem articulates a sticky problem of bodily regulation by demonstrating that the governance of biological urges is as much a function of internal management as of external or environmental awareness, since learning to urinate on command also requires the dog to recognize private property. To piss against the streetlight is allowable, though the "poor tramp" (*chiminot*) will be forced to clean it. To differentiate private from public property, the wall of a house from a streetlight, the dog must also become fluent in the conditional tense.

In contrast to the grammatically and urologically correct pet is the poem's speaker, who betrays a failure to live up to the high standards of decency he or she requires of the dog. We can glimpse this failure through the ironic usage of the vaguely uncouth word *pissez* to enforce a civilizing gesture. Here the language betrays the very propriety the command seeks to uphold. This word is lexically fuzzy. Not quite a curse and definitely not polite, *pissez* is slang that straddles the line between legitimate and vulgar linguistic domains. It implies something too about the poem's speaker, suggesting that this figure is more like the *chiminot* (Stein's malapropism for hobo, *chemineau*) than like the bourgeois dog-walker the poem suggests at first glance.[11] That *chiminot* is a telling intruder into this poem, a floating figure who seems to have migrated here from his pivotal role in, say, "Melanctha," the middle story of *Three Lives*. Tramps and dogs often come together in Stein's writing, existing on different kinds of margins in the social spaces her texts seek to narrate. In "Melanctha," railroad tramps dwell at the nether reaches of the community in which Melanctha uneasily lives, seeking to lure her out of it; in "The Good Anna" some dogs are established members of Anna's household while others are what Stein calls "transients."[12] And in *Ida,* Ida and her dog encounter "a man stretched out by the side of the road," who prefigures the sort of vagabonds Ida tends to marry (her first husband used "to sleep in a bed ["made of cardboard"] under a bridge" and "always carried his things with him."[13]

Like dogs, tramps pose interesting problems to domestic virtues—cleanliness and tidiness, self-control, the regulation of bodily functions. "Pissez Mon Chien" appears to align dog and tramp by suggesting that each will eventually be won over to obedience and regularity, if not by reason then by "force." The swift kick from the concierge's foot will exact what mere words fail to secure. If anything, however, dogs are more susceptible than tramps to the power of words. In fact, the dog in this poem is not aligned so much as contrasted with the *pauvre chiminot.* The latter is left cold by the property rights and linguistic authority that the dog has recognized as sacred.

The simultaneous alignment and contrasting of dogs and tramps is a routine juxtaposition in various contexts around the turn of the century. In *Tramping with Tramps* (1899), the reformer Josiah Flynt (who makes a guest appearance in *The Autobiography of Alice B. Toklas*) refers to the children of "the ambulanters" as a "ferocious pack" among whom "from morning to night it is one continual snap and bite." Even more telling is the language he uses to describe the discipline these children require: "To tame them is a task requiring almost divine patience. They obey their parents only when driven with boot and whip. They must be put under stiff rule and order, and trained strictly and long."[14] Borrowed from the lexicon of animal domestication, the language of "taming" and "training" points up the problem with tramps as Flynt and others construed it. Such persons were not so much degenerate as wild and unbroken, averse to the discipline of the parental home; their remediation lay not in medical treatment but in the "stiff rule and order" to be found in the dog show or the horse ring.

The ease with which Flynt can look at children and see a pack of wild dogs in need of handling reveals the extent to which the animal model circulated beyond the laboratory. His example suggests the readiness with which behaviorists were willing to blur the line between marginal persons and animals in the service of science. This blurring went both ways. Just as children for Flynt need to be broken like domestic animals in order to become obedient persons, so dogs, as Stein's poem suggests, require the mastery of human skills in order to become obedient pets. The point that dogs are a kind of person matters to Stein not because of any desire to elevate their ontological status but because of her much more intense and well documented interest in the idea of personhood, of what "makes" a person a person. If I seem to be stretching the credibility of this interest by dwelling on this middling poem, it is only because the idea that dogs could be anything but marginal to such interest in personhood seems an intuitive assumption. Yet for Stein and her contemporaries, something nearly the opposite was the case. Around the time Stein started to think hard about writing, many people thought that talking about the nature of personhood by way of the canine analogy made eminent sense. William James's *Principles of Psychology* (1890), to take an example relevant to Stein's formative years, devotes a number of its first hundred pages to the study of dissected canine brains. This is to say nothing of the literary dissection of canine consciousness found in such diverse writers as Jack London, Mark Twain, Rudyard Kipling, and O. Henry. These writers all tried their hand at a genre—let us call it canine life-narrative—that threatened to overwhelm the publishing world of the early twentieth century.[15]

Penciling in some of the characteristics of this genre and of its scientific antagonist allows us to see that a particular dimension of Stein's writing is less perverse or idiosyncratic than we may have realized. More exactly, Stein's experimentations with her culture's narrative forms and generative grammar turn out to have a locatable context in an intellectual milieu that is itself thoroughly perverse. Just as dogs find their way into popular and sentimental fiction, so legions of dogs find their way to the operating tables and laboratories of physiologists and psychologists. *Canis familiaris* becomes at once the most sentimental and the most clinical of subjects in turn-of-the-century culture, and this somewhat conflicted dual status becomes most acutely visible at the point where sentimentalism and science cross each other—in the discourse of antivivisectionism. If clinicians prize dogs for their consummate typicality—in that one canine body is as good as another, as likely to produce the same results as the next—sentimental canine literature pulls the dog in the opposite direction, toward home and family, seizing on the animal's specialness to interrupt the scientific agenda. However opposed, these discourses share an irresistible tendency both to personify canines and to juxtapose their personhood with undomesticated persons who never quite measure up to the high standard set by dogs.[16]

The immoderation of this personifying reflex is the defining attribute of dog stories. In canine literature, for example, the dog's vaunted fidelity at times escalates into full-blown theology, as in the case of Jack London's *White Fang*. "Unlike man, whose gods are of the unseen and the overguessed," London writes, "the wolf and the wild dog that have come in to the fire find their gods in the living flesh. . . . No effort of faith is necessary to believe in such a god; no effort of will can possibly induce disbelief in such a god."[17] White Fang's revelation that "man-animals" are gods rests on his discovery that they have built rather than merely found or been given shelter. The Indians are gods because they build tepees, and the white men are "superior gods" because their dwellings consist not of tepees but of "houses and the huge fort all of massive logs" (JL 305). White Fang's confidence in domestic existence recurs in virtually all accounts of canine consciousness, as if the dog could dispel any hesitation his human counterpart might have that such arrangements as one finds in the communities of Indians and white men are not innate. For White Fang and his kind, "no effort of faith is necessary" because the empirical evidence of the built environment dovetails seamlessly with a belief in home. Dogs help instill or renew faith in the given-ness of artificial relations—particularly domestic and hierarchical ones.

Recognizable for the close association of fidelity with domestic power and dependency, the canine memoir is just as conspicuous for the lapses in fidelity that form a staple of the genre. Take the dog described in meticulous if contradictory detail in John Galsworthy's *Memories*. "Naturally a believer in authority and routine, and distrusting spiritual adventure," we are told of this anonymous pet, "he yet had curious fads that seemed to have nested in him, quite outside of all principle."[18] Just as White Fang has spells of "distrust" (JL 9), so Galsworthy's dog is capable of a "sadly anarchistic" demeanor "for so conservative a dog" (JG 23). With routines that need constant reinforcement, dogs are not very convincing so far as creatures of habit go. Yet what looks inconsistent in this account of canine fidelity actually turns out to be the source of that legendary quality's durability. It is his basic inconsistency that makes the dog capable of rehabilitation, just as the dog in *Memories* has to break the rules occasionally in order to assert his commitment to good manners: "His eye and nose were impeccable in their sense of form; . . . people must be just so; things smell properly; and affairs go on in the one right way" (JG 20). Domestication begins with the dog's propensity to what London calls "adjusting" (JL 232). It does not avail a dog to be too staunch a "believer in authority and routine," given that both can change unexpectedly (as they do in White Fang's case on three occasions).

London's theory of adjustment permits us to witness another instance in which the literary dog, the sentimental pet, crosses paths with his clinical counterpart, whose tractable nature was subjected to "conditioning" or "engineering" in the experiments of Pavlov and his descendants. If controlling action is the end for behaviorism, adjustment is its essential means. According to canine life-narratives like *White Fang* and *Memories*, the best kind of dog is neither blindly loyal nor singularly faithful; he is capable of adapting, like Pavlov's salivating canines, to new situations of authority, new circumstances of dependency. Since key to the dog's sense of propriety—of "affairs going on in the one right way"—is an intuitive grasp of what rules apply and who is in charge in any given instance, the dog must be sensitive to any modification in routine. For turn-of-the-century canine enthusiasts, the dog becomes the most accurate barometer of the status quo world. And dogs not only reflect but also enforce this normative state of affairs precisely by misbehaving, since their misconduct licenses the master to reassert dominion over the dog (and so licenses the dominion of the norm itself). The dog is thus prized not because he is uniformly obedient but because his stretches of disobedience render him liable to continual correction, to a more or less constant "adjustment" to the rules of the house.[19]

II

Whereas canine memoirists strive via the canine analogy to banish any doubt about the centrality of domesticity and dependency to human existence, turn-of-the-century psychologists and doctors enlisted the dog to mediate the breach between consciousness and matter, between mental and physical life, between mind and body. We need not look far for evidence of the canine analogy where Stein's own intellectual interests are concerned. Those attributes that canine life-narratives impute to dogs—discrimination, respect for property and the built environment, domestic fealty, obedience to the dictates of the spoken word—form the basis for William James's account of consistent personhood in *The Principles of Psychology,* the shorter version of which Stein read as a textbook for an introduction to psychology at Radcliffe. James's commitment to property or possessiveness as the key attribute of the conscious self is well known; "*a man's self,*" he writes, "*is the sum total of all that he can call his.*"[20] I am less interested in rehearsing the particulars of this account of consciousness as ownership than in noting a different but related set of presumptions on which James builds the edifice of his psychology. *The Principles* relies on a strategic blurring of the line between domestic animals and persons in order to locate empirical proof that such eminently social beings as persons come about "naturally." The instinctive proprietorship and the sense of protectiveness the self has toward its own thoughts evolve from a model of property relations that James traces, in true Darwinian fashion, not just to primates, the "higher animals," but to "lower" ones like dogs.

"We all have a blind impulse to watch over our body," James writes, "to deck it with clothing of an ornamental sort, to cherish parents, wife and babes, and to find ourselves a home of our own which we may live in and 'improve'" (*PP* 280–81). From early on in *The Principles,* the impulse toward a general state of protectiveness is a feature of the mind-brain continuum that James is keen to advance. "Prudence" is the name James gives in the second chapter to the "functions" exercised by the "cerebrum."

> Wherever a creature has to deal with complex features of the environment, prudence is a virtue. The higher animals have so to deal; and the more complex the features, the higher the animals. The fewer of his acts, then, can such an animal perform with the help of the organs in question [the "lower" organs of the spinal cord and medulla]. In the frog many acts devolve wholly on the lower centers; in the bird fewer; in the rodent fewer still; in the dog very few indeed; and in apes and men hardly any at all. (*PP* 34)

The dog's prudence resembles the forethought and calculations associated with complex creatures, even if the dog does not quite rate so highly on the scale whose pride of place James assigns to "apes and men." "A strange person, and darkness, are both of them stimuli to fear and mistrust in dogs (and, for that matter, in men)," James writes, at once aligning and distinguishing the two species. "Neither of them alone may awaken outward manifestations, but together, i.e. when the strange man is met in the dark, the dog will be excited to violent defiance" (*PP* 91).

The equation of higher species with what we might call an aptitude for risk-aversion plays out repeatedly in James's book. In setting forth the species hierarchy, James gives the following example:

> Thus a tired wayfarer throws himself on the damp earth beneath a maple-tree. The sensations of delicious rest and coolness pouring themselves through the direct line would naturally discharge into the muscles of complete extension: he would abandon himself to the dangerous repose. But the loop-line being open, part of the current is drafted along it, and awakens rheumatic or catarrhal reminiscences, which prevail over the instigations of sense, and make the man arise and pursue his way to where he may enjoy his rest more safely. (*PP* 33)

Here and elsewhere in *The Principles*, consciousness has a "steering" function; it guides the self to its proper destination in the face of contrary impulses, desires, or "instigations." Consciousness arises as a check to the too fluid "complexity" of not just the environment but also the human mind by presenting the self with "a constant inhibition of the tendencies to stray aside" (*PP* 143).

When we connect this inhibitory function to the "tired wayfarer" or the dog's reaction to the stranger in the night, we discern a peculiar thematic tic of James's *Principles*. James's metaphors make unstinting recourse to what we might call fugitive persons—who, by virtue of their lack of virtue (which is to say their lack of "prudence"), vividly offset properly functioning consciousness. Whereas in one taxonomy James distinguishes between canines and "apes and men," elsewhere in *The Principles* he discriminates exclusively among persons, with specific attention to their quality of consciousness:

> In all ages the man whose determinations are swayed by reference to the most distant ends has been held to possess the highest intelligence. The tramp who lives from hour to hour; the bohemian whose engagements are from day to day; the bachelor who builds but for a single life; the father who acts for another generation; the patriot who thinks of a whole community and many generations; and, finally, the philosopher and saint whose cares are for humanity and for eternity—these range themselves in an unbroken hierarchy, wherein each successive grade results from an increased manifestation of the special form of action by which the cerebral centers are distinguished from all below them. (*PP* 35)

A not so tacit homology emerges in *The Principles* between "grades" of person, species of animal, and levels of brain function. Yet we should not let this mapping obscure for us what are nearly isomorphic positions—that of the tramp and the dog, each of whom stands well below the threshold of full human consciousness. "Since nature never makes a jump," James concludes after a long excursus on the limited "reasoning" of dogs, "it is evident that we should find the lowest men occupying in this respect an intermediate position between the brutes and the highest men" (*PP* 984). Though in one account of the species hierarchy the dog stands below his human counterpart, "the tramp who lives from hour to hour," his "violent defiance" against this creature—who often appears as a stranger in the night, an outsider to the home which it is the dog's task to defend—suggests another way of assessing the proximity of dogs and vagrants.[21] Naturally cautious and familial, the dog provides a foil to this chancy population. In this version of the hierarchy, whereby dogs instinctively grasp the prudence and propriety that tramps lack, the dog is not the tramp's inferior but an "ideal" (*PP* 130) for the latter to follow.

This is the role James assigns to domestic animals in his chapter on "Habit," which is anomalous in *The Principles* for the readiness with which it crosses the line between scientific detachment and moral imperative. "In wild animals," James observes, "the usual round of daily behavior seems a necessity implanted at birth; in animals domesticated, and especially in man, it seems, to a great extent, to be the result of education" (*PP* 109). The privileged status of "education" in this chapter licenses the crossover from "properties of matter" (*PP* 109) to the more nebulous realm of social theory and the various "ethical implications of the law of habit" (*PP* 124). After informing us that "domestic animals . . . seem to be machines almost pure and simple, undoubtingly, unhesitatingly doing from minute to minute the duties they have been taught," James announces aphoristically: "Habit is thus the enormous fly-wheel of society, its most precious conservative agent" (*PP* 125).

That James is ambivalent about this aspect of habit has long been observed. Such ambivalence is among the most interesting facets of The *Principles,* in which contradictory versions of mentality continually vie for James's attention. But one point is clear in this example: the domestic animal, trained not to doubt the work he undertakes, is indubitably superior to that "miserable human being . . . in whom nothing is habitual but indecision" (*PP* 126). Domestic animals are exemplary in the sense of setting a good example to persons who have trouble keeping "within the bounds of ordinance" (*PP* 125) or who live "hour to hour" or "day to day" in a morass of "express volitional deliberation" (*PP* 126) and existential doubt. Like his description of the "blind impulse" toward home which urges the wayfarer off the "dangerous repose" of the road and onward to safety, James's take on habit implies that consciousness at its optimum exerts a centripetal force that guides the self surely and safely to the "ordinance" of the "work-a-day world" (*PP* 129). In preventing its owner from "straying" too far from his best "interests," consciousness never loses sight of the fact that the best selves shun the risky world of the transient and the stranger.

Yet at least according to James and his contemporaries, it turns out that consciousness loses sight of this fact quite often. G. Stanley Hall, for example, alerted his readers to the perils of female adolescence in words that echo James's anxiety over the "indecisions" to which an insufficiently habituated consciousness was prone: "Women can remain in what is really a suppressed semi-erotic state with never culminating feeling, so scattered in their interests and enthusiasms that they cannot fix their affections permanently."[22] Just as James shares Hall's belief that adolescence is a particularly fraught period for the development of good habits, so Hall echoes James's sense of consciousness as liable at its most extreme to *too much thought.* Turning each moment of the self's existence into a matter of "deliberation," consciousness becomes the locale of an infectious and promiscuous desire that appears to undo the very agency James ascribes to it.

The unpredictable relation between consciousness and desire is one reason that psychologists after James considered the whole notion of consciousness problematic for their aspirations to exact science, and sought to displace it by returning to the morphological model in which physical behavior would subsume consciousness. In the words of John Watson, consciousness is a holdover from "medieval speculation," "an undefinable something" in whose analytic pursuit "there is no element of control" (*BB* 5). Watson banishes consciousness and its uncontrollability from consideration, declaring that thought is "largely subvocal talking" carried on "with the whole body" (*BB* 40). Watson's effort to reinterpret consciousness as a "device" of bodily "manipulation" (*BB* 40) answers the problem that James and Hall see in the tendency of consciousness to stray or to veer from its course by implying that such waywardness is a function of physicality and environment. By readjusting the self to its bodily propriety, Watson argues, one can rectify what look like diseases of the mind by retraining "the visceral components of a total bodily reaction"; in particular, this can be accomplished by "conditioning the intestine simultaneously with the verbal and manual components" (*BB* 33). Watson borrows from Pavlov the understanding of food as the stimulus par excellence for the canine subject. Yet extrapolating dramatically from Pavlov's research (though Pavlov resisted the application to persons), Watson converts problems of human consciousness—fear, anxiety, anger—into matters of physical hunger. What looks like a flaw in the mind is simply due to an "intestine" that hasn't been properly "conditioned" (*BB* 32). For Watson, there is no such thing as unfixed "affections" in Hall's terms; there are only appetites that have yet to be trained to their proper objects. Watson reconstructs the problem of desire not as a subject for introspection but as a problem of the environment, or more accurately, the problem of finding the right relation between the appetitive self and the exterior world.

The tendency of "mentality" (*PP* 21) to oscillate between wandering and concentration is a recurring dilemma which James, as if enacting his own theory of an overly stimulated consciousness, has difficulty resolving. Early on in *The Principles,* James tries to fuse these incompatible tendencies into a model that appears to balance human unpredictability against the need for self-regulation: "The pursuance of future ends and the choice of means for their attainment," James writes in chapter 1, "are thus the mark and criterion of the presence of mentality" (*PP* 21). Defining "living" beings as possessed of "fixed ends" and "varying means" (*PP* 20), James draws on Romeo and Juliet's example to illustrate this point: "Romeo and Juliet, if a wall be built between them, do not remain idiotically pressing their faces against its opposite sides. . . . Romeo soon finds a circuitous way . . . of touching Juliet's lips directly. . . . With the lover it is the end which is fixed, the path may be modified indefinitely" (*PP* 20).

This is not a good example of human desire at its "teleological" (*PP* 21) best, however. To exemplify the contrast between human agents and "inanimate" (*PP* 20) phenomena whose appearance of motion or action is simply "accidental" (*PP* 21) in the absence of a guiding mentality, James must forget that Romeo's desire—for "touching Juliet's lips directly"—is hardly coincident with his "best interests," given the consequences of his attraction to her. At most these interests can be construed in sheerly immediate terms, though

James spurns such terms elsewhere in *The Principles*. The "circuitous" methods that Romeo devises of course ensue from the opinion voiced throughout Shakespeare's play that such desire is not—could not possibly be—straightforward. Propriety and family pride both chafe at the idea of Romeo and Juliet belonging to each other. James's enlistment of Romeo and Juliet to assert the contrast between living "mentality" and inanimate phenomena is peculiar not only because the characters are fictitious, nor simply because their mutual pursuit is marked through and through by "accidents" that thwart their union despite their "varying means," but also because their example seems to unravel the very point that James seeks to make with it. That point is, of course, that consciousness provides human agents with a vehicle of self-control, of self-possession. Romeo and Juliet's mutual attraction is not aligned with the inhibitory aspect of consciousness that James has advanced as the means to curb waywardness or dispossession; it is instead synonymous with that waywardness or dispossession. In refusing to be "thwarted," this desire is capable of disastrous social consequences—not least of which involves the failure to keep either lover where he or she officially belongs.

The relation between desire and consciousness in *The Principles* turns on just this issue of belonging. If, as James writes, "My thought belongs with my other thoughts, and your thought with your other thoughts" (*PP* 220), then desire even at its most normative feels like a breach of the protocols of belonging crucial to James's theory of consciousness—domesticity, family loyalty, respect for status. To borrow a term James uses in a different passage of *The Principles,* Romeo and Juliet "go astray," (*PP* 232) even as their attraction induces James to promote them as the bearers of a "fixed end." Straying is opposed both emphatically and precariously to "belonging." But both categories come in handy when talking about dogs in both *The Principles* and in the literary examples I have been canvassing. Even when canine life-narratives understand the dog as liable to stray, the dog's disobedience never interferes with its real priorities, its sense that things belong together in a certain way. James echoes the canine memoirists toward the conclusion of his book in chapter 22, "Reasoning," in which he produces a lengthy excursus on the difference between brutes and persons regarding the faculty that gives the chapter its name. Dogs do not reason, James argues, because in them "thoughts will not be found to call up their similar, but only their habitual successors" (*PP* 977). Operating according to what James calls "mere contiguous association" (*PP* 973), which he opposes to the human capacity to have "groups of ideas break across in unaccustomed places," the dog's mind allows no room for disagreement among thoughts, no room for difference: "one total thought suggests to them another total thought, and they find themselves acting with propriety" (*PP* 977). The dog thus "takes the world simply for granted, and never wonders at it at all" (*PP* 977).

Though here James disparages as insufficient for full intellect the contiguities by means of which canine consciousness grasps the world, elsewhere in *The Principles* the dog's lack of "ruptures of contiguous associations," its inability to substitute a concept or thought with a like one "far off" (*PP*981), becomes the model of social stability, since the power to substitute the objects of our desire with things beyond our environs raises sticky problems for order. To say that James is ambivalent about this capacity of persons not only to want but also to be engrossed by things outside their purview would understate the matter. However vigorously he might champion the powers of "dissociation" (*PP*979) in the chapter on "Reasoning," throughout *The Principles* he is just as leery of the mind's tendency to become distracted, to move away from what he calls the "resting-places" (*PP*237) of consciousness in favor of the vertiginous pull of scattered objects. James sees the ability to desire what one doesn't have as both what makes a person fully conscious and what needs the most careful policing, since the pursuit of "far off" desires results in the untying of the social bond. "No one need be told how dependent all human social elevation is upon the prevalence of chastity" (*PP*35), James writes. But if this "factor" is what "measures . . . the difference between civilization and barbarism" (*PP* 35), it is a factor whose precepts must be taught through the example of the very brutes whom James would use to distinguish the civilized from the barbarous. "It is surprising how soon a desire will die of inanition," James claims, "if it be *never* fed" (*PP* 128). This theory of desire, of course, presumes that the desiring self, like the dog, is absorbed only in its "contiguous associations," whereby "each sign is drowned in *its* import, and never awakens other signs and other imports in juxtaposition" (*PP*981). Desire here is obliged to focus on the objects lying closest to it, the only objects on which it "feeds."

Even on James's own terms, this is a grossly counterintuitive account of desire, since human consciousness is set off from that of other species by its ability to transcend the contingencies of place, to be not local but "remote" in casting about for objects for its delectation. Yet insofar as it restates the threat to orderly belonging and routine that underlie the coherence of persons, desire necessitates this reactive recuperation on James's part. Though James comes to stand in for the failure of introspective psychology in the reaction-formation of behavioral theorists like Watson and Thorndike, his own view of the corrective to mentality's excesses—an alignment of desire with the physiology of hunger—predicts their physicalist approach to the problem of unruly conduct. Where the dog "takes the world simply for granted," including its status hierarchy and its property arrangements, the human person is far too liable to "wonder why the universe should be as it is" (*PP* 977). Endowed with the power to substitute one thing for another, persons have a knack for recombination and rearrangement. All that keeps them from "breaking up" "the actual" (*PP* 977), either by acting out their desires or by straying from their "resting-places," is the brute fact of habit. Habit makes what are otherwise questionable provisions and social structures feel as if they belong together in just the right way.

III

It is at the intersection of canine consciousness and the preservation of social order that Stein's interest in dogs most insistently imposes itself onto her larger project. In both her early and late writing, Stein exploits the customary proximity of loyal domestic pets and disloyal, shifty, or undomesticated persons. This combination, which we have observed as a structural element in the hierarchy of consciousness in *The Principles*, also has a lengthy pedigree in the intricate canine discourse I have been parsing. In London's *Call of the Wild* (1903), Buck's forced departure from the cozy Southland estate of Judge Miller ensues from an act of treachery on the part of a gardener's helper excessively marked as alien and vicious (a Mexican with a gambling addiction whose domestic economy is out of balance by virtue of his having proliferated too many mouths). In Mark Twain's peculiar and somewhat morbid talking-dog story, *A Dog's Tale* (1903), written expressly for an antivivisectionist organization, the heroic narrator, a mongrel named Aileen Mavourneen, rescues her master's baby from a fire started by a careless servant only to have her own offspring executed by that same master during an optics experiment.[23] In Kipling's "The Dog Hervey," that eponymous canine becomes the possession of a woman whose personal fortune is derived from her doctor father's illicit practice of "rescuing" indigent and dissipated men "in the repentant stage," rehabilitating them enough to take out lucrative insurance policies on them, and finally cashing in on those policies when his patients lapse into their old habits. Miss Sichliffe, the doctor's daughter, expects that nurturing the dubious runt Hervey back to health will serve as penance for her father's profiteering from the recidivism of the "stormy young men" he "patched up."[24] Like Twain with his unfeeling vivisectionist patriarch and Kipling with his disreputable father-doctor, the authors of canine life-narratives conjure drifters and illegitimate medical men in equal parts, just as Stein populates "The Good Anna" with (among others) two disobedient dogs, a succession of wayward servant girls, an abortionist, and a midwife who specializes in delivering the babies of unmarried women.

Reading Stein's texts through the lens of popular representations like Twain's and Kipling's, with their problematic mingling of illicit persons and irregular behaviors, allows us to move beyond the formalist accounts of Stein that have dominated discussion of her work. Because they focus criticism of

Stein on form rather than on content, on what Cary Nelson calls "language's representational claims" and "its signifying power," critics have made it hard to accommodate the idea that Stein's work might have interpretive value at the thematic level.[25] Though able Stein critics have explored the connection between her work and James's, for instance, they have viewed it largely in formal terms, nimbly positing how Jamesian habit is transformed into the arithmetic-like prose of Stein's texts.[26] Dogs have thus proved hard to read in Stein; they don't fit neatly into the abstractive calculus of most Stein criticism because they embody a sort of obdurate content, a sheer presence that doesn't necessarily "mean" anything.

In one sense that is exactly how Stein wants us to read dogs. Their very familiarity appears to put a brake on the endless interpretive abysses—the "indecisions"—toward which consciousness at its least domesticated was thought to tend. Though dogs mean a great deal to the diverse participants in Stein's culture, these figures are unanimous in seizing on the relation between the dog's regularity and the illicit, irregular, or undomesticated behavior of human persons. Restoring a sense of content to Stein's seemingly aleatory and nonnarrative texts allows us to look past the linguistic formalism her work has invited. A crucial narrative her work recounts is very close to the one I have been describing in modernist psychology and canine memoirs. This is the story of persons whose minds threaten to take their bodies astray and of dogs who meliorate this threat with their penchant for domesticity and equilibrium.

"I am I," Stein writes in "Identity: A Poem," "because my little dog knows me" (SR 588). The shoring up of human identity here seems to require the awareness that only a dog is privileged to provide. As it happens, this is an acknowledgment with an impeccable pedigree in Western literary tradition. The recognition that the dying Argos grants to the mobile and disguised Odysseus as he returns to his palace in Ithaca is the locus classicus of an act of knowing that essentially exhausts the dog's reason for living. Even as Odysseus strategically obscures his own identity by assuming the role of a beggar, the by now heroically aged dog in book 12 of the *Odyssey* acts as a chorus that hails Odysseus unequivocally, putting him in his rightful place as landowner, sovereign, and husband. The second sentence in "Identity" would appear to confirm the necessary supplement of canine recognition, without which, we are told, "the figure" in the poem, like Odysseus throughout much of the Homeric epic, "wanders on alone" (SR 588). Fixing or stabilizing the self, placing it in context and keeping it consistent, is unthinkable without the dog that serves as both the self's double and its steering mechanism. A creature incapable of being alone ("If it were alone it would not be there," Stein writes), the dog binds the human self to the world, keeping in check an otherwise perilously "wandering" consciousness:

"The human mind. The human mind by itself does play" (*SR* 590). This classical echo, I suggest, is quite intentional. Stein calls up not only the Homeric antecedent but also the tragedian's reliance on the chorus to negotiate the status of dogs in this poem.

Because they "rest" and "wait"—because that is the role they are assigned in this script—dogs ground the excess "play" to which the mind "by itself" is liable. "Play" here means both gaming and theatricality, implying a departure from a scripted role, an exchange of the real self for a make-believe one. Left to its own devices, Stein suggests, "mind" assumes that unfettered independence from constraint against which *The Principles* cautions. "Identity: A Poem" is infused with references to canine stasis in the midst of unreliable and anxiogenic human wanderings. "Yes there is a great deal of use in a man coming," Stein writes, "but will he come at all if he does come will he come here" (*SR* 590). In the context of such indeterminacy, it is the speaker's ability to predict the dog's behavior or to map out and to grasp its identity that matters most to the poem. "The dog listens while they prepare food" (*SR* 592) because the relation between the dog's hearing and the dog's eating is a functional one, reducible to necessity; all the dog hears is the preparation of food—since food, as Pavlov sought to prove, is the only thing a dog can be said to "care about." By contrast, Stein writes in the next sentence, "Food might be connected with the human mind but it is not." Where the relation between the dog and its basic needs and environment is certain and even natural (what James would call contiguous and what Pavlov would call reflexive), the relation between human need and "human nature" is much harder to calculate. Though the latter looks like a relation of necessity, as the speaker cautions, it is ultimately incoherent to claim an identity between "the human mind" and its bodily functions—to condense mentality to Watson's "intestine." Unable to achieve the consistency with which the dog inhabits his world, Stein implies, at best we can hope to illuminate our more obscure identities by the reflected light of canine order.

No sooner does "Identity: A Poem" introduce this scenario with regard to canine orderliness and human wandering, however, than it throws it into question by querying exactly what kind of acknowledgment a dog can provide to a human counterpart. This is so in part because the dog "does not write" (*SR* 590) and cannot "say" (*SR* 590); deprived of words, the dog can neither communicate the certitude of his existence, the self-evidence of his enviably static identity, nor help persons sort out the ambiguities of human language. Stein's poem draws out the implications for language of the canine analogy's basic conceit—its theory of correspondences, as in Pavlov's reflex studies. A stimulus-response theory of language would obviate the uncertainty of human relations by assimilating language to the natural realm of correspondence where each word, correlated to one determinate meaning, might become fully reliable and trustworthy. Furthermore, persons would be expected to follow each determinate meaning just as dogs reflexively obey environmental stimuli (or, for that matter, human commands).

Such hypothetical determinacy typifies language for what James sees as the equivalent to Stein's mute and illiterate dog, the "primeval man" in whom "a given emotion" induces "a natural interjection" (*PP* 981): "his mental procedure tends to *fix* this cry on *that* emotion; and when this occurs, in many instances, he is provided with a stock of signs, like the yelp, beg, rat of the dog, each of which suggests a determinate image" (*PP* 982). James's word to describe this state of "primeval" sign-grasping is "recall" (*PP* 981); "the reflex sounds" associated with states of emotion operate like the various commands a dog hears—"yelp, beg, rat"—to "remind" a person "of his own former experience" (*PP* 982).[27] That words are internally differentiated—that one sound can mean more than one thing—is a complexity to which dogs are indifferent. "What did a dog care to know whether know is no," Stein writes in a manuscript titled "Lesson I," "whether sew is so, whether read is red, what indeed did any little dog need to know."[28] That dogs are "stupid" to such concerns, to use Thorndike's term, makes them reliable interlocutors for a language understood exclusively as a set of imperatives. "With him," Galsworthy writes of his late dog, "words play no torturing tricks" (*JG* 56).

Yet because the dog unthinkingly obeys the words he hears without pondering their meanings, he offers no relief from language's tendency to produce misunderstanding as well as communication. In the realm of canine-human bonds all words have the status of imperatives—like the word "come," for example. In "Identity: A Poem," by contrast, the word "come" is aligned not with the imperative but with the interrogative. Like many sentences in Stein, the phrase "will he come at all if he does come will he come here" (*SR* 590) omits a question mark after a line that appears to demand this end punctuation, as if to emphasize that the interrogative has become hopelessly entangled with the most basic declaratives. The word "come" has a special place in the lexicon of canine-human bonds. It is the command that serves as shorthand for what dog-trainer jargon labels "recall." And recall turns out to be the crucial mechanism by which the dog does and does not steady human variability and disobedience. Unlike that of James's "primeval man," the world that "Identity: A Poem" envisions has lost the power to make words accord with "determinate" or "fixed" meanings, or to make persons "recall" those meanings intelligibly. Dogs in this poem serve as reminders to persons of how the latter should conduct themselves, only to be thwarted in this mnemonic assist. "No the dog is not the chorus" (*SR* 593), Stein writes. If the traditional place of the chorus is the place of tradition, of providing recall in tragic poetry, the dog has no such efficacy since, as Stein's poem abruptly announces, "There is no chorus in the human mind" (*SR* 592).

The dog is not a chorus because although "Nobody who has a dog forgets him," it is also the case that, as Stein writes in the following sentence, "They may leave him behind. Oh yes they may leave him behind" (*SR* 592). In denying that anything has a place in the "human mind" other than the mind itself, Stein introduces an extreme version of the aleatory relation among minds derived from James's understanding of consciousness as the exclusive property of its owner. "Leaving behind" becomes possible when minds are conceived as so exclusive that they can appear totally detached from one another. They don't line up; they don't cue each other the way a dog obeys human commands. Just as persons may not forget their pets even as they "leave [them] behind," so persons, unlike tragic heroes, may remember the laws of their societies yet choose anyway to disobey them without necessarily enduring the consequences—the divine wrath or judicial boomerang—that ultimately sanctify cultures in which tragedy matters. The Greeks, to whom such consequences indeed appeared to matter, called this sense of orderly necessity *dike*. The function of the chorus at its most reductive in classical culture is simply to remind the audience of *dike*, to remember for them that the hierarchical arrangement of persons and things is both necessary and just. In the dispensation of modernity, in which social reality follows what Anthony Giddens calls a logic of "disembedding" and what a more traditional school of sociology calls "anomie," to speak of *dike* feels at best naïve. The dependency that sociologist Edward Ross defined as constitutive of modern life in *Sin and Society* (1907)—"the mutualism of our time" "where the welfare of all is at the mercy of each"—coexists with that other modern innovation, limited liability, the legalized deniability enjoyed by corporate persons and practiced by real ones.[29] Indifferent to the classical correlation of drama and social order, Stein's plays emphasize dislocation rather than constraint, alternation rather than succession, because they are invested not in consequences but in their attenuation. Stein's plays stage the world as a place where neither things nor persons necessarily follow each other.

From one angle, the declaration "I am I because my little dog knows me" appears to resolve the matter of identity or self-knowledge so completely that it bears no further examination: "Yes there I told you human nature is not at all interesting" (*SR* 593). In another instance, though, Stein writes: "I am I has really nothing to do with the little dog knowing me, he is my audience, but an audience never does prove to you that you are you" (*SR* 593). Even with the loaded word "prove," which suggests the behaviorist goal of exacting human identity from human actions, it is hard not to read this comment as an autobiographical reflection regarding Stein's struggle with the discrepancy between her own self-understanding and that of her "audience." Indeed, the incongruity between audience and "performer" or player goes far back in Stein's career. Far from disabling her project, however, the failure of the audience to give "proof," to find common cause or identity with the thing it is forced to observe, is by her own reckoning the discovery that first energized Stein's writing of plays. "The thing that is fundamental about plays," Stein writes in her lecture on that subject, "is that the scene as depicted on stage is more often than not one might say it almost always is in syncopated time in relation to the emotion of anybody in the audience."[30] What a theatergoing audience "proves" to Stein (to use the word from "Identity") is such incongruity, the "difference in tempo" that forms the rhythm of staged performance. Stein describes this rhythm as "something that makes anybody nervous" (*LA* 95). "Nervousness," she further argues, "consists in needing to go faster or to go slower so as to get together. It is that that makes anybody feel nervous" (*LA* 95).

Nervousness originates in a desire to "get together" those experiences or relations which seem hopelessly out of sync—a theory not far removed from how James and later psychologists understood the physiology of the nervous system during the early days of its exploration. "So infinitely complex, so continuously in flux, are the conditions in the world around," writes E. L. Thorndike in *Animal Intelligence,* "that that complex animal system which is itself in living flux, and that system only, has a chance to establish dynamic equilibrium with the environment" (*AI* 13). Thorndike's is a potentially contradictory model of homeostasis, in that "flux" and dynamism are introduced into the system as the means to achieve consistency and balance. As if reacting to this potential discrepancy between means and end in the behaviorist doctrine, Stein's "Identity: A Poem" ultimately denies equilibrium, the settling or resting of the wandering self, in favor of nervousness. And its proliferation of different views of the relation between dog and person rehearses the defiance of stable identity, mutual recognition, and belonging that the poem also at times appears to solicit. The dog straddles the line between chorus and audience in that, like a chorus, the dog's example looks sufficient to ground the human self in place while, like a "nervous" audience, the dog is a helpless onlooker to a human "play" with whose syncopating movements he tries but fails to "get together." Whereas the chorus knows its place and sticks to it, the dog makes for an inadequate chorus because although he too "knows" his place, such knowledge does not provide any guarantee that human beings will follow his example. This is because modern culture calls the very idea of following into question. In "Identity: A Poem" as in other Stein works, following cedes readily to displacement—to wandering, straying, leaving home, and (not coincidentally) to surrendering, losing, or abandoning dogs. In Stein's plays, to which I now turn, what matters is the syncopation whereby things appear to "get together," to attain what physiologists call homeostasis, but in which the pull in another direction—away from belonging and correspondence—is finally too strong to resist.

Stein spent a good deal of energy not only dramatizing this syncopation between order and dislocation but also casting dogs in key supporting roles in her plays, the earliest of which were collected in *Geography and Plays* (1922). Stein registers drama's "nervous" rhythm in this book, first through the now familiar juxtaposition of dog and unruly persons. In the play "Do Let Us Go Away," Stein begins one scene:

> Conversation. I asked him did he like to hear the dog bark. He said he would shoot at him. I said did he like to hear it. We were ashamed of his servants. They talked together loudly. We hoped he would control them. He wrote it. So did they together. Please have peace.[31]

The barking of the dog is explicitly aligned with the loudness of the shameful "servants"; both dog and servant make noises that exceed the "control" and the peaceful decorum of the genteel conversation that brings them up. But in fact that conversation is anything but controlled. As in all Stein plays, the rhythm of the dialogue is couched in what we might call intense syncopation, in that its speakers seem barely to follow one another. ("I asked him did he like to hear the dog bark. He said he would shoot at him. I said did he like to hear it.") The non sequitur that governs the syntax of Stein's dramatic dialogues suggests at the most elemental level of communication that these characters do not follow one another; they do not obey the rules of polite discourse, any more than the dog's bark or the servant's loud talk does. More important, the play's title—"Do Let Us Go Away"—suggests that getting things in order or putting them in their place is the last thing on the speaker's mind. In this play the plea for "peace"—what another character calls the "habit of closing up" (*GP* 220), of turning inward against the clangor of the world—competes with the urge to depart or stray. In "For the Country Entirely: A Play in Letters," this urge is spelled out when the protagonist writes to a couple with whom she is friends: "we promised to go into the wind and not take shelter" (*GP* 229).

Stein's plays insist on foregrounding problems of alignment and consistency. One sees this insistence taken to its extreme in the broken dialogues of *Geography and Plays*, which not only record fragmented conversations but also dwell on the comings and goings, the endless visitations and departures, of cosmopolitan travelers. The breakdown both in linguistic progression and in keeping persons in place is so severe in *Geography and Plays* that dogs serve as the only recognizable conservators of order, the only custodians of a regular social world. When Stein wrote the pieces collected in this book, or so "Alice" tells us in her *Autobiography*, "we had a dog, a Mallorcan hound" whom the couple named Polybe and who "comes into many of the plays Gertrude Stein wrote at this time."[32] Polybe turns out to be the fixed element in these errant dramas. As in "Identity: A Poem," the dog's predilection for "following" is meant to compensate for the dramatic non sequiturs that infect each dialogue, just as its superior domestic habits keep persons mindful of their own. Hence in the play "Turkey and Bones and Eating and We Like It," the character Minorca observes, "I like a dog which is easily understood as I have never had the habit of going out except on Sunday" (*GP* 239). Dogs keep people inside and prevent them from venturing forth. In the same play, Polybe is shown appraising "straw seats which are so well made that they resemble stools" (*GP* 239). This is not only because Polybe is made for sitting ("he does not like to stand" [*GP* 239]) but also because, given the dog's traditional role as the weaver of the social fabric in sentimental canine literature, he is able to appreciate as only a dog can the fine craftsmanship that goes into the seat. Stein named her first and second poodles Basket I and Basket II as if in homage to a literary heritage that saw the dog as helping to plait the domestic containers in which we settle both our belongings and ourselves.

Yet in *Geography and Plays* even dogs ultimately fail at their customary duty to guarantee faith and belonging. In "A Collection," Stein writes of "Polybe in Port," "Polybe does not remember. Me. Yes. The house. Yes. The servant. Yes. You are not mistaken" (*GP* 25). As "Alice" informs her readers in *The Autobiography*, Stein and Toklas left "Polybe behind us in the care of one of the guardians of the old fortress of Belver. When we saw him a week later he did not know us or his name" (*AA* 165). The perdurable bond between pet and person meant to shore up the person's sense of the world at large turns out to be impermanent after all. Hence an exchange in "Every Afternoon" runs, "What did you do with your dog. We sent him into the country. Was he a trouble. Not at all but we thought he would be better off there" (*GP* 256). This instance illustrates that however deep one's affection for a pet may be, that pet can always be transferred or even *substituted* for another. The romanticized attachments between owners and pets are paradoxically inseparable from the real impermanence such attachments entail. Pet ownership is almost always serial, for example, given the different life cycles of dogs and persons (hence canine memoirs are typically concerned with dogs who have passed on, with a dog one "had"). A dog is a loved one both totally idealized and wholly replaceable.

"So we tried to have the same and not to have the same," Stein writes of the death of "Basket the First" in *Paris France* (1939), "and then at last we found another Basket, and we got him and we called him Basket and he is very gay and I cannot say the confusion has taken place but certainly *le roi est mort vive le roi*, is a normal attitude of mind."[33] The idea that one can transfer one's cathexis from one object to another without any loss of feeling finds its basis for Stein in the model of sovereignty—the king's two bodies—that grounds the reproduction of political orders and political loyalty.[34] For Stein, such substitutions form a "normal attitude of mind"; indeed, they are not only "normal" but also necessary if a regime's authority is to endure. By "confusion" in this paragraph, I take Stein to mean the awareness during moments of transition that power, however charismatic or durable, does in fact change hands, is dynamic and porous and liable to drift in a way that those who exercise it seek to conceal. "Confusion" ensues momentarily because what we might call the habit of obedience to one charismatic authority figure has been tampered with by that figure's death. In Jamesian terms, habit then comes to restore the seemingly oxymoronic speech acts—"*le roi est mort vive le roi*"—to sensibility, not to say propriety. Habit also translates what look like potential non sequiturs—the king is dead; long live the king—into the syntax of common sense. The habit of obedience to authority smoothes the passage of what might otherwise be an unstable and incoherent transfer of power.

Despite Stein's upending of the sacred hierarchy on which sovereignty is contingent, grafting onto a pet the authority of a king makes more sense than a first glance suggests. As the allusion to Odysseus's greeting by Argos alerts us in "Identity: A Poem," kings and dogs share a privileged relation to status recognition insofar as both are creatures who *embody* rank, who communicate power differentials through their bodily forms. Kings are creatures to whom one pays allegiance by bowing or genuflecting, physical displays of deference that naturalize the social artifice of hierarchy. Dogs enact dominance or submission through a detailed body language in which all dogs are instinctively fluent. As Darwin points out at great length in *The Expression of the Emotions in Man and Animals* (1872), when a "dog suddenly discovers that the man he is approaching, is not a stranger, but his master," "the body sinks downwards or even crouches, and is thrown into flexuous movements; his tail, instead of being stiff and upright, is lowered and wagged from side to side; his hair instantly becomes smooth; his ears are depressed and drawn backwards, but not closely to the head; and his lips hang loosely."[35] With dogs and kings, one always knows where one stands, and such knowledge is inscribed into the very corporeal environments kings and dogs inhabit.[36]

In Stein the problem of how to induce obedience to authority, how to make authority intelligible to its subjects, finds its modern rejoinder in a behaviorism whose idiom is taken from the body language of dogs. "The student of human behavior," Watson writes in *Behaviorism*, "works with the whole body in action"—by which he means a body "built around" "reactions to simple and complex stimuli."[37] The instability of power and the inco-herence of its reproduction are conditions of modernist culture, with its prolific mobility, its rapid turnover, and its propensity toward ever more par-ticularized divisions of labor and function. Yet modernity's impermanence and dynamism do not cancel out the science of social control so much as they pose acute new problems for it. Its volatile market economies and po-litical upheavals intensify the need for a mode of social control flexible enough to keep pace with modern culture's irregular rhythms—a need that behaviorism attempts to satisfy. I conclude this chapter by reading *Three Lives* in terms of the sustained tension between habituation and syncopation, be-tween correspondence and incompatibility with the social environment, that early twentieth-century behaviorism insistently understands through the canine analogy.

The elasticity and impermanence of social life in Bridgepoint, where *Three Lives* is set, operate at all times in tandem with bids for domination and struggles for power. From the first sentence in *Three Lives*—"The tradesmen of Bridgepoint learned to dread the sound of 'Miss Mathilda,' for with that name the good Anna always conquered"—we begin to glimpse the peculiar vicissitudes of power that energize these three loosely connected tales. We learn first that the "dread" of these merchants is an acquired habit, rein-forced over time through the name that Anna wields at them; and we learn that Anna herself, a mere delegate of Miss Mathilda, in fact assumes pride of place in the chain of command she invokes here. If Anna "always con-quered," that conquest nonetheless needs continual backing. Just as the prices of these tradesmen's goods are not fixed—"they could give things for a little less" (*TL* 3)—so the economy of power that operates in Bridgepoint at large remains in flux, its hierarchical coordinates liable to be shuffled or reorganized unpredictably. Just as Anna conquers the tradesmen with the force of will by which she masters her employers ("Anna's superiors must be always these large helpless women, or be men" [*TL* 14]), so other kinds of relations are prone to inversions of dominance and submission. Miss Mary, for example, "yielded docilely to the stronger power in" Jane, the niece she has adopted, a "little girl" distinguished by her "gentle force" and "sweet domination" (*TL* 14). And Mrs. Lehntman, "the romance in Anna's life" (*TL* 18), "was the only one who had any power over Anna" (*TL* 19)—though their relation consists in the oscillation of power between them. "It had been plain to see in the six years these women were together," Stein's narrator observes, "how Anna gradually had come to lead. Not really lead, of course, for Mrs. Lehntman never could be led, she was so very devious in her ways" (*TL* 26).

Power is ambiguous and unstable in "The Good Anna" because the rela-tions that would anchor it are constantly slipping away from Anna; these hierarchical arrangements are, like Miss Mathilda, "given to much wandering" (*TL* 50). In a rare aside in *Three Lives,* the narrator breaks from her myopic recording of the story at hand into a didactic lesson which seems to have only a faint bearing on the surrounding narrative. "In friendship," Stein writes,

> power always has its downward curve. One's strength to manage rises al-
> ways higher until there comes a time one does not win, and though one
> may not really lose, still from the time that victory is not sure, one's
> power slowly ceases to be strong. It is only in a close tie such as marriage,
> that influence can mount and grow always stronger with the years and
> never meet with a decline. It can only happen so when there is no way to
> escape. (*TL* 35–36)

The narrator's point is that once the standard channels of power cease to apply—once marriage no longer obtains as a means of "influence"—power does not evaporate so much as it becomes unpredictable; with no institution to contain them, nothing keeps relations between individuals in the home-ostasis that marriage promises. In this account of marriage, the "close tie" acts as a closed system from which "one can surely never break away" (*TL* 36) and in which "influence" can thus take the form of "a steady march." Marriage steadies individuals by making power flow evenly and in the proper direction; according to the obtuse narrator of *Three Lives,* husbands and wives are spared both the failure of their affection and the dangerous incursion of other influences, other desires, by the marital bond that ex-cludes all other considerations.

Why this concern should appeal to the narrator at this point, of course, has everything to do with the fact that marriage is precisely what Anna her-self cannot abide; she absents herself from employment situations, for ex-ample, in which the household passes into the control of a married couple (as with Mary Wadsmith, who goes to live with her married niece, Jane; or with Dr. Shonjen, whose wedding forces Anna to resign). As unsteady as the power relations may be among these unmarried households, Anna cannot thrive without them. Homeostasis, we might say, is her enemy. What Anna seeks is not domestic fulfillment but a continual administration of the dis-orderly creatures—the "stray dogs and cats and people," as Stein refers to them—"who all asked and seemed to need her care" (*TL* 53).

If power arrangements in *Three Lives* tend toward disarray, continually re-versing the ordained hierarchies of master and servant, then the means to negotiate this fluctuation derive from a managerial style that was perfected first in the husbandry of domestic animals—dogs and horses—and later in the behavioral research laboratories of Pavlov, Thorndike, and B. F. Skinner. We see this style most obviously in the frequent use of the term "obedient" to describe the servants and children who populate Bridgepoint. Anna's friend Mrs. Drehten has "hard working obedient simple daughters" (*TL* 29), and her brother's daughters are likewise "well trained, quiet, obedient, well dressed girls" (*TL* 32). Mrs. Drehten's face has the look "that comes with a german husband to obey" (*TL* 29); and in "The Gentle Lena," Herman Kreder "was always obedient in everything to his mother and father" (*TL* 180).

This language of obedience is notable not only because it shores up traditional family pieties—the dutiful children, the loyal wife—but also because it appeals directly to the animal model of behavioral control, as when Anna muses over the litany of those she "could scold": "Now it was not only other girls and the colored man, and dogs, and cats, and horses and her parrot, but her cheery master, jolly Dr. Shonjen, whom she could guide and constantly rebuke to his own good" (*TL* 23). Mrs. Lehntman, over whom Anna "had come to lead" (*TL* 26), is as "devious in her ways" as one of Anna's stray dogs; like a pet who never takes well to the leash, Mrs. Lehntman "had her unhearing mind and her happy way of giving a pleasant well diffused attention" (*TL* 27) that keeps her oblivious of Anna's efforts to "have direction" (*TL* 26). Even Anna's "scoldings" appear borrowed from Pavlov's investigations; she always accompanies them with "good things to eat" (*TL* 52) as if in adherence to Pavlov's dictum that food is the only incentive strong enough to condition the dog's reflexes.

"The Gentle Lena" takes this experimental conceit even further. Unlike the first two stories in *Three Lives*, "The Gentle Lena" is structured around a marriage plot. Yet Stein writes that marriage plot as a behaviorist experiment carried out by Mrs. Haydon on her "docile" (*TL* 176) niece Lena. Having failed to "make" her own children "behave well" (*TL* 175), Mrs. Haydon goes to Germany and brings Lena back to train her for domesticity: "It was all coming out just as she had expected," Stein writes. Unlike Mrs. Haydon's own "stubborn daughters" (*TL* 175) or her son, who is "very hard to manage" (*TL* 174), "Lena was good and never wanted her own way" (*TL* 179)—though the tractability that her aunt values in her is, according to her uncle, just as likely to land her "in trouble" (*TL* 177). The docile malleability Lena embodies could go either way; the same elasticity that molds her for marriage could also lead her astray. Stein points to the uncertain agency that behaviorists concealed at the heart of their project; to argue that persons could be made better than they were was also to cede that they were liable to be worse than one would have liked. "Sometimes a little girl, sometimes a big one was in trouble," Stein writes, "and Anna . . . helped them to find places." She treats them as she treats "the collection of stray creatures," the "dogs and cats," whom she also "places" (*TL* 45).

Melanctha Herbert gets into more "trouble" than any other figure in *Three Lives*. Melanctha shares with Anna an indifference to marriage, and likewise shares her "uneasy" (*TL* 63) relation to her environment. But where Anna "knew so well the kind of ugliness appropriate to each rank in life" (*TL* 25), Melanctha is wholly lacking in such confident judgment. "Too complex with desire," she is "less sure" (*TL* 61) about where things go and how they fit. And where Anna gravitates toward dogs and persons whom she imagines she can govern, Melanctha moves outward, toward the margins of her social world, the "railroad yards" and "the shipping docks" (*TL* 71). Whereas Anna tries to prevent others from escaping environments that cannot hold them down, Melanctha by contrast "would always make herself escape" (*TL* 70).

These stories invert each other. If "The Good Anna" narrates the terminally flawed system of management by which Anna tries to control or "place" persons "in trouble," "Melanctha" looks at management from the other side and suggests that its futility does not void so much as intensify its coerciveness. The continual need to rein in excess desires and behaviors takes its toll on Anna by "thinning" (*TL* 16) her physical form to a "strained" hardness, rendering her body "full of the stiffness, the bridling, the suggestive movement underneath the rigidity of forced control, all the queer ways the passions have to show themselves all one" (*TL* 17). The word "bridling" suggests that the proper analogy for understanding Anna's self-discipline comes not from handling dogs but from breaking horses. (And it is horses to which Melanctha gravitates before she seeks out railroad yards and shipping docks—"Melanctha had to come to the stable joyous" [*TL* 65], Stein writes, as if this inclination were irresistible.) The pun on "bridal" also suggests the link between taming and marriage that the stories in *Three Lives* continually evoke—the relation that will prevent the "movement" of "passions" away from their proper anchorage. Anna's "passions" slip as if tectonically and against her will from their moorings within the closed system of her body. Even her "firm fixed" habits are subject ultimately to the displacement that characterizes the market economy against which she "saves" (*TL* 42) and the "stray" creatures who pass through her household.

The endlessly elastic economies of market culture and personal conduct here create less a freedom from control than an acceleration of it. The strangely redundant phrase "forced control" in "The Good Anna" points to the odd logic at work in "Melanctha," a story in which control seems directed at those processes and behaviors least disposed to it. "Rose Johnson made it very hard," the story's first sentence runs, "to bring her baby to its birth" (*TL* 59). The paragraph suggests counterintuitively that Rose is responsible for keeping her baby from being born, as if the subsequent "careless and negligent and selfish" behavior that presumably leads to the baby's death could be retrofitted to the involuntary physical act of delivering a newborn from the birth canal.[38]

The status of the verb "to make" in *Three Lives* is at issue here. "Making" in this opening sentence implies that giving birth is a matter of behavior subject to modification and choice, an implication that other moments in "Melanctha" both bear out and complicate. If Rose makes it hard for her baby to be born, Melanctha by contrast "worked hard" for her sick mother "to . . . make her dying easy" (*TL* 77). In the context of the first sentence, this action becomes estranged from its common-sense bearings and drifts toward the aberrant construction found in Rose Johnson's delivery. In rendering such straightforward statements as "Rose Johnson had a hard labor" or "Mrs. Herbert had a peaceful death" into the suspect syntax of the auxiliary case, Stein attributes a weirdly misplaced agency to these affairs—a sense that birthing or dying, subject to volition or management, is also subject to disobedience. Persons become responsible for their own or other persons' involuntary actions. Throughout "Melanctha" reflexive or automatic acts are referred to as self-chosen ones through the peculiar usage of the verb "to make," as when Stein's narrator describes Jeff Campbell's facial expression thus: "he made his face get serious" (*TL* 84). Making is always associated with domination in "Melanctha," but just as throughout *Three Lives* power is unstable or fluctuating, so in this story making as a mode of domination is hard to pin down; its provenance is uncertain, its authorship obscure. When we are told that Melanctha is "made by white blood" (*TL* 76), making seems to partake of a biological process, however discredited; when we are told that "the things she had in her of her mother never made her feel respect" (*TL* 63), making appears to be a function of interior feeling, of introspection. When we are told that "Melanctha made herself escape" (*TL* 67), making is defined as a sort of conditioned reflex, somewhere between instinct and volition. Making stands between all these categories, like an adhesive binding them together, because in Stein's culture the concept of "making" provided the alibi for moving from a morphological to a behaviorist understanding of persons.

This peculiar conjugation of the verb "to make" with states of being conventionally understood outside the realm of the artifactual might usefully be termed the "coercive tense." This tense infects not only individual behavior but also the borders of human experience—birth and death—in "Melanctha." In the world this text elaborates, nothing is natural or given. As the terminal artificiality of these framing experiences implies, the coercive tense always posits a disjunction between the self and its environment that "making" must force into equivalence. The failure of alignment we have witnessed in other Stein texts—the failure of speakers to follow each other's meanings in her plays or the tendency of places not to stay still, of territories to erode their boundaries, and of persons to cease to belong where they should—summons the corrective "making" that will compel these dispossessed persons and drifting arrangements back into order. With regard to the disheveled domestic space of the Lehntman household, we are told, Anna "struggled to make things go here as she thought was right" (*TL* 24).

In "Melanctha" the problem of making intersects with the fact of desire as in the instance in which "Melanctha had not found it easy with herself to make her wants and what she had, agree" (*TL* 62). Desire—what one "wants"—is precisely that feature of the self which will not submit to equivalence, despite not only Melanctha's efforts but also Jeff Campbell's implorations on her behalf. Jeff finally abandons Melanctha because of her "way of not being ever equal in your feeling to anybody real": "You never can be equal to me" (*TL* 136), he writes to Melanctha. He means not equality in the political sense but the fact that he cannot make Melanctha—who "was too many for him" (*TL* 124)—add up correctly, without remainder. This remainder clouds the version of love that matters to Jeff, the "always living good and being regular" (*TL* 86) that he promotes as the goal for "the colored people." Jeff's plan for "always trying to make it right, the way they should be always living," distinguishes between this disciplinary familialism, "the way it is good to be in families" (*TL* 111), and "the other way of loving," which he calls "having it like any animal that's low in the streets together" (*TL* 87). In this Jeff mirrors Anna, who is tortured by irregularity, "worn out . . . with her attempt to make the younger generation do all it should do" (*TL* 7). Making, then, is necessary to transmit behaviors from one generation to the next—which is to say as a form of social reproduction. Hence Anna "scolded hard . . . to make young Julia do the way she should" (*TL* 24).

Distinguishing between "kinds of love" (*TL* 87) from the vantage of the physician, Jeff Campbell asserts the position of the scientist who believes that desire can be harnessed or tamed, made "right" or "regular," by domestication. And he also believes that desire can be reduced to necessity—the condition he demands, finally, of Melanctha before his break with her. "To think that Melanctha ever would give him love, just for his sake, and not because she needed it herself" (*TL* 124), turns him into a "beggar" (*TL* 124); her "bounty" ironically reduces him to that state of dispossession which, as we have seen, frequently accompanied those who resisted the necessities of domestic life in Stein's culture. Melanctha's problem, according to Jeff, is that her desire is too profuse to be compassed by the laws of property. It doesn't know where to stop and it doesn't know where it rightfully belongs. In likening the wrong kind of love to "animals . . . all the time just with each other" (*TL* 111), Jeff voices the Jamesian theory of civilization as founded on "chastity." Yet in aligning the untamable Melanctha with a "low" animal whose insatiable need for "wandering" excludes her from the possibility of domestication, he glosses over what he knows all too well: her desire is less a matter of physicality than of an excess of the very consciousness that brutes lack. This is what Stein means when she invokes the term "wisdom" to describe Melanctha's rail-yard sojourns. "More and more," we are told of her encounters with the men who congregate there, "Melanctha was learning the ways of wisdom" (*TL* 103).

In presenting Jeff and Melanctha as antagonists in a sustained debate on the nature of desire, Stein replays the dominant concerns of the psychology of persons through the most widely available strategies of the period: the antithesis between desire and habit, between wandering and regularity, between disobedience and obedience. Domestic animals, and dogs above all, anchored this debate over persons in a network of behaviorist assumptions that interwove the most sentimental canine memoirs with the most hard-nosed clinical theories. In Jeff's reiteration of "family living," of "animals," and of "making it right," Stein reveals the knots of domesticity and coercion that bound dog stories to psychology textbooks and physiology experiments. For these disparate discourses, conditioning and domestication become cognate terms. Assumptions about conditioning in early behavioral theory always lapse into assumptions about the superior integrity of animal habits as well as the certitude one can glean from that integrity. Repetition acquires value in behavioral theory because it is the supreme index of predictability, and animals can be counted on to repeat themselves.

Though it appears central to her style, Stein explicitly denied the claim that her own work involved repetition. "If anything is alive," she writes in "Portraits and Repetition," "there is no such thing as repetition. I do not know that I have ever changed my mind about that" (*LA* 174). Repetition is similarly defined through its negation elsewhere in the same lecture: "If it had been repetition it would not have been exciting and it would not have been exciting but it was exciting and it was not repetition" (*LA* 179). Excitement figures likewise into the argument between Melanctha and Jeff Campbell: Jeff reveals that "colored people" worry him because of "their always wanting new things just to get excited" (*TL* 83). But for Stein newness per se does not bring on excitement. Excitement derives from that sense of "nervousness" we have observed in Stein's plays, the syncopation whereby a person tries and fails to "get together" with her surroundings or herself. For Stein, simple repetition cannot describe "living" beings because the very fact of addition, of doing something more than once, implies a principle of accretion that changes the self's essential composition. "Excitement" is another name for the function of not being able to put the self into agreement with itself, to make the self equal to itself in any direct way. In Stein's view, Jeff's assumption that excitement for "colored people" derives from the unfamiliar is mistaken, as is his assumption that familiarity and family life will beget an end to excitement when they are in fact its basis.

"Sometimes the thought of how all her world was made," Stein writes, "filled the complex, desiring Melanctha with despair" (*TL* 149). For William James, such questioning "despair" at the simultaneously arbitrary and immutable nature of the world is a double-edged sword. On the one hand, *The Principles* exalts figures capable of extravagant leaps and ruptures of conventional thought; on the other hand, the book requires a stable hierarchy, an arrangement about which complete consensus exists, in order to advance even the most basic psychological claims. In James's account, the fact that we can think our way out of conventional understandings of the world we inhabit, altering in our mind its economies of property and rank, does not license us to do so. James's caveats against such alterations lead him to a defense of habit that, I argue, requires a blurring of the hierarchical divide between persons and animals. In a development he could not have anticipated, James's theory of consciousness as consistent and habitual found its way into the behavioral science of the new century, which confronted on its own terms the same problem that puzzled him: how to make people do what's expected of them in a world that appears made up and so capable of being broken down. The key verb in Stein's "Melanctha"—to "make do"—specifies the constructionist grammar that descends from James's account of habit through Pavlov, Thorndike, Watson, and Skinner: the belief that one can, through the force of one's own or another's will, artificially engender states of behavior that will over time become regular if not quite natural.[39] This grammar both concedes the irreducibility of consciousness to behavior and attempts to recuperate that irreducibility by turning consciousness to account, making it account for itself by "steering" persons toward equilibrium with an environment for which they feel no natural affinity.

Dogs are crucial to behavioral theory less because of their biological connection to a static natural world than because of their dynamic aptitude. Their capacity for "adjustment" allows behaviorists to work out an environmental model of conditioning that bypasses the problem of consciousness. Conceding that environments are neither natural nor given, behaviorism relies on domestic animals to argue for domesticity as an environmental default. To correspond to one's environment is just to be domesticated, to obey the rules of kinship, hierarchy, and reproduction that obtain in the domestic sphere. In its view of the animal as malleable and tractable, early behavioral psychology owed more than it cared to acknowledge to the sentimental culture of pets, just as that culture had an implicit kinship with the medical science whose use of animal models it abhorred. As Harriet Ritvo informs us, the pressing trend in the pet culture of Stein's time was the increase in breeding programs contrived to engineer perfect specimens of domestic animals from cows to dogs.[40] Ritvo shows how this vogue for "prize pets" dovetailed with early twentieth-century eugenics. As laboratory animals were

crucial to the development of reproducible and predictable scientific principles, so dogs in Stein's culture were valuable insofar as their breed traits
conformed to an ideal. "An American," the eugenicist Andre Siegrid wrote
in 1928, "looks on reproduction from much the same angle as a breeder of
dogs."[41]

Stein herself was fond of standard poodles, and the ease with which she
could replace Basket I with Basket II testified to the success of the standardization of breeding. In "Melanctha," however, standardization is out of
the question because reproduction is not an option. The separatist racial-
ism of Stein's culture imagined persons like Melanctha as sterile. In representing her mixed-race protagonist, Stein draws on pernicious stereotypes
concerning what Sterling Brown has called "the tragic mulatto"—the mis-
cegenational figure who, as the product of black-white coupling, was widely
construed in U.S. society as incapable of reproduction.[42] This is because mu-
lattoes were assimilated in the racist imagination to mules, those hybrids of
horses and donkeys which, however productive their domestic labor might
have been, could not spawn their own kind. Stein draws on this stereotype
of the mulatto as infertile beast of burden in order to twist it in another direction. What is important about this stereotype for Stein is that Melanctha's
desire turns out to be utterly divorced from the possibility of reproduction.
Her "complex" desire exceeds engineered breeding, or what Jeff Campbell
would call "regular family living," in which regularity and family life are
equated with husbandry. If at the beginning of the story "Melanctha Herbert had not yet been really married," by the end of the story "Melanctha
wanted Rose more than she had ever wanted all the others" (*TL* 166). Just
as she breeds "more and more" desire in Jeff Campbell the longer she stays
with him, so her desire always ends up attached to the wrong objects, like
Rose Johnson and Jane Harden. Melanctha cannot be standardized, made
equal to the imperatives of her culture or harnessed to the object—a husband—that would make her agreeable.

From early on in her adult life, making persons fit in places that did not
necessarily agree with them was a problem Stein felt keenly. "Long before
there is any rationale for a sex distinction," she told a Baltimore women's
club in 1897, "we try to make little men and women in their cradles at a time
when they ought normally to be only human beings." Around the time she
gave this lecture, Stein had her first meaningful encounters with black
Americans in her capacity as resident at various Baltimore-area hospitals. "It
was then that she had to take her turn in the delivering of babies," Alice's
autobiography informs us, "and it was at that time that she noticed the Negroes and the places that she afterwards used in the second of the Three
Lives stories" (*AA* 82). Soon afterward Stein left medical school, claiming
that she was "bored, frankly openly bored" (*AA* 81). However self-serving

this rationale for leaving medical school may have been, Stein's drift away from science surely had something to do with her experience in black Baltimore. "Tak[ing] her turn in delivering babies" there hints at something like a rote process, a routine that revealed the heady promise of medicine as a form of business as usual after all. If persons were capable neither of reproducing correctly nor of coordinating their desire to "right" living, then medicine would settle for the next best thing and reduce delivery to the exactitude of an assembly line. While standardization might work for poodles, Stein might have argued, its methods were boring when it came to persons.

Chapter Four

Hart Crane's Epic of Anonymity

Episode of Hands

The unexpected interest made him flush.
Suddenly he seemed to forget the pain,—
Consented,—and held out
One finger from the others.

The gash was bleeding, and a shaft of sun
That glittered in and out among the wheels,
Fell lightly, warmly, down into the wound.

And as the fingers of the factory owner's son,
That knew a grip for books and tennis
As well as one for iron and leather,—
As his taut, spare fingers wound the gauze
Around the thick bed of the wound,
His own hands seemed to him
Like wings of butterflies
Flickering in sunlight over summer fields.

The knots and notches,—many in the wide
Deep hand that lay in his,—seemed beautiful.
They were like the marks of wild ponies' play,—
Bunches of new green breaking a hard turf.

And factory sounds and factory thoughts
Were banished from him by that larger, quiet hand
That lay in his with the sun upon it.
And as the bandaged knot was tightened
The two men smiled into each other's eyes.[1]

This 1920 Hart Crane lyric provides us with a cluster of associations that resonate throughout his poetry: the understanding of physical contact as close to violence, the understanding of this violence as erotically desirable, and the sense that the most desirable form this violent contact takes is among men of different classes. "Boxing matches always make me feel homosexual," Crane told an acquaintance in Paris in 1929; and in 1920, he wrote to Gorham Munson of how "I get a real satisfaction and stimulant" from "a real knock-out."[2] One might infer that Crane's interest in boxing parallels Hemingway's mystification of *aficion*, the passion that accompanies watching a bullfight. But this modernist cliché appears to include an element of bad faith, given that the phallic prowess attached to bullfighting or boxing often turns on a wishful but inevitably fraudulent identification of the sedentary writer with what Crane calls the "sublime machines of human muscle-play."[3]

Yet Crane differs from Hemingway in two vital respects. One is his refusal of the inviolateness that accompanies Hemingway's life and aesthetics.[4] The boxing ring extends beyond the two fighters to encircle Crane's whole existence in the form of violent shocks that can intrude on him at any time, whether from an attractive man, an "Apollo in gob blue" (*SL* 335) whose beauty assaults Crane as he passes him on the street, or through the potential violence that same figure might and frequently did exercise on Crane if the latter's overtures were not graciously received. Boxing made Crane feel "homosexual" less because he took a voyeuristic pleasure in the fighters' bodies than because that pleasure, like many pastimes toward which Crane gravitated, was an outlawed one.[5] Not only risking violation to satisfy his desires, Crane desired risk itself.

The other difference between Crane and Hemingway—vital because of the difference it makes in their practice of modernism and in our understanding of that modernism—consists in the emphasis Crane places on the laboring male body, the "sublime machine of human muscle-play." In contrast to many of his contemporaries, who are preoccupied with primitivism and ritualism, Crane is relentlessly materialist in a way that has eluded his critics, who have instead dwelled on the mystical, visionary, or psychological aspects of his writing.[6] In this chapter I seek to restore this materialism to an account of Crane's poetry. Skewed toward questions of identity, analyses of sexuality in Crane's poetry have slighted the intricate, historically specific class relations in which Crane's erotics were entangled.[7]

Mining his poems for the biographical evidence they disclose, even Crane's best critics continue to regard him through the optic of personal rather than collective history.[8] Yet reducing Crane's affinity for working-class men to his homosexual essence obscures the complex erotic and social relations among laboring men in the early 1900s. Dilating our view of working-class sexuality allows us to expand our restricted vision of Crane's sexual and poetic identity and to see in his work a political valence that critics often overlook. I focus on the link between Crane's erotics and his desire to excavate modernist aesthetics by restoring to the cultural map the hand of the laborer. Committed to an invidious distinction between mental and manual labor, modernists of a certain school all but effaced the working-class body from the making of culture. Crane's ambition in *The Bridge* is to undo this erasure.

If "Episode of Hands" is a first step toward recovering the hand of the laborer as that figure helped shape the world of modernism and modernity, then such a recovery proves stubbornly elusive. Contact with the laboring hand in the poem is an "unexpected," "sudden" encounter, a moment of heightened awareness implicitly aligned with erotic embarrassment through the "flush" on the worker's face. The poem is intent on associating these figures of temporal accident and erotic embarrassment with a double violence: the violence of the "gash" in the mangled hand of the worker and the violence done to rational time, the schedule of the punch clock. "Factory sounds and factory thoughts / Were banished" in favor of the time marked by the sun, whose "shafts" "Fell lightly, warmly, down into the wound." Yet for all the temporal freezing that this episode implies, the poem finds it hard to keep these hands in stasis; the hands of the owner's son are "wings of butterflies / Flickering in sunlight over summer fields" while the worker's hands remind the owner's son of "wild ponies' play . . . breaking a hard turf." The hands at the focus of this episode flicker out of focus and break the ground of concentration. In this sense they also break off the discipline to which hands are understood to submit. Equipped with a "grip for books and tennis / As well as one for iron and leather," the hands of the owner's son are converted to butterflies, just as the worker's hand is concealed with white gauze and so concealed from the hands-on exertion of factory labor. Though the "knots and notches" that have calloused those manual implements seem "beautiful" and are reconfigured by the owner's son as objects of contemplation and desire, this aesthetic conversion does not frame those hands so much as further displace them into a maze-like realm where tracing the "many" lines they contain becomes an exercise in infinite regress.

Amid these temporary transformations, the poem ends with the "two men smil[ing] into each other's eyes," another temporary transformation in which the hesitancy and distrust that the injured worker directs at the owner's son in the first stanza give way to the reciprocal and harmonious gaze of the last. Even as it desires this harmonious reciprocity, the poem also suggests through its frequent references to the ephemeral or sudden or unexpected state of things that such longing gazes will not last long. As the poem's title suggests, this instance is episodic, a moment in time detached from a narrative sequence. Though Langdon Hammer suggests that the poem's last stanza "announces a new experience of continuity," this is not a sustainable encounter.[9] The episodic quality of the poem doubles the hands occupying its center, which appear detached from the bodies of which they are extensions. Because the hands feel more like hovering ("flickering") fragments than like continuations of the body, their prehensile dexterity—their power to grasp the world around them—breaks down as well.

"Episode of Hands" actively aestheticizes this state of affairs in opposition to an "experience of continuity." The poem's fragmentary and ephemeral narrative calls attention not to the utopian bond between these men so much as to the brevity of this encounter and to the different, less sustainable connection cruising implies. Like all cruising scenarios, this poem's depends on intensity rather than durability, on reducing to a minimum the distance between initial "interest" and ultimate "consent." Like all cruising scenarios, this one turns the self into sheer body and the body into a surface to be read or interpreted: hence the concealment of the hands stands in for the palmistry that the owner's son must enact on the "marks" embedded in the worker's hand. And like all cruising scenarios, at least as Crane construes them, this one takes place in the obligatory presence of working-class men. The larger narrative that would fill out this episodic poem is one that Crane strived to articulate over the course of his career. It is a narrative about the primacy of manual labor and manual laborers in the manufacture of a specifically modern desire averse to continuity, durability, or reproduction.

To claim that "Episode of Hands" is a poem of discontinuity rather than relatedness or wholeness brings one into the vicinity of terms where most Crane criticism invariably traffics. The difference between my account of these terms and their use by generations of Crane critics bears emphasizing. Whereas most critics take the ruptures in Crane's poetry to reflect or to confirm a biographical truth about his poetic or sexual self, I take this interest in rupture as confirmation of Crane's essential indifference to the search for literary or cultural identity. The "search for identity" has informed all manner of Crane criticism, from the most idealizing to the most progressive. In *The Homosexual Tradition in American Poetry,* Robert K. Martin asserts that Crane "looked for a poetry that could express a particularly American identity, as was to be found in the work of Whitman and his successors."[10] While this heuristic has proved fruitful for getting hold of his slippery poems, it has ceased to be a critical method and become an orthodoxy. If identity is the "Platonic" ideal in Crane's work, to use Martin's word, its inaccessibility to Crane becomes the agon on which successive generations of critics focus.

In reiterating this struggle, even critics carefully attuned to the various social contexts of Crane's career have unwittingly repositioned him as the idealistic and mystical poet their accounts seek to revise. Early critics frequently ascribed to Crane, as both person and poet, "the distraught but exciting splendor of a great failure," in R. P. Blackmur's memorable phrase. This judgment, which for decades informed the just barely submerged homophobia of Crane's literary companions and correspondents, survives to this day in his most fervently pro-gay supporters. Thomas Yingling's *Hart Crane and the Homosexual Text* distills Crane's career to a clash of values he could never quite reconcile: his sense of himself as a homosexual and his calling as a poet. Yingling argues that in Crane's "Voyages" cycle,

> we must see that the inability to sustain homosexuality as an absolute value in the text results from two things: a) the value the text ascribes to homosexuality is not congruent with the culture's more general devaluation of it; b) that value is ultimately incompatible with Crane's other privileged term of absolute value, "poetry."[11]

I would like to undo this judgment of Crane by putting forward two hypotheses. One is that far from feeling driven to disguise or to disavow his homosexuality, Crane neither sought a rationalization for his sexuality nor treated it as incompatible with the rest of his life.[12] The second hypothesis is that while maintaining a vivid same-sex expressiveness and orientation, Crane did not equate homosexual self-definition with the fulfillment of same-sex desire. Crane, I suggest instead, held definition itself in suspicion. Definition and certitude—summed up in Yingling's notion of "absolute value"—were antithetical to the erotics he sought for important reasons that his poetry and letters reveal to us.

We can get at this neglect of "absolute value" by noting a word that Crane routinely invokes as his highest honorific—"dynamic." Crane's letters recur to this word to define what he most prizes about his poetry and that of others. "You will forgive me for feeling my method as inherently more 'dynamic' than Williams'" (*SL* 322). Because of this dynamism Crane rejects Yvor Winters's work, which "suffers from such arbitrary torturings—all for the sake of a neat little point of reference" (*SL* 319). "A poem should have its own legs," he writes to Winters, "no matter what it's carrying" (*SL* 329). A poem, in other words, is measured less by its "point of reference" than by its mobility. "I wish I had a lyric or so to circulate, like Allen [Tate]" (*SL* 235), Crane writes, as if the poem itself would be a proxy or surrogate for his own motion. What is desired is the circulation, the trajectory of the lyric, rather than the lyric itself. The poem cruises. Not only in form but also in content, poems require dynamism. As Crane writes in "Modern Poetry" (1922), poems should not be about picturing things or setting them in place—what we would call the pastoral or the loco-descriptive—but rather about "the familiar gesture of a motorist in the modest act of shifting gears."[13]

"It is to the pulse of a greater dynamism that my work must revolve" (*SL* 137), Crane writes to Gorham Munson in 1923. This letter is significant because it includes the first reference Crane makes to *The Bridge,* and is also one of the few letters to his heterosexual correspondents in which he openly discusses "my sexual predilections": "I am all-too-free with my tongue and

doubtless always shall be" (*SL* 138). As this letter illustrates, "free" movement, dynamism, figures importantly in another register in Crane's life
work, for Crane is attracted almost exclusively to men on the move, and he
describes this attraction in the vocabulary of travel. Crane's alias on his sexual prowls, for instance, was Mike Drayton, "one of my Elizabethan enthusiasms—though all I know of him is his *Unfortunate Traveller*" (*SL* 360).
Adopting this name, Crane defines himself as the "unfortunate traveler" at
risk in an unstable world of erotic encounter. What contributes to the dynamism of this world is the drifting population by which it is inhabited: a
"most affectionate red-haired mariner" whose tryst with Crane the latter describes as "a night with Circe" (*SL* 363) (which casts Crane as that other unfortunate traveler, Odysseus); "some sailor" who "gives me a jolt" (*SL* 379);
"Apollo himself . . . sojourning in Gob blue" (*SL* 335); "a wild Irish red-
headed sailor" with whom Crane "went flying back to Brooklyn" (*SL* 318);
"a blue-jacket from the Arkansas" (*SL* 412). Crane is oriented to sailors because sailors are oriented toward movement, toward cruising itself (as in
"the cruising of warships" [*SL* 360]), which he notes in a letter employing
an obvious pun on his erotic activity: "the number of faggots cruizing [*sic*]
around out here is legion" [*SL* 373]). "After a good deal of 'sailing' since
arriving here," Crane writes of California, "I am now convinced that 'flying'
is even better" (*SL* 355).

Even in his most sustained relationships, as with Emil Opffer, Crane resorts to metaphors of drift and transience:

> I have been able to give freedom and life which was acknowledged in
> the ecstasy of walking hand in hand across the most beautiful bridge of
> the world, the cables enclosing us and pulling us upward in such a
> dance as I have never walked and never can walk with another. (*SL* 187)

Despite his claim that this is a relation unlike any other he has experienced,
Crane sees his intimacy with Opffer as a more intense, more freeing and mobile version of the cruising to which he would soon return (indeed in Opffer's company). What really distinguishes this relation is the heightened
newness Opffer provides to Crane, an episode of particularly charged erotic
encounter which the poet will seek again and again. This rhapsodic initial
contact with Opffer will be repeated in a darker but no less "exciting weekend" foray several years later in California, when the two fall in with a group
of "merry andrews" who beat and rob Crane and his "goldy-locks" (*SL* 365)
in a hotel room where the party has finished up a night of drunken carous-
ing.

Crane's interest in cruising is inseparable from the interest in hands
found throughout his poems. Hands are less the "parts of the body that fashion bonds in Crane's poetry" (as Langdon Hammer argues) than the parts

that draw attention to the frailty and danger of such bonds.[14] Hands often have a groping relation to cognition in Crane's poems, as when the speaker in "My Grandmother's Love Letters" "would lead my grandmother by the hand / Through much of what she would not understand; / And so I stumble" (P6). As the "stumble" indicates, what sort of apprehension the hands provide is both uncertain (hence a matter of questioning) and clumsy. In "For the Marriage of Faustus and Helen," Crane writes of the "bleeding hands" which "extend and "thresh the height / The imagination spans beyond despair" (P32). And in "Voyages" I, the urchins' "fingers crumble fragments of baked weed / Gaily digging and scattering" (P 34).[15] In these diverse episodes of hands, their extension into the world at large—whether into the past, or to "heights" of "imagination," or below the surface of the shore they dig—coincides with their fragmentary, broken, "bleeding" nature. Hands collect or hold on to knowledge, memory, or experience at the same time as they risk "scattering" or losing it. In Crane, knowledge is continually posited as tactile and ephemeral, as materially firm and epistemologically wavering.

Crane's interest in hands further reveals an understanding of relations as physically intimate at the same time as they are interpersonally opaque, even alien. And this understanding applies equally to a cognitive grasp of the material world and to contact between persons. In Crane's work, the intensity of physical touch is separated—and at times even radically distant—from personalities. Both Crane's logic of erotic disorientation and his attention to the dynamics of risk are mirrored in the unsettling of both sexual and visual mastery found in his hand poems. (We might want to remind ourselves also of the centrality of hand-to-hand contact in Crane's description of his first among many intense, intermittent flings with Opffer.) With their confusion over exactly what or whom hands can apprehend, these lyrics point to a broad set of concerns with working-class agency in early twentieth-century America. The wavering apprehension found in Crane's hand poems implies an instability in the realm of knowledge or value; this implication derives from Crane's acquaintance with a culture of manual labor defined by a high level of insecurity and epistemological doubt. Crane's hand poems chronicle the displacement of hands from the world of work and the rise of the new premium of working-class life—the physical mobility that overtakes the primacy of manual labor, as products once made by hand are now made by machine. In this milieu, the only thing the laborer has left—his portability—is at once his most important asset (in that it gives him an edge over stationary machinery) and his biggest liability (in that he can always be replaced with another, equally portable worker). The emphasis on the episodic that we find in a poem like "Episode of Hands" turns out to define working life in the new century. And this emphasis on the fragility of hands

(Crane's code for—among other things—manual labor) is also intimately connected to the sexually perverse erotics of the migratory or outcast working-class man, the casual laborer.

Consider Sherwood Anderson's aptly titled story "Hands," in which Wing Biddlebaum, a disgraced former schoolteacher, "worked as a day laborer in the fields, going timidly about and striving to conceal his hands." Biddlebaum's desperate attempt to control his hands results from their having been implicated in Wing's pederastic embrace of "a half-witted boy of the school" who "became enamored of the young master." Reduced from the relatively plush status of "master" to that of hired hand as well as forced to change his name (from Adolph Meyers), Wing condenses several tropes of the early twentieth-century hobo. It is fitting that "the name of Biddlebaum he got from a box of goods at a freight station as he hurried through an eastern Ohio town"; his "hurried" flight from scandal and his alias recall the clandestine, anonymous movement along freight lines at the center of hobo existence. The origin of Wing's loss of caste in a perverse episode of hands recalls another pattern of hobo existence less recognizable to contemporary readers: the strong association of the casual laborer with both pederasty and pedagogy in early twentieth-century America.[16]

Of course pederasty and pedagogy have gone hand in hand (as it were) for millennia.[17] What is striking in this period is the association of seductive knowledge with hired hands. The cognitive uncertainty implied by hands in Crane's lyrics becomes easier to grasp when we observe the close affinity in his culture between improper knowledge and day laborers like the itinerant Wing Biddlebaum. "Vagabondage is a veritable University of Vice," Edmond Kelly writes in *The Elimination of the Tramp* (1908), "for if the university is correctly defined as a system for the acquisition of useless knowledge, vagabondage may be defined as a system for the acquisition of unnecessary vice."[18] By "seduc[ing] the young into sharing his fortunes," Kelly warns, the tramp "diligently undoes what little our compulsory education contributes to good citizenship."[19] Even if the widespread corruption of youth by vagrants who tutored them in the pleasures of "wanderlust" was more fanciful than real, reformers like Kelly were nonetheless certain that the young were continually being tempted by the sort of things that Wing Biddlebaum got "from a box of goods." In alighting on the academic peril that tramps allegedly posed, Kelly displaced the fading patrician generation's anxiety over the self's proper development onto the tramp—a target more visible and hence more manageable than what he and his contemporaries took to be the real threat to individual cultivation and maturation. That threat had its source in consumer culture, which endowed youth with the potential not only to remake their identity according to commodities but also to choose such things over the tried and true objects of value that traditional schooling brought about. "In America," one contemporary reformer argued, "the great educator is the spending of money."[20] The objects of mass culture were degraded precisely because of their association with a bowdlerized version of the good life, a vision of leisured happiness that inverted the protocols of reflection and edification by fostering a world of temporary pleasures and renewable yet disposable experiences.

One way of making this dichotomy clear would be to describe it in terms of the split between what Kelly calls the "university" of "useless knowledge" and the "university" of "unnecessary vice." A university education was crucial to the self-identity of modernist authors in a way that it wasn't, say, to Henry James (who dropped out of Harvard in 1861 without much ado). Yet as essential as they considered higher education for their own development, writers like Eliot, Pound, Winters, and Tate were deeply ambivalent about university life, always haunted by the suspicion that such education was "useless knowledge." This ambivalence was resolved finally through a profound overcompensation of the university as the proper seat of cultural value, a community insulated against the depredations of mass society. As John Guillory points out, Eliot's overwhelming interest in "a *total* culture, inclusive of belief," developed in reaction to what he and his New Critical heirs viewed as the "secular authority of a derogated mass culture."[21] The spiritualization of the modernist canon (vividly captured in Eliot's Catholic conversion) proceeded under the aegis of the university in violent reaction against a commercial world that advertised itself by appealing directly and quite shamelessly to consumer bodies. Against this backdrop, Crane's successors infamously berated him for his lack of university education—and Crane tried to make his way by writing ad copy that endowed the banal objects of daily life with an erotic mystique.[22]

With his lack of schooling, Crane was implicitly someone who, like Anderson's Wing Biddlebaum, had lost caste. The name "Wing" figures prominently in Crane's coded acknowledgment of his own social lapse, if we recall the "hands" "like wings of butterflies" of the factory owner's son in "Episode of Hands."[23] Crane appears to have learned from Anderson the association between wings, hired hands, and wayward sexual desire. In his copy of Anderson's *Poor White* (1920), Crane underlined a passage that itself underlines the intimate link between these various figures in Clara Butterworth's reverie about an "old and unmarried" "farm hand" named Jim Priest. Clara cannot help thinking "how strong his hands were" and how, despite being "gnarled and rough, there was something beautifully powerful about them." As she connects these hands with "the song of labor that arose out of the beehives," "[i]t got into her blood and her step quickened. The words of Jim Priest that kept running through her mind seemed a part of the same song the bees were singing." What makes Clara flush (just as the factory worker flushes in "Episode of Hands") is her perception that Jim's "words" are "connected with the idea of love." As if to leave us in no doubt that this is a masturbatory reverie, the focus of which is Jim Priest's gnarled laboring hands, Clara notices two "birds in a tree nearby ma[king] love. The female flew madly about and was pursued by the male bird. . . . [H]e flew directly before the girl's face, his wing nearly touching her cheek."[24]

This chapter in *Poor White* is notable not just because of its commingling of the signifiers we have observed throughout Crane's poetry but also because of its focus on the crossing of class lines. The daughter of an affluent farmer, Clara encounters the hired hand in the summer before she is bound for the "State University at Columbus." Jim Priest becomes a sort of alternative tutor for her, his name an ironic reminder of the clerical function that schooling has always subsumed. Clara requires such schooling because, according to her father, she "has been too much among the rough workmen who work on my farms and had become a little rough."[25] By "get[ting] her acquainted with the right kind of people," schooling will polish her up to "meet and marry some young man."[26] The "song of labor" that Jim Priest evokes in her thoughts is a siren song that will draw her away from marriage and family life, away from "the right kind of people."

Unlike the fictional Clara Butterworth, forced by her father to abandon the promiscuous sex life down on the farm, Crane did not shed the rough contact of hired hands for university life. And unlike the fictional Biddlebaum, forced into social decline because of his own busy hands, Crane actively curried his own lapse in standing with his refusal to tread the path his class and status had ordained for him. It is almost as if Crane were suggesting that the writing of poetry could proceed without the "system for the acquisition of useless knowledge" that Pound saw as the essential basis for poetic production. For his own poetic apprenticeship, Crane embraced the "system of unnecessary vice" that his culture indiscriminately associated with working-class and underclass men as well as with consumer society. It was schooling in guiltless pleasure or "unnecessary vice" that both vagabonds and copywriters taught—like the otiose transports that baths promised in the advertisements Crane wrote for the Pittsburg [*sic*] Water Heater Company in 1922. These vignettes paint the water heater in terms that highlight that object's ability to gratify the senses and to spur carnal delights. In "Bathsheba's Bath," Bathsheba's "reckless" "open air plunge" incites King David to such passion that he has her husband killed and takes Bathsheba as his bride.[27] In "Bathing by the Kalendar," the emphasis is on the "immediately available" bathing that moderns enjoy, compared with the long wait "a Roman aristocrat like Pliny" endured "while a flock of slaves lugged water enough from nearby brooks and wells to fill one of his pools." By delivering a bath *when you want it* (Crane's slogan), the water heater promised a world of bodily pleasure to which the bather could surrender without inconvenience or shame.[28]

Though it begs credulity to argue that Crane's copywriting was other than facetious in its use of biblical and classical antecedents, the erotic treachery in the one advertisement and the decadent indulgence in the other were features too often present in Crane's more canonical work not to take seriously. (For instance, Crane's Bathsheba possesses the sexuality on public display that will define Pocahontas in *The Bridge*'s section II, the epigraph of which refers to the "wanton yong girle" whose sexual charms "get the boys forth with her into the marketplace.") Baths have a special place in the history of migratory men in the United States, and it is hard to read these bathing stories of Crane's without calling up the history of illicit sexuality that baths connote. Originally designed to purify their charges, the baths at charitable institutions like the YMCA catered not only to drifters' souls but also to their sexual whims.[29] And just as the reformer's zeal for cleansing could tip over into an unwitting license for transient sexual contact, so advertising's powers of persuasion could tip easily into corruption. Or so Sherwood Anderson thought. Anderson spent over twenty years making his living in advertising before turning on the business in a disgust that emanated from what he took to be advertising's inevitable misuse of language. "I would be compelled, as an advertising writer, to corrupt these words," Anderson says in a remarkable moment in his memoir. "I will be corrupt, but, God give me this grace. When I am being corrupt, perverting the speech of men, let me remain aware of what I am doing."[30] Advertising and perversion go hand in hand in the world that Crane and Anderson shared. And Crane's advertisements for the Pittsburg Water Heater Company participate in this perversion by turning the home into a locus of sheer indulgence beyond domestic decorum—a site of public exhibitionism and adultery in one instance, a sort of bachelor paradise in the other. This perversion of domestic norms was closely tied not just to advertising and its milieu—mass culture—but also to the denizens of that mass culture. The anonymous voice of the seductive copywriter is matched to the anonymous legions of men and women whom advertising wooed with the immediate and transitory pleasure of a bath (if not immersion in a less wholesome medium).

Though Crane's neglect of proper schooling as well as proper behavior was a source of frustration and pity to his literary friends, these opinions did not ultimately count for much in Crane's view. After falling out with the Tates, for instance, he wrote to Wilbur Underwood, "I'd rather lose such elite for the old society of vagabonds and sailors—who don't enjoy chitchat. . . . With the sailor, no faith or such is properly *expected* and how jolly and cordial and warm the touseling [*sic*] is sometimes" (*SL* 261). When it came to defying married life and its ostensibly permanent ties, Crane relied on assumptions about the dubiousness of sustained attachment he acquired in the working-class venues where he spent much of his time.

Yet we can also gloss Crane's dismissal of "faith" in terms of the community of belief that Eliot most famously associated with poetic tradition. Turning to Eliot briefly before examining *The Bridge* is illuminating, since that poem was written at least partially in reaction to Eliot's view of poetic value. Crane inverts the priorities of the Eliotic school by discovering within the degraded and prosaic precincts of mass society the very elements on which high modernism pins its hopes for redemption. The term "redemption" is in keeping with the religiosity of much of Eliot's thought on poetic value, if we credit Guillory's claim that Eliot's "revaluation" of "tradition" stemmed from the desire for "such doctrinal contents as Christian belief (or some other belief) would provide."[31] Guillory's account encompasses a latent assumption concerning the way Eliot reconstructs the clerical role of the poet—the preserver of spiritual content—against the backdrop of a material world. In Eliot's view, the world is grossly contaminated not only by mass consumption but also by the laboring bodies who do the consuming. Putting self-interest ahead of all else, such persons threaten the poetic enterprise with their lack of interest in the supreme dividend to be gained from literary tradition—that of "sacrifice." In "Tradition and the Individual Talent," Eliot writes: "The progress of an artist is a continual self-sacrifice, a continual extinction of personality."[32] It is no surprise that in a period when the charismatic performance of "personality" was becoming ever more valued as a way of getting ahead in business and in private life, Eliot would aim to separate poetic vocation from the daily grind of bureaucracy or the service economy on just this point. Eliot implies that poetic tradition must do away with "personality" because poetry is a privileged form of labor, irreducible to the theatrical self-presentations that executives and department store clerks must constantly enact for those around them.[33]

What is distinctive about Eliot's model of "tradition" is the strenuous rhetoric of production in which he chooses to couch its unfolding. Hence the artist who would succeed to tradition "must obtain it by great labor" (*SW* 47). Eliot further specifies the labor involved in depersonalization by referring to scientific method: "It is in this depersonalization that art may be said to approach the condition of science" (*SW* 53). The analogy goes even further, however, for the method Eliot has in mind is the act of "fusion" (*SW* 56) or condensation, the "action which takes place to a piece of finely filiated platinum when introduced into a chamber containing oxygen and sulphur dioxide" (*SW* 53). This process names precisely the form of labor most attractive to Eliot—one that, through a process of filtration, gathers "the standards of the past" (*SW* 50) comprising the "mind of Europe" (*SW* 51) from Homer on.

Eliot's model of impersonality is predicated on an account of labor in which physical bodies serve no real purpose except as conduits for an intellection that preexists and subordinates any other form of work. "Depersonalization" above all means disembodiment, the process of yielding one's physical being in order for one's mind to join "the mind of Europe." Impersonality is the prerequisite to artistic undertaking because artistic undertaking is contingent on the absence of particular identity, the peculiar mark of the individual worker or craftsman, which vitiates the potential for universalism toward which Eliot's aesthetics aspire. "The more perfect the artist," Eliot writes, "the more completely separate in him will be the man who suffers and mind which creates; the more perfectly will the mind digest and transmute the passions which are its material" (*SW* 54). Such a separation corresponds to the historical division between manual and intellectual labor which Eliot's account of artistic labor misreads. One need not be "erudite" (*SW* 45), for example, to observe that there is something peculiar about Eliot's view of manual and intellectual labor as allegorical doubles, respectively, for particular experience and universal creation. Committed to the universal labor of the mind, Eliot reverses what is a given to Homer or Hesiod: what is universal is precisely the physical exertion and toil that defines all human existence.[34] Well into the modern period, poetry declared itself a record of physical labors, whether military (as in epic) or agricultural (as in *Works and Days*) or the labors of birth (as in *Theogony*).

The first example Eliot gives in his essay of a properly depersonalized poetics is most telling in light of this understanding of the intellect laboring on behalf of the universal and against the bodily. This example, which is meant to confirm the principle "that the poet has, not a personality to express, but a particular medium" (*SW* 56), is canto 15 of the *Inferno,* the encounter between Dante and his "teacher," Brunetto Latini. Latini inhabits that circle of hell reserved for sodomites, and it is precisely this feature of Latini's life that Dante cannot square with his noble lessons, the pedagogy transmitted to the young poet through Latini's texts. Torn between sympathy and judgment, Dante falters in the sinner's presence until forced on by Virgil. Dante's reaction, as Eliot puts it,

> is a working up of the emotion evident in the situation; but the effect, though single as that of any work of art, is obtained by considerable complexity of detail. The last quatrain gives an image, a feeling attaching to an image, which "came," which did not develop out of what precedes, but which was probably in suspension in the poet's mind until the proper combination arrived for it to add itself to. (*SW* 55)

The quatrain Eliot refers to is rendered thus in Robert Pinsky's translation: "And he went off, / Seeming to me like one of those who run / Competing for the green cloth in the races / Upon Verona's field—and of them, like one / Who gains the victory, not the one who loses."[35]

Keeping in mind the division between physical and intellectual, particular and universal labor on which Eliot's essay turns, we can draw several lessons from his reading of Dante's canto 15.[36] The first is the unusual choice Eliot makes in claiming Dante as the poet who divorces experience and poetic practice, "personality" and "medium," given that Dante is the star "personality" written into his own poem. My second point concerns Eliot's effort to stage just this agon, the breaking of Dante from experience and his assent to being the "medium" of experience. This agon could not transpire except through the negative example of the sodomitical and hence all too embodied Latini, who, running away from Dante at the end of the canto, reminds the poet of the naked boys who raced in competition at Verona. To see the mentor as the youth unclothed is a bit of infernal *contrapasso*, given Latini's pederastic crimes; he has become a version of the bodies he corrupted, and so his own soul is condemned to an eternal embodiment. Seen as such, Latini is competitive but on the wrong terrain. While "victory" will be his, it is not the victory of the poet, which is mental and universal, but the limited reward of a shred of cloth in a contest of mere bodies. This is the vision of Latini that Eliot imagines "came" to Dante with the inexorable force of a closure to that chapter of the poet's life. Chained to the body and forever desiring it, Latini will never occupy the company of the blessed whose ranks Dante is by his poem's own admission destined to join.

That such blessed company is synonymous with the "mind of Europe" is clear once we realize that Eliot sees Dante's "vision" of Latini as a thinly veiled conversion narrative for the poet himself. Dante will not compete for mere trifles, the sham prizes of earthly victory; rather, he defines himself against Latini insofar as he allies himself with "the one who loses" personality, including embodiment. Discovering the lesson that sodomy and poetry do not mix, Dante is "added to" the tradition that enforces this lesson, even as his own response to it "adds" a refreshing pathos to a breach that repeatedly evokes melancholia in the blessed. To learn this larger lesson, or so Eliot would have it, Dante must unlearn the lesson of his sodomitical tutor. Latini's error during life was to imagine that sharing minds with another is qualitatively indistinct from sharing bodies; but his larger error, at least in Eliot's view, was to imagine that his life is what matters to his writing and in his writing, that writing is the "medium" for the survival of the author's "personality": "I live in my *Tesoro*—your judgment being won for it, I ask no more," he tells Dante before leaving him. Though Dante's judgment is not given, Eliot renders it on his behalf. Putting his body where it doesn't belong (in writing or in another man), the sodomite in Eliot's version of the *Inferno* gets what he deserves. He is finally all body, like another sodomite to whom canto 15 refers, Andrea de' Mozzi, who "left his body distended in nerve and muscle."[37] Because they cannot or will not occlude their desires, the likes of Latini and de' Mozzi draw excessive attention to their excessive selves. They are bloated with personality, swollen nearly to the point of rupture; and just as Dante must forget them in order to forget himself, so in their eternal state of overembodiment they are doomed never to leave themselves well enough alone.

In contrast to these "distended" figures, according to Eliot, real artistic labor is essentially conservative, fusing rather than disseminating the objects of its production. Mental labor is "concentration" (*SW* 58), in the sense of both convergence and reflection. And the mind of Europe is a self-regulating system that tolerates no real difference, though like any closed system it paradoxically requires a principle of change: "[W]hat happens when a work of art is created is something that happens simultaneously to all the works of art that preceded it" (*SW* 49–50). This is because, like the artists who make it, "the emotion of art is impersonal" (*SW* 59). Art's simultaneity and uniformity differ sharply from the "distended" bodies of failed artists or thinkers, who cannot "surrender to the work to be done" and instead yield themselves exclusively to sensual experience. Such men and women make bad art, Eliot claims, because they don't know how to *work:* "[I]n this search for novelty in the wrong place," Eliot writes, the bad poet "discovers the perverse." Poetry is not, ultimately, "an expression of personality, but an escape from personality" (*SW* 58).

What is strange about this axiom is how close it comes to the definition of impersonality implied by Bessie Van Vorst, a society woman who, along with her daughter, posed as a textile worker around the turn of the century: "Here we were," she reports, "working from seven until six, with as little personality as we could, with the effort to produce, through an action purely mechanical, results as nearly as possible identical one to the other." For all its transcendental striving, Eliot's account of poetic tradition feels similarly mechanistic. Yet where for Eliot impersonality names the transcendence of bodies and their partialities for the sake of a pan-European mind, for labor theorists in the early 1900s, impersonality named exactly that perversity for which Eliot condemns the over-embodied and intemperate Latini. Van Vorst notes that the "life of mill drudgery" turns the factory girl into an "egoist," and that "her whole effort is for herself." The impersonality of her work paradoxically bestows on her an "independent" status free from "domestic cares."[38]

This is impersonality as perversity rather than its cure. For the manual laborer, such impersonality leads inexorably away from the mind and its pursuits and into the body and its baser pleasures. The impersonality of industrial life, Carleton Parker argues in *The Casual Laborer* (1920), makes persons neglect the fruits of "contemplative thinking"—"art, poetry, evolutionary speculation, behavior study, philosophy"—in favor of "perverted compensations" that pass for the "gratification" of "instinct expression."[39] Parker attributes the perversity of working-class pleasures and pastimes to the "industrial psychosis" brought on by the irregular nature of a labor economy in which seasonal work, "hire and fire" policies, and transience were the norm rather than the exception. "Sex perversion" is the outcome of this state of affairs, Parker argues, citing "a widespread practice of homosexuality among the migratory laborers."[40]

"Nothing becomes the economic world so ill as their record under the touchstone of the sex problem," Parker writes. "The fact that ninety percent of migratory workers have no women awakens no train of thought."[41] The equation of working-class culture with a debased form of impersonality and with gross sexual irregularity was crucial to the labor history of the early twentieth century, in which (as Parker shows himself acutely aware) the casualization of labor portended the casualization of erotic ties. The Van Vorsts note this tendency in the working women whose ranks they infiltrate, claiming that the latter "trifle with love" and that "the accepted honesty of married life makes them slow to discard the liberty they love."[42] These associations between casual labor and casual sex were also crucial to *The Bridge,* which leans heavily on the version of impersonality found in industrial labor to change the valence that Eliot assigns to this quality. When in a letter to Gorham Munson Crane suggests that "it is perhaps good to become impersonal in the admiration of art" (*SL* 109), he has in mind a form of impersonality quite different from what Eliot would have condoned. Indeed, as Crane writes several months later to Munson, "I take Eliot as a point of departure toward an almost complete reverse of direction" (*SL* 117). Rather than conferring disembodiment, impersonality confers embodiment; rather than a function of the mind, it is a quality of manual labor; rather than transcending egoism by humbling the self with a sense of its fatal dependency on the past, it grants the ego autonomy; and rather than deflecting desire in the service of lasting permanence, it is the path along which the most transient of desires proceeds.

I want to return now to Crane in order to tease out the implications of anonymous embodiment and decadent pedagogy in *The Bridge.* In that book's inaugural lyric, "To Brooklyn Bridge," Crane's speaker, addressing the bridge, refers to "Thy guerdon . . . Accolade thou dost bestow / Of anonymity" (*P* 43–44). Critics have glossed this cryptic phrase in terms of the reward ("guerdon") of sexual gratification, a meaning borne out by the last stanza of the proem, where a lone figure stands underneath the bridge at night in what to all accounts appears to be the expectation of a nocturnal tryst: "Under thy shadow by the piers I waited" (*P* 44). Less readily noticed, though, is that far from restricted to this moment, the "accolade" signals the general form of communication crucial to the poem, a mode of call and response based largely on the channels of an anonymity that finds its way into almost all the poem's sections, from the "incognizable word" in "Ave Maria" to the "whispers antiphonal" of "Atlantis." Despite their spiritual overtones, these instances of voice in Crane's poem are not disembodied. They have everything to do with bodies, though the connections among those bodies are far from clear. These instances of "anonymity" engage a form of contact that is simultaneously intimate and public. "Accolade" suggests this communication in that it connotes a sense of collective recognition, like the applause given by a nameless audience to a performer. Yet Crane's poem also relies on an archaic meaning of this term to designate even more precisely the kinds of bodies associated with this recognition, in that "accolade" refers to a "ceremonial greeting" performed by medieval knights upon meeting. Crane's often antiquated rhetoric has a deliberate referent here. The medieval cheek of terms like "guerdon" and "accolade" summons up the specter of those laboring men who had the temerity to dub themselves "knights of the road," a common epithet for hoboes in the first third of the twentieth century.[43] Although such figures do not appear in the flesh until "The River," which presents three "men still hungry on the tracks" (*P* 57), their importance to *The Bridge* is signaled in this early allusion to the "accolade," a term evoking the archaism, the cultural belatedness, that these "hobo-trekkers" (*P* 58) embody.

Both the reference to the "accolade" in the proem and the self-conscious positioning of these hobos as holdovers from another era signal the importance of these sidelined and obsolete figures to *The Bridge* as a whole. Their importance in fact rests on their temporal irregularity, their tendency to be in the wrong place at the wrong time. Always bringing up the rear—"Caboose-like they go ruminating" (*P* 58)—these men are categorically left behind. For instance, the speaker in "The River" first notices them "[b]ehind / My father's cannery works" (*P* 58). As these references to "behind[s]" alert us, their "ruminating" is never far from that sodomitic vice which Eliot's Dante pitied in Bruno Latini. Though at first glance Crane's "wifeless or runaway / hobo-trekkers" are too "slow" (*P* 58) to keep to the race of life, they are facilitated by an episodic and impersonal logic that Crane views as inescapably modern. "From pole to pole across the hills, the states," the speaker tells us, "[t]hey know a body under the wide rain" (*P* 59). Oriented by the compass points of the physical body, the hoboes experience this body as both insufficiently individuated—indefinite even ("a body")— and physically intimate: they "*have touched her, knowing her without name*" (*P* 59). Anonymity is the means to lay a "body bare" (*P* 59), as if the absence of a name confers a privileged access to nakedness and intimacy.

The "body under the wide rain" of course is a reference to Pocahontas, "Powhatan's Daughter," the presiding spirit of the section of *The Bridge* that includes "The River." How Pocahontas is depicted in *The Bridge* is worth noting: "a well-featured but wanton yong girle," as the epigraph to Section II from William Strachey reminds us, who would *"get the boyes forth with her into the market place, and make them wheele, falling on their hands, turning their heels upwards, whom she would followe, and wheele so herself, naked as she was, all the fort over"* (*P* 51). As this lurid description suggests, it is Pocahontas's "wheel[ing]" promiscuity rather than her gender in which Crane's poem is invested, a promiscuity it aligns with her anonymity ("without name"). As the upsetting effect she has on her admirers implies, the cartwheeling Pocahontas reduces the "boyes" to prostrate bodies, their upturned heels priming them for a sexual encounter that is misplaced in several senses: it occurs in public, in the "market place," and it illegitimately positions "the boys" as penetrable and exposed, their hands on the ground and their backsides in the air. The danger Pocahontas embodies consists less in her heterosexual licentiousness than in her far more treacherous knack for upsetting orthodox gender roles, for turning good boys into "fall[en]" women like herself, for infecting those around her with a collective, excessively mobile desire.

Pocahontas gives *The Bridge* a "wheel[ing]" vehicle with which to introduce the "perverse" and equivocal desire, Eliot's "novelty in the wrong place," that infects virtually every erotic moment in the poem. The reference to "wheeles" suggests the "wheels" in "Episode of Hands" among which "shafts of sun" "glittered." Crane frequently associates this evanescent light with the evanescent labor of the factory floor. Both of these features in turn link Pocahontas with the "hobo-trekkers" of "The River," because like them, she is *"time's truant"* who will *"lead you by the hand"* (*P* 55). That "hand" is a telling sign that Pocahontas exemplifies not only the equivocal desire but also the irregular temporality that Crane's culture understood as characteristic of migratory laborers. It bears noting that hobo men did not discriminate fastidiously between "wheel[ing]" women and other men in terms of object choice; the gender of hoboes and their sexual partners counted less than the casualness and informality of their contact. As Nels Anderson reports in *The Hobo: The Sociology of the Homeless Man* (1923), "Though he does enter into transient free unions with women when the occasion offers, all studies show that homosexual practices among homeless men are widespread."[44] Anderson is even more specific than this about the "practice" favored most by "hobo-trekkers." It is that dreaded pederasty from which Eliot spends such energy defending the mind of Europe. "The boy does not need to remain long in hobo society," Anderson remarks, "to learn of homosexual practices" (*H* 144). And though the "duration of an intimacy" between men and boys "is seldom more than a few days" (*H* 145), such a connection suffices to train the young recruit in the ways of what Josiah Flynt in *Tramping with Tramps* calls "the turf." "A crowd of gamins gazes up at him with admiring eyes," Flynt writes of the tramp's scene of seduction.

> Somehow, little by little, there is a favorite who is getting more and more than his share of the winks and smiles. Soon the most exciting parts of the stories are gradually devoted to him alone. . . . It is not long before he feels his importance. He begins to wink, too, but just as slyly as his charmer, and his little mouth curls into a return smile when the others aren't looking.[45]

The tutelage that proceeds here through storytelling is also an erotic initiation, as the young boy's discreetly flirtatious reciprocation of the tramp's attention implies. It is this doubling of pedagogy and pederasty that Crane's speaker has in mind when he notes the "youngsters with eyes like fjords, old reprobates / With racetrack jargon" among the "hobo-trekkers" (*P* 59). In "hobo society," men traveled with boy companions, and in the hobo argot of the day, men were jockers and boys were punks. The pun on jockey and jocker (a bit of "racetrack jargon") indicates Crane's awareness and exploitation of this terminology. Like that "jargon," the rules of social life among hoboes are transmitted, passed from "old" to "young," through a cycle of erotic induction; as Flynt relates, "[I]n this way the number of boys in Hoboland is always kept up to a certain standard. Every year a number are graduated . . . immediately to find younger children to take up the places they have left."[46] Pederasty forms the means by which an otherwise ephemeral and barren, "wifeless" group perpetuates its kind.

Crane's sense of the importance of the hobo in *The Bridge* concerns what sort of knowledge he understood the hobo as capable of teaching. That Crane in fact saw these irregular men as teachers and workers is by no means a truth self-evident to readers accustomed to viewing hoboes in a sentimental light (not least, it might be added, because this is the light in which hoboes have liked to paint themselves). As Nels Anderson reminds us, the idea that hoboes were idle or unemployed was largely a myth. "We can hardly overestimate the importance of [the hoboes'] interim role," Anderson writes, in the building of the transcontinental infrastructure of modern America. Working "in places where no labor supply existed," hoboes "multiplied when railroad building began and when other types of firm structuring were needed" (*H* xix). "The true hobo was the in-between worker," Anderson contends, whose migratory, seasonal, and piecemeal employment was indispensable to closing the gap between East and West. Hoboes, then, were a population in the limbo between America's agrarian-capitalist heyday and its triumphal corporate future, a transitional as well as "transient" (*H* 108) group whose absence from the historical record Anderson traces

to their lack of organized solidarity and their "mobility tradition" (*H*xix).[47]
In slowing down the hobo-trekkers in "The River," Crane's poem seeks to
get hold of this portable and sexually irregular population long enough to
take stock of what kind of labor they might be seen to embody.

Thomas Yingling argues that Crane's use of the "hobo-trekkers" in *The
Bridge* demonstrates the poet's attachment to a "marginalized masculinity
romanticized by the homosexual from childhood." For Yingling, these "wifeless" figures with their rootlessness and isolation represent the abjection of
same-sex desire that deforms the poem. They signal Crane's failure to articulate a homosexuality based on integration with the normative world
"dominated by commerce." The hoboes are thus synecdochic for what Yingling reads as *The Bridge*'s inability to reconcile homosexuality with the
larger culture, to surmount what he calls "the utter unmarriageability of
Crane's homosexual desire." The first poem of Section II, "Harbor Dawn,"
which Yingling sees as contrasting homosexual union in the privacy of the
harborside bedroom with the "traditionally masculine world outside it," in-
augurates a ban on homosexuality that becomes more severe as *The Bridge*
progresses. Homosexuality is the thing that waking life relegates to the
dream-state of innermost reverie. "The lovers, barely awake, hear the beginnings of morning activity in the harbor," Yingling writes of "The Harbor
Dawn, "actions that announce the end of their harbor in one another and
assert the primacy of economic harbors where other forms of male behavior take precedence."[48]

Yet to reduce the poem's narrative logic to an antagonism between the
world of manly labor and a homosexuality it proscribes is to ignore the ways
in which working-class sexuality encompasses same-sex desire—and, more
important, to ignore the continuity between sex and work that *The Bridge* un-
derscores. "The Harbor Dawn," for example, collapses the distinction between the "fog-insulated noises" of the speaker's presumably homoerotic
fugue and the sounds of truck drivers, winch operators, and "the drunken
stevedore." The sounds outside the room and the "tides of voices" that come
to the speaker in his sleep are intimately connected; they bind inside to outside in the poem. The "fog" in which the speaker is immersed as he resists
wakefulness and which the poem appears to understand as an interior substance—a means of "insulat[ing]" the self from the invasive sounds of the
working world—originates in that exterior world, turning the latter into a
"pillowed bay" in which "steam / Spills into steam, and wanders, washed
away / —Flurried by keen fifings, eddied / Among distant chiming buoys,
adrift" (*P*53).

The pun on boys ("buoys") reinforces the promiscuous same-sex erotic
fantasy implied by this hydrodynamic vision of "steam / Spill[ing] into
steam": laid out as if in bed on the "pillowed bay" of the harbor, these "chim-

ing buoys" ("charming boys") serve as the nodal points for an undetermined, collective eros that "washes" over them all indistinctly, no matter how "distant." In fact it is the lack of proximity that adds to the charm of the buoys/boys. Though several critics have seized upon the phrase "signals dispersed in veils" in the first stanza of "Harbor Dawn" as a reference to the elaborate coding that serves as currency to enter the gay world, the "dispersed" nature of these signals is equally important to the poem's erotic atmosphere.[49] This is sexual contact imagined as extensive, disseminated, "adrift," and tidal in both senses: it is multiple (as in "a tide of voices") and it is subject to withdrawal and return: "And if they take your sleep away sometimes / They give it back again" (*P* 53). This is the dream from which the lover chooses not to awaken and yet which waking also brings home to him in the form of the "sirens," the captivating songs of masculine labor that "stealthily weave us into day" (*P* 53). Compared with this fantasy of plural and public sex outside the insulated precincts of domesticity, the speaker's "merge[r]" with the single partner in the bed "beside me" feels anticlimactic, except that their union implies less the reversal of this polymorphous eros than its prolongation. "While myriad snowy hands are clustering at the panes— / *your hands within my hands are deeds*" (*P* 53), Crane writes, as though to confirm the undisrupted segue between outside and inside, the multitude and the couple, the hands groping at the window and the hands groping in bed, that the poem entertains. The word "panes" points us back to the association between brutality and pleasure that we find in the vicinity of busy hands throughout Crane. As the screen that mediates between the hands outside and the hands inside, this word (pointedly echoing "pains") reinforces the sense that such intimacy is in danger of being violently ruptured at any moment.

The sounds of working life are not antithetical to this complex and at times painful promiscuity but rather are "whispers antiphonal" (*P* 108) to it, to use the phrase from the last line of "Atlantis." The "accolade," the greeting or public recognition that belongs to hobo society, finds its way into "The Harbor Dawn" through the "sirens" and the "chiming buoys" and the "howl and thud" of working-class life, which calls this desire into being and responds to its appeals. What makes this continuity between labor and sex difficult to see, and what Crane's poem takes pains to disclose, is the fact that both the labor and the desire attached to these bodies are discontinuous, casual rather than purposive, impermanent rather than sustained. We might revise Yingling's reading of this poem by arguing not that the masculine economies of labor are opposed to same-sex desire but that they are closely bound up with it. "Longshoremen usually lifted heavy burdens in pairs and became so accustomed to each other's movements that they needed no verbal communication to coordinate their efforts," David Montgomery notes.[50]

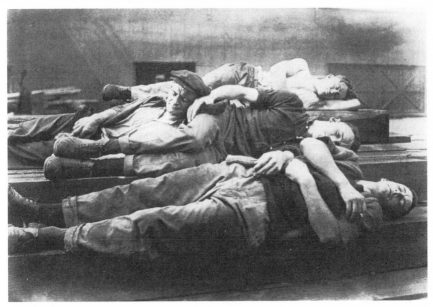

Lewis W. Hine, *Dockworkers Taking a Siesta,* circa 1922

"For such a working couple to part company created a scandal among their workmates." Lewis Hine's photograph of longshoremen touching bodies during a "siesta" indicates the level of intimacy that was customary among early twentieth-century working-class men.

Just as it makes sense to note the continuum between working-class labor and working-class intimacy, so it avails us to note that far from being opposed to the "traditionally masculine world" of labor, the category of the hobo was historically an ambiguous one. In a culture where two-thirds of unskilled laborers spent up to six months a year unemployed while mills and factories were idle, anyone who worked with his hands might become a hobo. His "pariah" (*P* 44) status notwithstanding, the hobo's irregularity was less the exception than the rule in an economic order that kept virtually all labor erratic by design in order to keep wages low. In immigrant communities during the early decades of the century, laborers lived in conditions that bore closer resemblance to the "wayward plight" of tramps than to the well-settled homes of their employers. The laborers often lived in crowded boardinghouses far from immediate relations, worked seasonally, and spent months at a time in a state of what one contemporary informant called the "leisure enforced by the shutdown in the mill . . . with neither the pleasures nor restraints of home life."[51] Their status did not conform to any recognizable pattern of domestic regularity. The "male behavior" pursued by working-class men was thoroughly irregular and perverse by the standards of genteel culture.[52]

What Crane's poem demonstrates is the mutual parasitism between the world that produces tramps and that tramps help produce. This world not only turns irregularity, underemployment, and insecurity into systemic features of working lives, but also incorporates the restless, risky, and anonymous pleasures found in working-class culture into its own consumer venues. The structure of desire in hobo society—its "termless play," its "wayward plight"—has come to look suspiciously like the structure of desire of market culture itself. Rather than representing an isolated moment of pathos in *The Bridge*, then, the hoboes in fact might be seen as embodying a sensibility that radiates throughout the poem as well as throughout the culture in which Crane composed his poem, a culture in which "casual labor" was the norm rather than the exception and in which workers' own relation to this casualness fell somewhere between compulsoriness and choice.[53] Crane was hardly alone in forging this association between tramps, casualness, and culture. "Aside from the indispensable labor of his hands," sociologist Robert Park writes of the hobo's "casual and seasonal labor," "the only important contribution which he has made to the permanent fund of our experience which we call culture has been his poetry."[54]

For Crane, "casual and seasonal labor" is inseparable from the *casualization* of personal ties, particularly those ties that bind men to women and generation to generation. In "Van Winkle," for example, the upright figures of Priscilla and Captain Smith, "all beard and certainty," give way to "Rip Van Winkle bowing by the way" (*P* 55). Despite his cramped and marginal status on the road to courtship and marriage, Van Winkle overtakes the happy couple on the "macadam" (*P* 55) or road that matters to this poem: the world outside the generational memory provided by familialism. "And Rip forgot the office hours," Crane writes, "and he forgot the pay; / Van Winkle sweeps a tenement / way down on Avenue A" (*P* 55). In turning Washington Irving's famed character into a custodian and a denizen of the slums, Crane elaborates the resistance to social conformity embedded in Irving's tale into class terms.[55] Van Winkle's "truant" status and amnesia, his being out of time with the imperatives of both national and generational continuity, are aligned with the indifference and neglect that Crane's culture imputed to working-class irregularity.

The relation between the casual laborer and the breakdown of normative social customs was a frequent topic of discussion among early twentieth-century social thinkers. "There is here," Parker notes in *The Casual Laborer,* "a great laboring population experiencing a high suppression of normal instincts and traditions. There can be no greater perversion of a desirable existence than this insecure, undernourished, wandering life, with its sordid sex expression and reckless and rare pleasures."[56] The intimate link be-tween the riskiness of the "insecure" labor economy and the riskiness of la-borers' "reckless and rare pleasures" was a pressing concern even with regard to workers who weren't what Parker labeled "migratories." "The cre-ation of genuine interests below the security line is a hopeless task," Mary Simkhovitch writes in *The City Worker's World* (1917). For those without "se-curity," "the most highly stimulating forms of amusement" keep them "sub-merged" in "the most mechanical forms of chance" and "a mere titillation of the senses." The chanciness of laboring life reinforces the chance or ran-dom amusements that workers appear to favor, and thus reinforces their lack of "security" by "making dissipation easy" and "true concentration" im-possible. Simkhovitch is most distressed by the fact that the "overwork" caused by industrial society leads to "abandon" rather than to the discipline that industrial time ostensibly curries. "Exhaustion demands stimulants," she concludes; when labor is not its own reward, the latter must come from "the most highly stimulating forms of amusement."[57]

The idea that "overwork" in industrial life leads to overplaying outside the factory walls, that leisure time flouts the discipline of work time, finds a parallel in the textile worker and her "life of mill drudgery." In keeping with the temporality that disturbs Simkhovitch, this worker's machine-driven la-bor is paced in such a way that it leaves her ego free to roam outside the do-main of a work routine, the habitual rigor of which results paradoxically in moral lassitude. This perpetual cycle is exacerbated by aspects of working-class life—games of chance and music halls—that Simkhovitch finds re-gretful because they remove the working man or woman from any active engagement with culture. Such diversions cloud the mind of the working classes and prevent the uplift through education and edification that the so-cial gospel preaches. The "nickelodeon entertainment," Simkhovitch writes, "is fed out to the auditors, whose reaction is but slight. No concentration or sustained interest is demanded."[58]

Yet something is missing from this picture of working-class leisure time and its numbing effects. Far from making their participants over into pas-sive drones, the venues of working-class life (saloons and casinos, movie halls and cabarets) tended on the contrary to be sites of the most raucous and unruly forms of expression. According to a feminist reformer in 1910, nickelodeons "are the recruiting stations of vice," because of which, she argues, "there should be a police woman at the entrance of every moving picture show and another inside."[59] We have already noted the clash be-tween competing modes of education in Crane's culture—the fight be-tween the university model and the consumer model, we might call it, or the school of Eliot and the school of J. Walter Thompson. The culture of the cinema figured importantly into the calculus of immoral pleasures that vexed Simkhovitch, Parker, and other high-minded observers. Crane knew as much as anyone that before it became a respectable corporate industry, the movie business was vulgar working-class entertainment. And in keeping with this class dimension, nickelodeons shared in the general casualization of personal life that defined working-class experience after 1900. It is fair to say that in the early years of motion pictures, nickelodeons functioned as illicit gathering places. The darkness, revolving crowds, and continuous screenings central to the milieu fostered an informal environment where persons could flirt with one another not only without having their presence or conduct policed but also in the absence of sustained expectations of commitment.

Thus when in the proem to *The Bridge* Crane's speaker refers to "cinemas" and "panoramic sleights," we must assume he has in mind not only the visual illusion presented by the bridge's wires and the constant stream of pedestrians over the bridge but also the tricks that occur in the cinematic realm itself. "Sleights" here encompass both the sexual tricks that movie theaters allow to take place and the sleights of hand that moviegoers play on the world at large by masking a potentially illicit encounter with the veneer of mute and frozen spectatorship. This is another way of reading the "accolade" of "anonymity" further along in the proem, since the reward of a darkened, busy nickelodeon is that of a protected place in which to have something like sex in public. Movies have always served as a cultural alibi for those who would rather not get caught in the wrong place at the wrong time—a feature of movies that from their inception provoked endless worry over how to classify or justify time spent in nickelodeons. Most reformers were suspicious enough of what went on in such venues to want to shut them down.[60] Seen in this light, the sexually explicit situations on the screen were much easier to control than what went on in the back row. Whereas censorship codes could cleanse movies of explicit erotic themes, there was no analogous code to curb the lurid scenes that took place in the theater itself.[61]

Crane's abiding interest in Charlie Chaplin is worth pursuing in connection with this *Kulturkampf* in the teens and twenties not only because Chaplin was the supreme avatar of mass entertainment but also because to reformers and university types the content of his films reflected exactly what was wrong with mass entertainment. Crane's "Chaplinesque" is a poem written in response to the 1921 film *The Kid,* in which Chaplin's "little tramp" raises an orphan boy he finds in an alley. As Crane notes in an astonished letter to Gorham Munson soon after he saw the film in Cleveland, *The Kid*'s release in Ohio was delayed by a year "on account of the state board of censors" (*SL* 65). What Crane saw, naively perhaps, as the "brilliant subtleties of this picture" Ohio's censorship board saw more keenly as the overt subversion of domestic pieties at every level. In the film, Chaplin's fatherly tramp tutors Jackie Coogan's kid in breaking windows in preparation for Chaplin's character to fix them; encourages Coogan to box with a neighborhood youth; and eventually smuggles Coogan away from juvenile authorities who want to institutionalize him with "proper care and attention." If the window-breaking scam symbolically equates both tramp and kid with home wreckers, the lengthy kiss that comes at the climax of Coogan's rescue by Chaplin puts on the screen a vision of pedophilic bliss—the cross-generational desire that found its way into hobo culture and from there into Crane's long poem. Like the "hobo-trekkers" in *The Bridge,* Chaplin's tramp carries his labor on his back. Each morning he straps glass plates onto his shoulders in order to repair the domiciles that do not otherwise admit him. The tramp's profession highlights his itinerancy; as the cycle of broken and repaired windows suggests, there is something terminally unsettled and unsettling about this entrepreneurial glazier. As if confirming the link between tramps and locomotion, our first glimpse of Chaplin's character shows him on what the film's inter-title calls "his promenade," which consists of sidestepping the garbage that housewives throw out their windows into a back alley. After being doused with one such discharge, Chaplin is referred to as an "awkward ass," a phrase that combines the unease and ill fit of hobo existence with the physical part most frequently associated with "bums," the anus or backside. With his sizable derriere and waddling gait, Chaplin's tramp summarizes the social peril of hoboes in American culture: their adoration of little boys, their "awkward" and overexposed backsides, their irregular and even illegal labor. The tramp's improper movement and status outside the home were not so much exceptional as indicative of modern socialization—an intuition reflected in the fact that *The Kid* was the highest-grossing film of its time.

The success of Chaplin's film consisted to some extent in its power to circulate back to its mainly lower-class audience a version of itself in the form of a sentimentalized but no less potent deviation from middle-class domestic and cultural norms. The film condenses crucial features not only of casual laborers but also of the casual leisure such laborers preferred, incorporating elements of the all-too-relaxed and promiscuous culture of the working classes into its narrative structure. Hence the mother who abandons her illegitimate child turns out to be a theater star, and the film's finale reunites mother, tramp, and kid in an ironic tableau that suggests that tramps and loose women are obverse and reverse of each other: A child born out of wedlock is destined to grow up the protégé of a tramp, and a woman who has sex without marriage is destined for celebrity. The film not only fails

Jackie Coogan and Charlie Chaplin reunited in *The Kid,* 1921

to punish the kid's mother for her sins but actively rewards her with success in the very medium—mass entertainment—deemed to lead women astray.

One reason for that success is of course the different sort of identity that mass culture allows its participants—the ability to disown a disgraced past by assuming, as Sherwood Anderson's Wing Biddlebaum does, an alias. Just as Chaplin's kid and tramp are nameless figures, so the moviegoers themselves form an anonymous body of viewers. Contemporary reformers understood the anonymity it allowed its audiences as one of the most perilous features of early cinema. Here was an impersonality that seemed to make not only proper names but also propriety irrelevant. Crane perceives in this realm of anonymous congregation a potential for social contact and relatedness that critics of *The Bridge* and of the status of "cinemas" in it have never quite put their finger on. In his astute analysis of linguistic doubling in Crane's poem, Paul Giles repeats a general critical assumption that Crane's attitude toward motion pictures shares elite culture's sense that movies breed something like false consciousness in their viewers. In a gloss of the proem's lines "With multitudes bent toward some flashing scene / Never disclosed, but hastened to again" (*P*43), Giles concludes that the "cinema-audience" is "trapped in" a "cycle of illusions" perpetrated by "cinema-owners" who "exploit" this audience "for profits."[62] Yet given the morally ambiguous status that movie houses had in Crane's world, his interest in why persons return again and again to movies seems to have less to do with the cycle of "illusions" perpetrated on the screen (which Giles likens to the shadows on "Plato's cave") than with the possibilities for encounter that movie houses furnished.[63] In other words, movie houses, like other venues in working-class culture, facilitated an impersonality that dispensed with the decorum of tradition and longevity central to both modernism's creed and the narrative of social uplift. Although preachers of the social gospel sought to redeem the (largely poor, often immigrant) motion-picture audience by encouraging distributors to supply educational, spiritually uplifting, or patriotic fare, these reformers remained painfully aware that working-class entertainment was popular because it endorsed without qualms those qualities of instant and transitory gratification that we have come to associate with a by now hegemonic consumer culture.

The context of working-class pleasure has implications for parts of *The Bridge* that we have been accustomed to seeing primarily as abstract and timeless dimensions of the poem—its oblique and disembodied language, its emphasis on a mythical or legendary past. The central coordinates of this working-class pleasure are not very different from those informing working-class labor in the period: transience and anonymity. Despite protests to the contrary from reform-minded social theorists, these features of working-class leisure experience were not meaningless. Instead, their real meanings were all too apparent and threatening, for they suggested that desire might be indulged in the absence of the protocols that society had evolved to legitimate desire—the most important of which were companionate marriage and child rearing. Likewise, the "flashing scene / Never disclosed" can be read in a different light from the one Giles sheds on it; such a scene may have less to do with anything on the screen than with what transpires in the back row, where "flashing" turns out to have a more erotically charged valence than a first glance implies. Throughout the poem, "flashes" of light evoke the physical materiality that seems to matter most to Crane, the particulate matter that is also, as Einstein revealed, a wave or stream. Like the wavering, never quite steady bodies of casual laborers, this insoluble yet floating matter encodes a notion of sexual desire unencumbered by the dictates of identity or value. The uncertain status of light as matter doubles the uncertainties of both working and erotic life in the culture that Crane inhabits.

Crane picks up on the radical potential embodied by the circulation of desire in working-class life—desire as circulation, as both particle and wave. Above all, this desire is distinguished by its episodic temporality, its "flashin[ess]," by its heightened investment in a moment that may be repeated indefinitely and in different circumstances but that need not add up to a narrative of sustainable attachment or enduring expectations. This is the temporality that "cinemas" deliver to their repeat viewers in the early twentieth century, the temporality of return and departure that the tidal drifts in "Harbor Dawn" evoke, as well as the ships "complighted" in "Atlantis." This is a time measured by suddenness and accident rather than by the permanent settlement that Crane's poem associates with the dead "friends" in "Quaker Hill." As that poem morbidly details it, such a bonded and bounded community of faith can be procured only by a cessation of movement that Crane and the other writers in this book frequently associate with interment.

At the center of *The Bridge*'s episodic temporality we yet again find hands. From "Episode of Hands" to the late poems in *The Bridge*, the hand becomes the means for grasping or getting hold of the episodic. This is a power the hand possesses by virtue of the fact that hands in Crane's culture were seen as liable to vanish at a moment's notice, whether in the form of manual labor displaced by machinery or in the guise of hired hands and day laborers taking off for new frontiers. The structure of episodic time is embedded within the material life of working-class labor in the early twentieth century—when employers manifested a widespread indifference to the identity or continuity of their workforce from day to day. In "The Tunnel," a section of *The Bridge* concerned with the virtues and liabilities of circulating in modern mass culture, Crane writes of how "hands drop memory" (*P* 101). If memory shores up social identity, then episodic time, because it is unconcerned with right relations between self and world, because it is indifferent to the ontological demand that who you are today bears a close connection to who you will be tomorrow, allows a respite from this normative requirement. Hands drop memory in "The Tunnel" because memory—either your own or other persons' about you—does not count for much in the calculus of cruising, which thrives on momentary intensities and the absence of both expectation and explanation. The liability attached to the vanishing hand in one domain (secure employment) becomes a kind of virtue in another (the cruise). The cruise divests the body of the marks of "memory" and so of the narrative coordinates by which memory places the other according to social caste or role. In the poem "A Name for All," Crane writes, "I dreamed that all men dropped their names," a fantasy of anonymity that the speaker sees as rectifying what the poem earlier construes as the violence that naming entails. Names are what "we pinion to your bodies to assuage / Our envy of your freedom," the speaker argues to the nonhuman creatures the poem addresses. Yet this account of naming as "maim[ing]" could just as easily apply to Crane's understanding of human relations, for the "usurp[ing]" that naming entails is described in the poem's middle stanza as "tak[ing] the wing and scar[ring] it in the hand" (*P* 119).

The "hands like wings of butterflies" from "Episode of Hands" are clearly on Crane's mind here. "A Name for All" was written very close to the completion of *The Bridge*, and its concern with the dream of "drop[ping] names" resonates into that complex cycle of poems. The matter of naming matter in "A Name for All"—and the fantasy it entertains for men to "drop their names"—returns us to a crucial problem in Crane: the dilemma of how to get hold of matter that flutters on the brink of intangibility. We have noted that Crane chided Winters for his "arbitrary torturings" "all for the sake of a neat little point of reference." Here the torture seems to be the violence that inheres in a poetic project that, at least according to Crane, posits the material world as graspable on conventional grounds. For Crane, the problem with this poetic model is that the material relations of the new century appear radically ungrounded, abstracted from solidity. As demonstrated by the suspension bridge that gives the poem its title, infrastructure to Crane looks more like a bird on the wing than an unwavering bulwark against the elements.[64] This "dynamic" matter thus demands a different poetic approach. Nowhere does the problem feel so acute as in "Atlantis," the culminating lyric of *The Bridge*, a poem that in its relentless abstractness threatens to substitute the "arbitrary torturing" Crane disdains in Winters for an equally "arbitrary" and tormented obscurity. Based largely on the evidence of "Atlantis," for example, Alan Trachtenberg has concluded that Crane "refused to—could not—acknowledge the social reality of his symbol, its concrete relations to its culture."[65]

One way to recover "Atlantis" for analysis would be to piece together its matter with clues abounding throughout Crane's poetry. Taking seriously the figures of winged hands in Crane's work allows us to see "Atlantis" as an insistently materialist poem. The "seagull's wings" in the proem, for instance, are figures for the kind of hands that matter to Crane—those that come and go, that "dip and pivot," touching earth momentarily while always holding out the option of "shedding" encumbrances. Since the proem also imagines these "wings" as "building high / Over the chained bay waters Liberty" (*P* 43), it is no stretch to claim that these wings are figures for manual laborers engaged in the construction of the bridge itself. Like these workers, birds represent a sort of matter that defies material grounding, defies location or placement. The "seagulls stung with rime" (*P* 105) and the "agile precincts of the lark's return" (*P* 106) in "Atlantis" reconnect the avian imagery of "To Brooklyn Bridge" with the dilemma of matter in motion that *The Bridge* as a whole takes up. Along with the continual return of spectators to the cinemas, the continual "return" of birds to the bridge has invited the claim that Crane conceives of time in Nietzschean terms—a cyclical trap that the poet must expose. On this reading, the freedom of the flying bird is a false transcendence betrayed by the "blinding cables" (*P* 107) of repetition and eternal return.[66]

As compelling as this account of the poem may be (since *The Bridge* is keen to reveal how its central figures from Columbus on mistake their dead-end movements for progress or discovery), I argue that it is not the account of time most germane to Crane. What we might call *The Bridge's poetics of amnesia* should be regarded not as a disabling of the self in its unwitting repetition of the past but as an enabling respite within the larger confines of normative temporality. In other words, rather than subsuming its various moments of apparent liberation under a concept of fatal timelessness, *The Bridge* opposes the momentary interstice to the structure of reproductive time that memory serves. This amnesiac potential is inseparable from the dynamic matter of birds and hired hands, and inseparable as well from the bridge itself, which, "[k]inetic of white choiring wings" (*P* 107), partakes of the fluttering motion it facilitates. Because the bridge facilitates "migrations," it "must needs void memory" (*P* 107). Like the "hands" that "drop memory" in "The Tunnel," the bridge proves indifferent to memory's prerequisites, encouraging instead "Unspeakable . . . Love" (*P* 107). This cluster of terms—"unspeakable," "love," "migrations," "void memory"—indicate that, for all its monumental stature, the bridge is most notable for sustaining not mythical but episodic time. For Crane, the Brooklyn Bridge sustains the time in which unspeakable love might unfold because the bridge itself is a kind of episodic matter, the kind of body in motion that he associates with hoboes and sailors. Insofar as it consists of "transparent meshes," insofar as its parts (like the "voices" it hails) "flicker" in and out of vision and "waveringly stream," the bridge is a negation of solid matter. Its woven metal strands and lattice structure give the illusion of nonexistence even if its basic matter is obdurately tangible—"granite and steel" (*P* 105). The flexible materiality of the suspension bridge makes it a form without an intrinsic content, a body without an essence, and so a body to whose "fleckless," "gleaming staves" (*P* 105) nothing can be made to stick.

That the bridge is a sort of body to Crane (and, with its "staves," a phallic body at that) becomes plausible when we recall that Crane uses the word "gleaming" to describe the merchant marine the speaker encounters in "Cutty Sark": "I saw the frontiers gleaming of his mind" (*P* 72). In one sense what the speaker sees in these "frontiers gleaming" is a "mind" irradiated with knowledge and enlightenment—"rum was Plato in our heads" (*P* 71), as he puts it. But from another angle the "frontiers gleaming" is Crane's way of saying that the sailor has a dirty mind, a mind full of slime—since "gleim" is an archaic word that the *Oxford English Dictionary* defines as "[t]o smear with a sticky substance . . . to be infected (as with a disease); to be attached *to* something." Though Giles suggests that Crane uses "gleam" as a veiled term for excrement or detritus in "Virginia" (since "gleam" is a falconry term that means to "disgorge filth"), this derivation misses something in

Crane's fastening on the word not only in "Cutty Sark" but also in "Atlantis."[67] "Gleam" is doing double and perhaps triple duty in *The Bridge*. It means not only a flash of light but also, in its medieval connotation, something like the opposite of this luminous brevity: a sticky substance that contaminates the self, signifying not fleeting light but "attach[ment] to something." I take Crane to mean both states at once. The transitory "wisdom" that "Cutty Sark" associates with the sailor's "mind" is entirely compatible with the infectious attachment that "gleaming" also encodes.

An examination of some of the terms crucial to Crane makes such speculation seem less intemperate. For example, the reference to "Plato" calls on the sodomitic pedagogy that Western culture has traditionally assigned to the Socratic method—just as "frontiers" recall the migrant population of homeless men whose labor, according to Nels Anderson, was closely aligned with the vicissitudes of the "firm structuring" of a transcontinental nation. The sailor in "Cutty Sark" isn't far removed from the complex of irregular desires and pedagogic and erotic tricks that early twentieth-century society imputed to hoboes; the "frontiers gleaming of his mind" evoke the overwhelming association of tramps with diseased affections in Crane's culture. The particular scourge the hobo was understood to bring with him, as we have noted, consisted in the deranging of proper attachments among young men and boys, whom he smeared with his seductive fantasies of a life without attachment or obligation, a life in which boys might immerse themselves in the filth of temporary erotic connection, say, and yet take wing, having disgorged any consequences from such illicit connection.

"Cutty Sark" might best be read as an enactment of the cruising scenes to which Crane was accustomed, in which extemporaneous sexual attraction (the flash of attachment between two men) was inseparable from the fleeting nature of such attraction (a flash in the pan). The poem depicts an encounter with a lover who both insists the speaker "remember . . . / to put me out at three" and yet himself "forgot to look at you / or left you several blocks away" (*P* 71). The drift of this erotic fugue is inseparable from the drift embedded in the sailor's own wandering mind, whose "frontiers" turn out to be "gleaming" because they are always off to another place—and so nothing sticks there—and because his refusal of placement or permanence ("I can't live on land" [*P* 72]) allows him to sully his mind and body with the wrong kind of sex. If such sex is hazardous for men who sail—a liability where male power is concerned—its threat becomes defused when it can be imagined as a momentary gamble or a "lark," not as a fixture of one's identity. This is how the "crap-shooting gangs in Bleecker" may imagine it when they turn male-male sex (one way to construe shooting the crap) into a game of risk.

"Fleckless" bodies are ones that by virtue of the cover of anonymity do not have to yield themselves to any other narrative script than that of episodic desire. One way to reassess "Atlantis," a poem that appears to include no persons or bodies, would be to suggest that the poem's intensive abstraction is not so much a de-peopling as it is Crane's way of signaling the divestment from peculiar individuality and social role that places like the bridge occasion. Because the bridge is not a resting place but a place to move through or past, it is not really a place at all—or rather its function as a place, like its substance, is at best equivocal. In this regard it is a utopia for desire that circulates outside the sheltered confines of the domestic sphere. And while it is clearly associated with men throughout the poem in general, the radical form of impersonality, of "drop[ped] memory," that the bridge underwrites is often gender-neutral. The impersonality that the poem designates at the heart of the structure of migratory labor and migratory pleasure does not distinguish between genders. Crane understands this alternative, episodic temporality as something like a cultural universal. We need only recall Pocahontas and the "nameless woman of the South" in "Southern Cross" (*P* 87) to see that episodic sexuality is not confined to one sex.

If this structure of impersonal desire applies equally across gender lines, so do the risks it entails. There is of course the "pariah" status attached to the casual laborer, a figure understood to stand more or less permanently outside the garden of normative existence, just as the "homeless Eve" in "Southern Cross" "[u]nwedded, stumbling gardenless" (*P* 87), is permitted no truck with that Edenic realm. As this lyric suggests in recurring to the crucial Crane term "stumbling," the price one pays for "unwedded" bliss is a continual loss of footing, a continual trek along the uneven "macadam" that "Van Winkle" invokes. Just as "Southern Cross" implies that "homeless Eve" is less nameable than subject to epithets—"simian Venus" (*P* 87), for example—so *The Bridge* as a whole entertains the suspicion that such naming or identification of the working man or woman as "pariah" forces a kind of categorical violence. Such violence aims to deny the abundant ways in which ordinary time proceeds along the vectors of irregular desire and seasonal labor epitomized by working life. Naming is problematic because it seeks to eliminate unexpected, random, sudden events by the fiat of identity. Thus the largest risk that episodic time entails, where Crane is concerned, is the ingrained assumption that such sporadic or transitory time seemingly cannot endure. Just as the larger culture circumscribes the hobo or casual laborer within a narrative of normalcy, so this temporary temporality is all too often inscribed as a "phase," a momentary detour in a career understood as having an otherwise "straight" path. Since they slip away as suddenly and easily as they arrive, the brief and intense experiences of episodic time become the primary object of another, socially sanctioned form of amnesia—the narrative of desire that erases any accidental or chance sexual interlude to smooth the way for an immemorial and predestined heterosexual norm.

Embedded in the new order of labor that Crane sees around him, the narrative of impermanence at the heart of *The Bridge* is an intensely materialist vision. If this is a materialism we don't see, it is because material culture in the early twentieth century hovers so close to the immaterial and ephemeral that it is in constant danger of disappearing, of dissipating its essence. Crane retrieves from the object-world of consumer culture (in which things are made to be disposed, replaced, and exchanged) a radical possibility both latent and continually thwarted by our society's abiding commitment to sustainable value, to permanent attachment, to the logic of identity. By a similar token, when Crane's critics are disappointed not to find the evidence of homosexual identity or "value" in *The Bridge,* one can't help thinking that they have been the victims of a "panoramic sleight" not unlike the poem's transposition of material life into an ostensibly mythical register. This mythical register is the pretext—or the alibi—for what I argue is the different material culture that Crane's poem explores. In this culture, matter is conceived of as dynamic and substitutive in the same way that those who labor on this matter are understood to be portable and disposable.

Recognizing that the frequently homoerotic cast to working-class sexuality during the period in which Crane composed poetry is secondary to its casualness, brevity, or transferability requires us to reposition our view of *The Bridge* in such a way that we look less for traces of the homosexual identity that the poem refuses to speak than for the figures of class difference through which the poem continually announces its understanding of desire. This understanding involves the radical possibility that desire might be experienced in the absence of the cultural obligation to anchor its energies in the stabilizing cement of true love and monogamy. Even as the mass entertainment of Crane's time often recurred to this bonding agent in its own narratives of illicit passion, its venues catered to a restless and independent working audience that reacted somewhat ambivalently to the family romance. That desire could be detached from a narrative of permanent attachment, that it could go by other names—by aliases or even by no name—is Crane's utopian proposition. The episodic structure of desire in the poem is intimately tied up in the erotics of anonymity, which becomes the poem's article of faith. Religious faith is traditionally seen as a driving component of *The Bridge*. "To keep the faith but not close his eyes to reality was Hart Crane's chief struggle in composing *The Bridge*," writes Alan Trachtenberg.[68] The reference to "the incognizable Word" in "Ave Maria" calls to mind religious devotion—the ineffable mysteries of Catholic doctrine. Yet when in "Virginia" Crane writes, "It is / God—your namelessness," we might hesitate to take the devout stance before the Almighty too seriously. It is likely that this supplicating figure is kneeling with an altogether different object of devotion in mind. Or in hand, to be exact.

Chapter Five

Willa Cather's Catechism

I

When he first appears in the eponymous home of Godfrey St. Peter, Tom Outland proves his mettle by reciting some lines in Latin from Virgil. Just as his appearance in *The Professor's House* is belated, so the lines he quotes from the *Aeneid* are not the poem's beginning, but Aeneas's monologue from book 2: "*Infandum, regina, jubes renovare dolorem,*" he begins, "and steadily continued for fifty lines or more."[1] Two things make this Latin descant unusual. The first is that Outland's recitation positions St. Peter as Dido, Queen of Carthage, in a move that the professor either does not notice or chooses to deflect. "You have a good pronunciation and a good intonation" (*PH* 93), he tells Tom, as if his focus on the formal elements of Tom's Latin might elide the indecorous cross-gendering implied by this excerpt. In hearing only Tom's cadences the professor avoids listening to what Tom is saying. The second is Cather's choice of this moment in Virgil's epic, where *infandum,* which translates into the "vulgar tongue" (*PH* 50) of English as "too deep for words," suggests the ineffability and trauma at the heart of erotic desire. Seen in this light, Tom's citation lends credence to the claim that what Cather called "the thing not named," "the overtone divined by the ear but not heard by it," is a transparent code for homoerotic desire.[2]

But I suggest that Tom's recital functions less like a password inviting the professor into a shared identity based on homoerotic feeling than as a rebuff in which Tom, because he has taken stock of St. Peter, wants to clarify the erotic contrast between them. Cather's readers have spent much energy trying to map her all too elusive sexuality onto her all too "accessible" fiction by focusing on those moments in her work that contribute to her erotics of namelessness, which she is assumed to have inherited from the fin-de-siècle homophile culture of Wilde and Douglas (who coined the phrase "the love that dare not speak its name").[3] The move toward reclaiming Cather's sexuality on these grounds has been so pervasive, in fact, that it has spurred a backlash in the form of Joan Acocella's indictment of "politically correct" Cather criticism. In a polemic that is both informed and blinded by its author's devotion to a pristine view of her subject, Acocella argues that readers who focus on the issue of whether Cather was a sexually active lesbian or proto-feminist repeat a misprision not unlike that found in an earlier school of critics who took her as the nostalgic chronicler of prairie life. For Acocella, Cather does not fit into any of the categories assigned to her. Her discontent with the barrenness of frontier existence, her well-documented sexual repression (most evident in the injunctions her will placed on her correspondence), and her avowed Republicanism all refute the spurious scholarship that Acocella takes to task in a rescue of Cather from the hands of tenured radicals and into the arms of a phantom "common culture."[4]

If there is something to be salvaged from Acocella's reading of Cather, it would be her recognition of the categorical maladjustment that Cather's work evokes and endlessly dramatizes. The dominant mood of Cather's characters might be described as a combination of frustration, resentment, resignation, and anticipation with respect to where they are or might belong in a social order that forever reminds them of their displacement from it. This odd obsession with unbelonging is key to characters, like Tom Outland, who routinely construe their social role as exiles in modern society, usually through a combination of ethnic dispersal and economic deprivation. The orphan Tom is the son of "mover people" (*PH* 98), and so is marked from his origins as a mobile entity—and even in death he has yet to settle down. His legacy to the professor's family amounts to a mobile form of matter like those I have been considering throughout this book. Tom's invention of a "gas" that fuels jet engines demonstrates that we are in the vicinity of an immaterial materiality whose energy and dynamism are more salient than its obdurate substance. Like Milly Theale in her dissemination at the end of *The Wings of the Dove,* like Crane's kinetic bridge and kinetic laborers, the posthumous Tom becomes "a glittering idea" (*PH* 94) or "some fugitive idea" (*PH* 113).

While tinged with nostalgia, these postmortem descriptions recapitulate the flickering nonexistence with which Cather endows her character. If St. Peter "loved youth"—"he was weak to it, it kindled him" (*PH* 19)—Tom throughout the novel is animated by a very different sort of desire, which does not square with either the heterosexual domain or the pedophilic domain that St. Peter doubly, maddeningly occupies. Rather, Tom's eros is fundamentally antisocial, incapable of any cultural redemption and beyond the reach of any common cause. The sort of thing that satisfies Tom and other Cather figures does not reduce to either species reproduction or the kinds of pedagogic transmission that homophile writers began to idealize at the end of the nineteenth century. Like St. Peter, those writers relied heavily on a classical antecedent to defend the value of same-sex desire. In Tom's choice of recitation to St. Peter, we glimpse both Cather's tacit acknowledgment of this borrowing of antique glory and her refusal of that model's limitations.[5]

Aeneas's speech predicts the logic that both unites and separates Tom and his mentor. By casting Tom and St. Peter in the role of Virgil's star-crossed lovers, Cather conjures the same-sex erotics so palpable throughout this novel and produces a foretaste of the departure for Europe and battle that establishes the dynamic Tom's relation to the sedentary professor. Although he needs the tutelage of the older man, the "glittering," "fugitive" Tom finally abandons him and the domestic life for which he stands (or rather sits). It is ultimately St. Peter's dislike of the "vulgar tongue," his embrace of that scholarly sublimation of vernacular perversions like pederasty, that marks the essential difference between them. Whereas the cowboy-turned-scientist Tom likes dirt and gas, St. Peter prefers order and ideas. ("[K]eep it just an idea—it's better so," he tells his daughter of her plan to build him a study in her country house. "Lots of things are" [PH 47].) Whereas Tom chooses to wander, St. Peter opts to stay still. Like Aeneas's life, Tom's does not provide for a feminine respite; by contrast, St. Peter announces to his maid Augusta that she "shan't take away my ladies" (PH 12), as if keeping her dressmaker's dummies "right there in their own place" is necessary for St. Peter to center himself. These inanimate "ladies" are a telling index less of Cather's often cited misogyny than of a subtle critique she levels at her novel's ostensible hero. In this as in so many other Cather texts, settlement and conjugality appear to be the real objects of the author's hostility, and those who embrace them, male or female, come in for an undue share of her disfavor.

Dido's fate in Virgil's poem is not exactly buoyant, of course. Pining after the man who leaves her, she takes her own life. This detail too seems to play into Cather's understanding of her professor, whose death wish suffuses the novel. Her routine alignment of St. Peter's housebound existence with his virtual encryption inside his home implies that interment and domesticity are continuous states, inducing the same state of inanition. Though readers have often seen in St. Peter's death wish a melancholia attached to the foreclosure of homosexual possibility in his adult life, I entertain the suggestion that Cather takes a less generous view of the professor. For it is just his over-refined, claustrophobic, hothouse role that makes St. Peter a "queen" in Tom's eyes, a figure of attachment from whom Cather insists that Tom flee.

Tom is already biased against the sort of domestic existence the professor represents, as he reveals in the first-person account of his sojourn to Washington, D.C. "The couple I lived with gave me a prejudice against that kind of life," he recalls of the Bixbys, about whose "affairs" Tom "couldn't help knowing a good deal" (PH 209). Those affairs consist of a daily round of calculation and scheming on behalf of their own social advancement—a climb up the ladder that unmans Mr. Bixby, who cries out at a dinner party during which his wife's too-expensive skirt has been splashed with "claret-cup" (*PH* 210). Tom's life with the Bixbys reveals the sort of "slavish" (*PH* 209) entanglement he must disown—one, like St. Peter's, in which the ambit of heterosexual desire inevitably strays beyond the narrow domain of physical pleasure to encompass a whole set of social demands, a whole narrative train of events. In the sordid private life that Tom is forced to bear witness to involving this struggling couple, every action is so thoroughly planned, so carefully taken account of, that a red stain on a dress can figure as an unintended sex act—approaching assault, even—in which the husband feels more violated than his wife.

To Bixby and his wife, the realm of private pleasure attaches to the worldly round of "promotions in his department" and "how many new dresses [his coworkers'] wives had" (*PH* 209). But the home life that the Bixbys reveal to Tom suggests that those who domesticate desire in such a way end up paradoxically transforming desire into something outside their control. The compulsory heterosexuality that the couple models turns heterosexuality into a compulsion, a sort of addictive substance of which (like money) the Bixbys can never have quite enough. In light of Tom's realization in the nation's capital, it makes more sense that Cather would send Tom away from St. Peter rather than keep him in the arrested state of "filial piety" (*PH* 227) which the "Latin poets" have taught him. Like the Bixbys', St. Peter's life is fashioned after an insistently schematic calculus of desire. "Because there was Lillian, there must be marriage and a salary. Because there was marriage, there were children" (*PH* 240), he tells himself. Though this litany appears as a critique that Cather and St. Peter share of the inevitability of heterosexual existence, it does not obscure a moment early in the novel in which St. Peter himself presumes the very logic of predicable desire he laments in this reverie. "If there were an instrument by which to measure desire, one could foretell achievement," he muses. "He had been able to measure it, roughly, just once, in his student Tom Outland—and he had foretold" (*PH* 19–20). It is this equation of desire with predictability, with the rational planning in the service of "creation" (*PH* 19), as St. Peter sees it, from which Cather's novel seeks to cleave Tom. *The Professor's House* drives a wedge between this all too familiar and familiarizing concept of eros and the *infandum* one that Tom, who appears to have "reflected deeply upon irregular behavior" (*PH* 99), embodies.

Whereas Cather reserves her fiercest animus for heterosexual relations—focusing repeatedly on unhappy marriages, for example—she appears to be most vexed by the cultural tendency to subsume *any* sexual passion under a narrative of entropy. When desire becomes narrative, so her work argues, it is inevitably pictured as a conjugal experience that erases the line between bonding and bondage, attachment and suffocation. This is the story to which Cather's most beloved characters have the hardest time adjusting. And it does not seem to matter whether this desire is yoked to another person or to a self-identity (both alternatives to which St. Peter succumbs). The logic of coupling works the same, and inflicts the same sense of diminishing returns.

Cather's fiction thus continually makes recourse to men and women whose irregular motion and sense of displacement thwart the orderly narratives of monogamous desire. These figures tend to belong to the underclass populations of drifters, migrant workers, and outcasts I have tracked throughout this book. Rather than seeing these figures as criticism has trained us to view them—as ciphers for an implicit homoerotic desire—I take their social identity at face value. Positioning them in the historical context of shifting class relations in the early twentieth century, I argue that instead of allegorically transposing Cather's own tormented, closeted sexual identity, such misfits assume a different but related burden in Cather's fiction. Their main purpose is not to give voice to the "unspeakable" desires of their author so much as to help her interrogate the tight fit of sociality, sexual destiny, and middle-class security that American culture encodes in what Eve Kosofsky Sedgwick aptly dubs the "family romance of heterosexuality."[6]

II

Rather than tracing moments of potential erotic irregularity in her work to a thematic of authorial identification, my aim is to make salient a complicated textual revisionism operating across Cather's fiction. Cather's quarrel is with the prescriptive narrative logic whereby sexual identity becomes fated or naturalized in prose—the logic, that is, whereby a representation of social norms becomes indistinguishable from the norms themselves. Cather did not have to look far for an alternative to this discursive normalization, especially where the underclass was concerned. She was born into an America permeated by an anti-Catholic ideology in which the Catholic Church's intensive proliferation of regulations was understood by Protestant onlookers to coincide with the basest and most unlawful of practices. While the intensity of antipapal reaction fluctuated throughout the nineteenth and early twentieth century, its essential formula remained intact. In the anti-Catholic imagination, Catholicism as an institution thrived on the discrepancy between form and intent, between prescription and conduct. The only thing reliable about the notoriously degenerate Catholic clergy was the consistency with which they contravened their own vows.

The basic conceits of this anti-Catholic ideology (which Cather largely opposed) find their way into her fiction to buttress Cather's rewriting of the master plot of sexuality. It may seem counterintuitive to suggest that

Cather finds the most forceful revision of the romance of conjugal desire less in the field of homoerotic subcultures than in the Catholic Church—a cultural site almost synonymous with sexual repression. Yet such is the substance of the argument that follows. For Cather, Catholicism provides an entrée into the order not just of faith but also of *infandum* desire. The stereotypical association of American Catholicism with sexual deviance, with a prolific multitude of poor persons, and with ritual superstitions and doctrinal obscurantism becomes the resource from which Cather learns to represent radical erotic difference.

It should be stated at the outset that what I am calling American Catholicism is less a matter of doctrine or spirituality than a name for what largely Protestant America viewed as a *culture*—or, rather, an ethnicity—in its midst. Catholics by no means formed a linguistically or ethnically homogeneous group at the turn of the century, but such distinctions tended to be secondary, according to anti-Catholic nativists, to the shared faith that fused Irish with Bohemian and Italian immigrants. Cather was not vexed by the niceties of theological distinctions so much as she was invested in the representative potential of the generalized Catholic other that preoccupied her contemporaries. This preoccupation was of necessity biased and distorted—an ideological mixture somewhere between the reality and the perception of how Catholics lived in and ordered their world. What comes into play repeatedly in anti-Catholic literature is the duplicity of the Church. Its priests were double agents; its congregants were necessarily divided between loyalty to American and to Roman interests.

Cather came of age when American society was undergoing one of its fiercest revivals of anti-Catholic sentiment. She was at the University of Nebraska when the antipapal American Protective Association, which had spread into Nebraska from neighboring Iowa, was at its most powerful. Founded in 1887 as a secret society, the APA claimed between 1 million and 2 million members at its height—though the clandestine nature of the organization made a verifiable count impossible. Its main platform included preventing the public funding of parochial schools, excluding "Romanists" from teaching positions and political office, and revoking the tax-exempt status of the Catholic Church. The APA's commitment to the school question above all indicated the anxiety that Catholic authoritarianism spurred in the American psyche. The APA tapped into a long-standing American fear of a supposed Catholic mission that centered on "the overthrow and destruction" of "our public schools." Exposing what he called a papal effort to dismantle the public school system was the goal of the Reverend Isaac Lansing's *Romanism and the Republic* (1890). If "our schools teach loyalty" and "love for the state," Lansing argued, then the Catholic's purpose was clear: "Tear in pieces our whole system of schools" and the result would be "a dismembered and ruined country," a "drop back into barbarism" that would prime the American scene for papal dominance.[7]

"When the Roman Catholic Church enters the arena of political force," Lansing reasons, "it has no right whatever to claim the immunities of a religion."[8] Well into the twentieth century, ambivalence toward Catholics could still be felt as a problem with what Protestant observers saw as the duplicitous character of Catholicism—its religious doctrine serving as but a cover for what Lansing called "a political engine."[9] "It is a form of faith and it is a form of government," Winfred Garrison argues in a 1928 book regarding this "mysterious stranger in our midst." In the latter guise, Garrison writes, Catholicism means "a corporate control over the minds, consciences and moral conduct of its adherents—of all the world, if its hopes could be realized—by a very small self-perpetuating group, in the last analysis by one man."[10] Garrison's comments reveal that even when not expressly anti-Catholic, the Protestant majority took a dim view of "Romanism," extrapolating Catholicism's most extreme or conservative traits into their opposite. According to this counterintuitive logic, the iron-clad authority of the Roman Catholic Church tended to generate a state of chaos whereby the masses of lowly and ignorant Catholics would riot against and dismember the American social body under the inexorable direction of far-removed papal encyclicals.

A phony bulletin, "Instructions to Catholics," which the APA circulated in 1891, exhorted "the faithful to exterminate all heretics found within the jurisdiction of the United States of America." As this document indicates, in the anti-Catholic imagination the difference between docile submission and open revolt was nonexistent. Guided by the dictates of duty and faith over reason and fellowship, Catholics would turn violent at a moment's notice. And just as the rigid hierarchical mentality that determined the relation between the Church elite and the plebian parishioner could turn under the alchemical gaze of the anti-Catholic into a threat of anarchy, so vows of celibacy or chastity were seen as pretexts for erotic licentiousness, the likes of which ordinary Christians could scarcely contemplate. The seduction of female parishioners by priests in the confessional and molestation of the young by priests in the classroom were the usual outcomes that the vow of chastity set in motion.

The professed dogmas of the Church were subject to radical reversal and undermining by their very adherents—and to make matters worse, these dangerous corruptions of authority or chastity compounded and amplified each other. The threat of "corporate control" over the body politic was carried out, according to nativist thinkers, by means of an orgiastic free-for-all built into the very fabric of Catholicism, "whose theology is so vile that it cannot be translated into English," according to Lansing's *Romanism and the Re-*

public, "lest the translator be taken up for publishing obscene literature."[11] For the anti-Catholic writer Justin Fulton, the only viable remedy for the Catholic conquest of the American polity was to expose the Church's numerous sexual crimes, as the following passage makes clear:

> Washington, the center of political influence and activity, is in the lap of Rome, with the consent of the people. Let there be a protest. Unroof the monster, Jesuitism. Uncover the pollution, the scandal of the confessional. Unlock and throw open the doors of the convents and nunneries, the assignation houses, kept for a so-called celibate priesthood. Expose the conduct of those who have made prostitution flourish at Rome and in all the great cities in which they have control, and Washington will shake off the incubus.[12]

Fulton crystallizes a widely held belief among Protestants that Catholics elaborated their rigid codes of conduct only as a means to flout propriety under the cover of dogma. The trotting out of "ex-priests" and "escaped nuns" at APA-endorsed public events reignited an old equation between sexual illicitness and Catholic devotion. Typically recruited from the ranks of confidence artists, these alleged fugitives from the clergy would narrate (in as much lurid detail as decency allowed) the sexual degradations they either suffered or inflicted on others while in orders.[13]

The ease with which Protestants perceived priestly chastity as but a ruse for gross erotic trespass had partly to do with what they understood to be the arcane logic of the sacraments. Thus while in orthodox Catholic teaching the proscription of "venereal pleasure" raised the threat that every tempting thought, act, and moment of physical pleasure might be a sin punishable by damnation, according to the logic of confession one could repent of one's sinful acts and have one's erotic slate wiped clean on a regular basis.[14] To unsympathetic observers, Catholic sacraments looked like a way of cheating at virtue or striking bargains for salvation. "Such virtue as they keep is on tap . . . in the church itself," a character in Harold Fredric's *Damnation of Theron Ware* says of Catholics, "and the parishioners come and get some for themselves according to their need for it."[15] This penitential exchange economy—whereby, as William James writes in *The Varieties of Religious Experience,* the sinner who confesses "has exteriorized his rottenness" in a complex logic of admission and reparation—was anathema to mainstream Protestant culture.[16] Cather was attuned to this supposed softness in the Catholic attitude toward sexual sin, as a moment from *Shadows on the Rock* (1931) indicates. On a visit with her apothecary father to the Hotel Dieu, a Catholic infirmary, the young Cecile Auclair hears a tale about an exchange between Sister Catherine, a dutiful novice, and the spirit of an "abandoned sinner," "a *pecheresse* named Marie," who "fell lower and lower, and at last hid herself in a cave" before being "consumed by a loathsome disease."[17] Marie visits from Purgatory to let Sister Catherine know that "The tender Mother of all made it possible for me to repent in that last hour" by "having my punishment abridged," so that all that stands between this fallen woman and paradise are "a few masses" (*SR* 38). Saying these "few masses" retrieves the sinner's soul and redeems the irredeemable. While the fairness of this trade-off seems self-evident to Sister Catherine, who immediately prays for Marie, her comfort with the relative ease by which sexual sin could be "abridged" was shared by few non-Catholics in Cather's day.

Cather had little patience with the powerful anti-Catholic assumptions that swept the Midwest in the 1890s. She was outspoken, for example, about the question of parochial schooling, arguing in print for the right of Catholic schools to determine their own curriculum without public harassment.[18] Yet notwithstanding her own views, Cather's Republican surroundings were steeped in anti-Catholic feeling, and her position on the school question also indicates that her take on Catholic culture was informed by her awareness of groups like the APA, which made its greatest gains by working to shape Republican ballots in local elections in favor of anti-Catholic candidates. Indeed the APA's ultimate goal was to amass national influence by colonizing the Republican Party (evident in the group's ill-conceived plan to swing the 1896 Republican presidential ticket toward an anti-Catholic slate by smearing McKinley as a papal sympathizer).[19] As Harold Fredric's Theron Ware muses, "[T]his tremendous partisan unanimity" among Republicans regarding Catholic insurgency "took it for granted . . . that in the large cities most of the poverty and all the drunkenness, crime, and political corruption were due to the perverse qualities of this foreign people" and their "idolatrous religion."[20]

Given that Cather's father not only held town office as a Republican in Red Cloud but was also a reformer of the state and local Republican parties, it seems worth speculating how "politics"—partisan politics, in other words, rather than cultural politics or what Joan Acocella calls "the politics of criticism"—figures into Cather's aesthetic practice, shaping one of that practice's basic dilemmas. This would be the representation of those "perverse qualities" of licentious behavior that litter her otherwise serene texts.[21] Cather's writing frequently reaches for the Protestant-Republican assumption that Catholic obedience translates readily into Catholic defiance, and celibacy into perversity or promiscuity, when her work seeks figures to embody erotic excess and irregularity.

The prevailing American perceptions of Catholics during Cather's lifetime were dominated by one particularly vexing feature of Catholic alterity. This was the widely held belief that devout Catholics readily surrendered the sacred precincts of private life to the authority of the parish priest, a figure whose own vows placed him outside both family bonds and the conventions of American masculinity and individualism. Protestant America provides no normative equivalent for this anti-domestic and anti-individualist figure, and Cather's writing exploits this asymmetry. Her writing is suffused with Catholic figures who embrace their faith at the cost of private domestic attachments, and whose faith leads them into behaviors that are just barely guarded from the charge of indecency by their ostensible piety.

Among the many pages of criticism devoted to *The Professor's House*, one feature of Tom Outland's life that has largely escaped analysis is his having been raised by a Jesuit priest. The nurturing of children by priests is a regular enough topos in Cather's work to warrant generalization. And the common feature of these contacts between priests and boys is that the latter, reared or tutored by clerical "fathers," turn out somehow *wrong*. Such misguidance is implicitly linked to the priest's pedagogical function in "Tom Outland's Story." Not only is Father Duchene a "good Latinist," having taught Virgil to Tom, but his surmise about the ancient skeleton of "Mother Eve" which Tom finds in Blue Mesa depends on an assumption of her having been left behind by her tribe because of an erotic dalliance with a man not her husband. Duchene's theory of this "personal tragedy" (*PH* 201) is worth citing at some length:

> Perhaps when the tribe went down to the summer camp, our lady was sick and would not go. Perhaps her husband thought it worth while to return unannounced from the farms some night, and found her in improper company. The young man may have escaped. In primitive society the husband is allowed to punish an unfaithful wife with death. (*PH* 201)

Father Duchene's conjectural leaps are in keeping with the alleged tendency of priests to hypothesize the worst—which is to say the most "improper"—chain of erotic events. It is hard not to draw a link between the priest's dirty-minded explanation and Tom's habit of "reflect[ing] deeply upon irregular behavior," as if one habit of mind caused the other.

But this is only to say that in tending to think the worst about sex, priests tend to make all sexuality illicit—with the ironic effect that those who enter the priest's orbit cannot help being drawn into sharing the priest's assumption that all erotic experience is necessarily perverse. Throughout the nineteenth and early twentieth century, Protestant attitudes toward the scene of confession made clear this easy move from the proscription of sex as sinful to the embrace of that very sinfulness. In addition to treating the confessional redemption as a swindle, Protestants considered the confessional itself as the primary domain of sexual wrongdoing. In the formulaic account of confessional seduction, the priest becomes so worked up over the erotic secrets he is told that he cannot control himself. ("Priests," Lansing notes, "are compelled to ask questions of boys and girls in the confessional, that are not fit to be repeated even between grown men, unless they are physicians.")[22] And in recounting his or her trespasses, the penitent ends up in the same script. Rather than absolving the self of erotic sins, the confession paradoxically exacerbates those sins by replaying them with the priest cast in a leading role.[23] Fulton again is instructive on the anti-Catholic logic whereby clerics succumb to lust: "No men are tempted like priests. Their passions are often necessarily aroused. The demon of bad thoughts takes possession of them. Their ministry drives them into such relations with women, into whose most secret thoughts they are obliged to enter, that their virtue receives many shocks."[24]

III

Given that priestly prurience inevitably tampers with normal development, it may come as no surprise that in Cather's 1920 short story "Coming, Aphrodite!" Don Hedger, who as a boy of sixteen was adopted by "a Catholic priest . . . to keep house for him," ends up as damaged goods, living a cloistered and monastic existence as a painter in New York with no companion other than his dog.[25] And neither does it seem surprising that Cather stages Hedger's deviance by detailing his proclivity for watching his female neighbor perform calisthenics in the nude through a "knot hole" (CS 71) in the wall between their apartments—an aperture that Hedger happens upon one day while he is rummaging in "the enclosure" (CS 71) of his closet. "Day after day," Cather writes, "he crouched down in his closet to watch her go through her mysterious exercises" (CS 73). "Crouched" here is a revealing word, one that Cather has already used in reference to this voyeurism. "Hedger was crouching on his knees," she writes a page earlier, "staring at the golden shower which poured in through the west windows" (CS 72). The halo effect that bathes this room in light, together with the kneeling viewer, evokes an unmistakable resonance between Hedger's closet and the genuflection that occurs in the vestibule of the Catholic confessional. That "it did not occur to him that his conduct was detestable" (CS 73) only indicates how impaired Hedger has been by the priestly influence of his teenage years. He can make no distinction between proper and improper conduct, between the scene of repentance and the scene of the crime.

Hedger's "stoop[ing]" (CS 72) closet voyeurism is an extreme example of the dialectic of impurity and devotion that Cather's work frequently develops around Catholic figures. In *O Pioneers!* (1912), Marie Shabata, a married woman and "a good Catholic," falls in love with Emil Bergson, the brother of the novel's heroine.[26] What is interesting about the inevitable adultery between them is that while Emil has left the country (to make his fortune in Mexico), Marie spends her time going to "the French church, whatever the weather" (*OP* 181). In Emil's absence, Cather writes, "Marie found more comfort in the church that winter than ever before. It seemed to come closer to her, and to fill an emptiness that ached in her heart" (*OP* 181). The town's Catholic church becomes a surrogate for the adultery that will ensue between Emil and Marie on his return from Mexico, as though the building itself, with the sense of intimacy it tenders to Marie outside the marriage bond, were somehow the catalyst for the extramarital dalliance. This affair occurs not despite but because of Marie's professed faith; "a sincerely devout girl" (*OP* 181), Marie simply exercises her devotion in ways that routinely conjure the specter of erotic recklessness. "Why did she like so many people, and why had she seemed so pleased when all the French and Bohemian boys, and the priest himself, crowded around her candy stand?" Emil asks himself in an earlier moment of jealousy during the Catholic fair (*OP* 161). As the example of Hedger implies and that of Marie confirms, what is startling about this sort of sexual impropriety is that its proponents do not consider it improper—a misprision that is a function here and elsewhere in Cather of their Catholic background. Marie's sincere churchgoing and prayer temporarily take the place of her adulterous desire and exempt her from acknowledging it as adulterous.

Shadows on the Rock presents another illustration of this devotion masking what to non-devout eyes would look like "unnatural" acts—but this time from the priest's angle. The novel features a young boy named Jacques who, though not exactly a "foundling" (like Don Hedger), is treated as such by the community of colonists in "New France" by virtue of the fact that his mother is "a young woman who was quite irreclaimable" (*SR* 50). Jacques's mother, 'Toinette Gaux, belongs to "a large class of women" (*SR* 58) who, like the *pecheresse,* thrust their way into this otherwise virtuous novel about seventeenth-century Quebec. Indeed, *Shadows on the Rock* insists on joining figures of spiritual purity to those of physical corruption. Cather, as though deferring to the official anti-Catholic line on the short trip from sin to salvation in Romanism, cannot conceive of one state without the other. But an exchange between Jacques and the elderly bishop, Monseigneur Laval, clarifies some of the themes I have been glossing in Cather's Catholics.

Laval has come upon Jacques on a cold night, "crouching back against the masonry" of the "Episcopal residence" (*SR* 72). The bishop takes the boy home and puts him in his own room.

One strange thing Jacques could remember afterwards. He was sitting on the edge of a narrow bed, wrapped in a blanket, in the light of a blazing fire. He had just been washed in warm water; the basin was still on

the floor. Beside it knelt a very old man with big eyes and a great droop-
ing nose and a little black cap on his head, and he was rubbing Jacques's
feet and legs very softly with a towel. They were all alone then, just the
two of them, and the fire was bright enough to see clearly. What he remembered particularly was that this old man, after he had dried him
like this, bent down and took his foot in his hand and kissed it; first the
one foot, then the other. That much Jacques remembered. (73–74)

Whereas Jacques has trouble assimilating this experience to anything other
than "strange," the bishop perceives its meaning all too clearly: "this reminder of his Infant Savior" has visited the old man in the night as "a sign
that it was time to return to that rapt and mystical devotion of his earlier life"
(*SR* 75). There appears a discrepancy between this claim for a renewal of
faith and the loving caress of the boy's feet. But that fissure seems exactly
the point. The embrace of one position (that of "rapt and mystical devotion") excludes another from consideration (that of a pleasure by turns pederastic and fetishistic).

Far from an isolated occurrence in *Shadows on the Rock,* Laval's bathing of
Jacques's feet with kisses points to the logic of part for whole that Cather's
Catholic fictions understand as coterminous with Catholic culture. Foot
worship is not far removed from the normative mode of worship in Catholicism—which has historically relied on a subterranean traffic in relics and
artifacts distinctive for their portability, their ability to circulate faith and
meaning from one person to another across great stretches of time and
space. "There are so many sacred relics," Cecile notes, "and they are always
working cures" (*SR* 126). These relics—the scraps and remainders of persons long dead—not only flow throughout Cather's imagined Catholic land-
scapes but also bind their inhabitants in a general economy of corporeal
desire. *Shadows on the Rock* is a novel saturated in bits and pieces of bodies
and persons that their possessors cherish for their substitutive magic, their
ability to conjure the real presence of the absent object of desire on the basis of no substance other than a synecdoche.[27]

As Cather sees it, there is no qualitative difference between Catholicism
and fetishism. Thus, when the ships come in to port where the Quebecois
are waiting en masse, "a sailor would always make straight for the headdress
or bonnet or jacket of his own *pays*" (*SR* 204), since he takes the object of
apparel as an adequate replacement for the homeland he has lost. These
mariners are interesting because their shore leave is marked by "godless behavior" and "rough pleasures" (*SR* 208). The community allows them "a certain license during the few weeks they are on shore" (*SR* 210). Cather forces
a continuity between the sailors' bodily indulgence and the visceral economy of Catholic devotion, which has at its center the ravaged and perpetu-

ally consumed body of Christ. The latter body's eternal resurrection and return in the form of the Eucharistic sacrament reveal what Protestants have always considered the most troubling element of Catholic belief—the "miracle" of transubstantiation. Cather generalizes from the mystery of Christ's real presence in the wafer to depict a Catholic world in which absent, dead, or missing objects of desire (including Christ) can be restored or experienced as whole through the assimilation or absorption of their leftover parts.

Cecile thus tells her father of an "English sailor" who "lay sick at the Hotel Dieu" and was both healed and converted when the mother superior of the hotel "ground up a tiny morsel of bone from Father Brebeuf's skull and mixed it in his gruel" (SR 125). This story appears as a sort of photonegative of the fate of the beggarly Blinker, an exile from the court of the French king who occasionally lives with Cecile and her father and does menial chores for them. Blinker's existence in New France is revealed as a lengthy self-imposed penance for what he considers an unpardonable life of sin. He is a former royal torturer whose guilt has manifested itself in the form of a "suppuration in his jaw" (SR 161). What is interesting about Blinker's case is that the novel insists on construing his guilt in terms of a literal corporeality, according to the logic of stigmata: "These things would rise up out of the past . . . faces . . . voices . . . even words" (SR 161), and these psychic and linguistic ruptures manifest themselves on his body in the "pieces of bone" that "came out through his cheek" (SR 160).

What we might infer from Blinker's complicated embodiment of guilt is comprehensible only in the context of the ground-up bones that the sailor ingests. Cather means to draw our attention less to the moral economy of sin and salvation that these instances bespeak than to the almost vanishing line between feeling and physicality, between psychic interiority and bodily sensation, which determines Catholic faith. The point is not that Catholicism in Cather's view insists on sinfulness as the basis of its power over its subjects. It is rather that Catholic faith seems to work only through proofs that blur the distinction between mental and physical experience. Here we might refer to that moment in O Pioneers! when, in Emil's absence, Marie goes to church to replace her missing lover and thus to fill "the emptiness" she feels. This satiation can take place because, like the bones of the dead priest that the sailor ingests, the church is understood to reveal its mysteries through an epiphany or transport that its worshipers experience directly in their bodies. Marie's worship does not signal her repentance from her adulterous thoughts so much as it gives her a physical taste of what that adultery will feel like.

Cather's work privileges feet as the appendages that crystallize this specifically Catholic mode of worship. The passion with which Bishop Laval embraces young Jacques's feet recurs in another episode of foot worship—here involving not feet exactly but the shoemaker's lasts that Jacques and Cecile peruse in the shop to which Cecile has taken Jacques to outfit him with a new pair of shoes. "You have the feet of all the great people here" (*SR* 82), Cecile tells Pommier the cobbler, thus making the identification between tokens of feet and the real thing that Cather sees as a Catholic habit of mind. This is an identification that the shoemaker shares. Referring to a particular last that he "shall always keep" (*SR* 83), Pommier tells the children, "That foot will not come back" (*SR* 82). This last, belonging to "Robert Cavalier de la Salle," is significant because it is the imprint of a foot that "went farther than any foot in New France" (*SR* 83), its owner having been "murdered a thousand miles away" (*SR* 83). This last is special, then, because it represents a foot doing what a foot in Cather should do—keeping on the move, outdistancing its surroundings, rather than standing still. Throughout this encounter, the lasts and the shoes which they pattern are fetish-objects. Cecile "took the smoothly shaped wood in her hands and examined it curiously" (*SR* 82); earlier, she watches with "fascination" as Pommier drove "his awl through the leather, drawing the big needle with waxed thread through it" as Jacques "followed Pommier's black fingers with astonishment" (*SR* 81). A continuity exists between Laval's devotion to Jacques's feet and the children's "fascination" and "astonishment" with lasts and shoe leather. These acts of rapt attention to bodily details or to bodily accoutrements, or even (like the lasts) to replicas of body parts, speak to Catholicism's cult of paraphilia, in which the experience of material or visceral tokens of the love object satisfies as much as (if not more than) that love object itself.

The difference between a whole body and a partial, broken, or even dead one seems not to matter where Cather's Catholics are concerned. In fact, whole bodies may even get in the way of the desire and sensations these Catholic fictions seek to transmit, as another foot example in Cather suggests. In *O Pioneers!*, the hermitlike Crazy Ivar, an ascetic and visionary "who disliked human habitations" and is constantly subject to "temptations," explains that he goes barefoot "for the indulgence of the body" (*OP* 247). His anatomy of indulgence is worth citing at length:

> "From my youth up I have had a strong, rebellious body, and have been subject to every kind of temptation. Even in age my temptations are prolonged. It was necessary to make some allowances; and the feet, as I understand it, are free members. There is no divine prohibition for them in the Ten Commandments. The hands, the tongue, the eyes, the heart, all the bodily desires we are commanded to subdue; but the feet are free members. I indulge them without harm to anyone, even to tramping in filth when my desires are low." (*OP* 247)

Ivar's attitude to his "free members" helps us to place the exaggerated attention to feet and to foot objects in *Shadows on the Rock* more squarely in the context of Cather's own interest in the fetishistic body. Ivar's feet may be only a fraction of his body, but they are the fraction he allows to experience sensual pleasure and, more important, they are the parts that move. Far from testifying to Ivar's resistance to temptation, his shoeless state points to the structure through which Cather's work construes the circulation of "bodily desires." Like Ivar's "tramping," this dynamism is "wayward" (*OP* 107) (Cather's word for Carl Lindstrum in *O Pioneers!*). This dynamism does not follow a straightforward path and it is not anchored in a straightforward body. The partial or alienated body, the body in pieces, seems the requisite for a paradoxically corporate fantasy in which passion migrates from one person to another through the fractured medium of objects valued in excess of their plain substance. In contrast to the closed erotic circuit alleged to pass (as in an endless loop) between the members of a heterosexual dyad, the economy of desire that Cather's Catholics share does not stop at one love object but rather embraces the collective.

Shadows on the Rock depicts this logic of corporate eros through the role it assigns to miracles. "The people have loved miracles for so many hundred years," Cather writes of an angel's visit to the celibate recluse Jeanne Le Ber, "not as proof or evidence, but because they are the actual flowering of desire. From being a shapeless longing, [the miracle] becomes a beautiful image ... and the experience of a moment, which might have been a lost ecstasy, is made an actual possession and can be bequeathed to another" (*SR* 137). Like the relic or the shoemaker's last, the miracle's dispersal of "ecstasy" among "the people" partakes of the logic of the fetish, and does so again through a body—like that of old Bishop Laval—formally excluded from the ranks of normative erotic desire. "The miracle," as Father Vaillant defines it in *Death Comes for the Archbishop* (1927), "is something we can hold in our hands and love."[28]

The circulation of Jeanne Le Ber's story, which passes back and forth between the colonists, recapitulates the "flowering of desire" that inheres in the miracle itself. As such, this story and the numerous others about unmarried, illegitimate, unnatural figures in *Shadows on the Rock*—whether sacred (like Jeanne Le Ber) or profane (like 'Toinette Gaux) or both (like the *pecheresse* from Purgatory who is saved by Sister Catherine's prayers)—give a shape to "shapeless longing," inciting a schism in the consensus narrative that a culture dispenses to its members. "There are only two or three human stories," Carl Lindstrum tells Alexandra Bergson in *O Pioneers!*, "and they go on repeating themselves as fiercely as if they had never happened before" (*OP* 110). This is a state of affairs that Carl, "just a tramp" (*OP* 150), laments because his "wandering" existence essentially writes him out of the accepted narratives; between a life of marriage and a life of solitude there is no room to maneuver, no middle path by which to have a meaningful sociality. Thus Carl defines "freedom" darkly, as an intolerable state of unbelonging in which "one isn't needed anywhere" (*OP* 113). The world as it is written in Carl Lindstrum's view writes him out of it; only in marrying Alexandra can he achieve a fit. In *Shadows on the Rock,* by contrast, Cather offers at least an alternative to the sparse narrative economy that Carl despairs of in *O Pioneers!*. This alternative scenario involves the fetishistic, materialist culture of Catholic worship in which young men and women often grow up to defy marriage and family life in exchange for the experience of a "shapeless longing" that is by turns a radically private concern and an entirely shareable "ecstasy."

IV

One way to describe the difference this Catholic narrative makes to Cather is by contrasting the "flowering of desire" whose circulatory movement she chronicles among Catholics with the rectilinear narrative that, as Carl Lindstrum claims, aims to monopolize everyone. This story is of course none other than the marriage plot—an orderly procession from birth through marriage and procreation to death. Its pattern or likeness reappears in the chain of events leading from courtship to proper domestic settlement and prosperity that St. Peter muses over in *The Professor's House* and that Tom disparages in the Bixbys, a causal sequence from which one defects at the risk of simply disappearing from the social map. That Cather seeks to thwart this unswerving story line by any means necessary accounts for the strange intervention of "Tom Outland's Story" in *The Professor's House.* Like the tales Cecile frequently hears of recluses who renounce heterosexual bonds in *Shadows on the Rock,* Tom's story (what Eve Sedgwick has called the "gorgeous homosocial romance" [68] of his life on the Mesa with Roddy Blake) throws the heterosexual melodrama of *The Professor's House* off course.

If Cather's later fiction marks a turn toward the reactionary, as some critics have suggested, her appraisal of the Catholic Church becomes difficult to assimilate to the same trend. Cather's Catholic leanings are selective and strategic. She inscribes Catholicism by turns as a culture of the fetish, as a tutelary system in which priests or recluses encourage the young to resist normative sexual experience, and as a faith structured around a group desire in which collective passions supersede conjugal ones. All the energies that cycle through Cather's appropriation of anti-Catholic ideology converge in *Death Comes for the Archbishop.* This convergence, moreover, illuminates what I take to be Cather's disruptive narrative project in her late fiction.

In *Death Comes for the Archbishop,* pious Catholicism stands in such close proximity to its infidel obverse that it is scarcely possible to distinguish them as separate attitudes within one belief system. This equivocation is central to the book and central as well to Cather's larger ambivalence about the neatness or rectification of desire. *Death Comes for the Archbishop* is arguably Cather's most experimental novel not only because it actively aestheticizes the experience of unsettlement but also because it persistently disorients a forward narrative trajectory. The novel begins with a prologue, "At Rome," uneasily removed from the novel's primary setting, the New Mexico desert, before turning to Bishop Latour's story proper. Yet the novel's Roman prologue is meant to confer a sense from the outset that displacement is central to Latour's own story line. When we first hear Latour's voice in the novel, it is during his encounter with a young girl to whom he describes himself as "a priest who has lost his way" (*DC* 24). This self-appraisal recalls the missionary who has sponsored Latour's bishopric in the prologue—"a man of wide wanderings," "an Odysseus of the Church" (*DC* 5). For these priests there seems no alternative to dislocation—not only because the Church mandates their itinerant missions but also because the very concept of settlement is at odds with the vow of celibacy that excludes them from domestic and private life.

Latour's having "lost his way" in the desert articulates one of this novel's dominant motifs—the frequency with which priests lose their way and desert their office, their vows, or both. *Death Comes for the Archbishop* is remarkable for the sheer number of priests it includes who have stumbled on the path of spiritual righteousness and have fallen into bad behavior. The point of Latour's mission derives from the fact that the priests in New Mexico have become "dissolute" (*DC* 9) and "disobedient" (*DC* 8), "without guidance or discipline," even to the point of living "in open concubinage" (*DC* 7). The head priest in Albuquerque, Father Gallegos, has engendered "a scandalous state" (*DC* 86) in his parish. Another priest recounts to Latour the story of Fray Baltazar, a missionary from an earlier generation who exercised his "tyranny" by demanding from his Indian parishioners a succession of "serving-boys . . . who were even more minutely trained" (*DC* 113) than their predecessors. (Baltazar treats these servants so nastily that he is eventually executed for striking one of them to death with a piece of pottery.) Then there is Padre Martinez, a "plotting priest" who has incited a revolt against "the American governor and a dozen other white men" (*DC* 146). These instances of children held hostage in clerical houses and of open revolt against white Americans at the instigation of priests were staples in the repertory of anti-Catholic propaganda in the last half of the nineteenth century, when *Death Comes for the Archbishop* is set. The prologue functions as a way for Cather to set American Catholicism in its most lurid guise without the unsavory intermediary of anti-Catholic spokespersons. The authorities at Rome admit what the anti-Catholic nativists assume.

Yet if these stories of priests gone bad are cautionary tales, it is unclear whom they are meant to caution or what they caution against. The anti-Catholic position held that no priest could be trusted; and at a certain level Cather's novel bears out this supposition, if only to complicate and transform its implications. The problem the novel poses and explores might be summarized as the belief that the geographical dislocation that Latour undergoes—a function of the mendicancy built into the Catholic mission—seems indivisible from the loss of virtue so characteristic of New World clergymen. Or, to put the point more accurately, the novel draws an implicit yet forceful link between devout and dissolute priests by virtue of the fact that each is animated fundamentally by a logic of motion and migration, of propagating satisfaction (whether in the form of converts or concubines) that depends fundamentally on elements of seduction. Referring to "all missionaries from America" as "inveterate beggars" (*DC* 12), the cardinal who hosts the gathering in Rome relates the story of a "Franciscan" who connived his grandfather out of an El Greco painting of "St. Francis, of almost feminine beauty" (*DC* 13) that the priest sought "for the ornamentation of his mission church among the Indians" (*DC* 13). This priest, adept at "wheedl[ing]" "money" "as well as vestments and linen and chalices—he would take anything" (*DC* 13)—is the model for Father Vaillant, whose skill at raising funds from the poor Mexicans amounts to a confidence game: "Father Joseph opened his campaign, and the poor Mexicans began taking dollars out of their shirts and boots . . . to pay for windows in the Denver church" (*DC* 273). In these instances, the line between grift and petition, between what the cardinal calls the missionary's "covetousness" and what the missionaries themselves see as the glorification of God, threatens to disappear.

Embedded in the very structure of Catholic missionary life, according to Cather's novel, is the potential for every priest to become a renegade, a thief, or a con artist. In Catholic experience, as the missionary's choice of the El Greco "of almost feminine beauty" suggests, the charismatic conversion of the people is never quite separable from idolatry, the heresy of worldly desire. Father Vaillant likens "the temper of his parish" to "that of a boys' school; under one master the lads try to excel one another in mischief and disobedience, under another they vie with each other in acts of loyalty" (*DC* 123). The ease with which the parish vacillates from one state to another—and, more important, the role that the parish priest assumes in the changeability of this temperament—indicates the unpredictability, the instability, at the heart of Catholic experience.

Padre Martinez offers the best example of this equivocation. On Latour's way to Taos, where Martinez holds sway, the bishop recollects the padre's face, which is "so unusual that he would be glad to see it again" (*DC* 147). "His mouth was the very assertion of violent, uncurbed passions," Latour observes, "the full lips thrust out and taut, like the flesh of animals distended by fear or desire" (*DC* 147). Latour's focus on Martinez's lips and mouth is telling, insofar as the padre's mouth, with its "assertion of violent, uncurbed passions," is the source of the padre's greatest clerical successes and his most heinous apostasies. Martinez's mouth is an unsurpassed rhetorical weapon. He uses it to persuade Latour that "celibacy" is contrary to Church doctrine because "no priest can experience repentance and forgiveness of sin unless he himself falls into sin" and "since concupiscence is the most common form of temptation, it is better for him to know something about it" (*DC* 153). As distasteful as Latour finds this line of reasoning, he is at a loss to square Martinez's casuistry with a lack of devoutness. During the services that Martinez celebrates the next morning, "[t]he bishop had never heard the mass more impressively sung than by Father Martinez. The man had a beautiful baritone voice, and he drew from some deep well of emotional power" (*DC* 157).

Martinez ends finally in schism from the Church, but even this break cannot quite dispel the ambiguity that his brand of Catholicism embodies. Indeed, this schism testifies to a source of lasting anxiety within the Church's conversion practices themselves, in that Martinez can break with the Church only because he has a "devotedly loyal" (*DC* 164) following for whom his indiscretions are secondary to his personal magnetism. In establishing his own "Holy Catholic Church of Mexico" (*DC* 168), Martinez plays to the unspoken assumption that it is not revealed faith but rather the seductive machinery of the Church, its glamorous personalities and aesthetic satisfactions, that inspire the catechumen—or to rewrite the matter in terms of Latour's encounter with Martinez, that it is only the beautiful sound emanating from Martinez's "full lips" and "baritone voice" to which the faithful are responding. Not the truth his mass articulates but the sumptuous physicality, the alluring and earthly exterior, of the priest's body—this is the basis of worship. This suspicion about where passion is located in Catholicism cannot help evoking another privileged character in Cather's corpus: the diva. Like the priest, the female singer remains unmarried and unattached, makes a living by circulating, and makes her most passionate connections to collective audiences in whom her interest is episodic and transient, a tie lightly and necessarily severed.

Catholicism and opera go together, of course, as far as Cather is concerned. In the turn-of-the-century writer F. Marion Crawford, Cather had an unlikely model for narrating this combination. Crawford, a flamboyantly Catholic figure whose best-selling novels about Italian culture, and opera in particular, were the bane of Henry James's existence, advocated treating the novel as a "marketable commodity, of the class collectively termed 'luxuries,' whose first object is to amuse and interest the reader."[29] A youthful Cather reviewed Crawford's novels with disdain; what she disliked most about his work was its sheer consumability, which was indistinct from its sheer volume: "He publishes a new novel every few months," she writes in an 1895 review of Crawford's *Casa Braccio* (a novel set in part in a Carmelite convent in Italy circa 1840). In Cather's view, Crawford's "prolific rapidity" amounts to a repetition compulsion, a consequence of a "yearning in him" that devolves finally on his *audience,* whose praise he requires at the cost of "his own personal pleasure and satisfaction," which for Cather is equivalent to "reverence" for one's own "talent." "The curse of having sold oneself," she writes, "is that one is always branded with a trademark and can never escape from the habits of his vice."[30] That cultivation of an audience which Crawford has converted into a "vice" is striking above all because it mirrors the story he rehashes in his "seldom reread" novels. This is the story of the diva's star turn on a stage in front of an audience, replaying similar roles in performance after performance. Cather's early dismissal of Crawford on the grounds that he recycles the same book in order to satisfy a superficial and momentary audience demand paradoxically coincides with her own later appropriation of the story on which Crawford performed endless and minute variations—that of the diva who enters the public sphere to transport an audience with an intensity matched only by its brevity.

This transport of ecstasy is closely connected to the dynamic of transportation itself—insofar as the diva travels and disseminates her genius much as the Church depends on the circulation of its icons, relics, and persons in a fetishistic economy. What the diva and the Church share is the communication of a passion indivisible from public display and from the suspicion that the passion alone—rather than the edification it is meant to deliver, in the form of devotion to God or to aesthetic virtues—is what really matters. Crawford's books are particularly attuned to the disjunction between the experience of the performance and the performance's enduring meaning. Thus in *The Primadonna* (1908), "the audience would all say again what they had always said about every great lyric soprano, that it was just a wonderful instrument without a particle of feeling, that it was an overgrown canary, a human flute, and all the rest of it; but while the trills ran on the people listened in wonder."[31]

The defense of the novel that Crawford offers—that it is designed to "amuse" and nothing else—is like the temporary "wonder" that the soprano's voice induces. Cather rewrites Crawford's defense of the novel's disposability as an apologia for the temporal delights of Catholic experience and operatic performance alike. She radicalizes the disjunction between fleeting, all-encompassing wonder and permanent, sustainable meaning as a way to articulate a principle of desire. Cather's books use divas and Catholics to cleave the experience of desire or physical passion from the narrative of causality to which desire is inevitably yoked. "In religion desire was fulfillment," the narrator of *My Mortal Enemy* (1926) claims, referring to the Catholic Myra Henshawe. "[I]t was the seeking itself that rewarded."[32] This "seeking" is fulfilling, where Cather's Catholics are concerned, because they set "desire" along a decidedly errant path. The paths of irregular desire that weave in and out of *Shadows on the Rock* are traversed by fetishes, whose portability makes them ideal objects of diffusion, able to be possessed by multiple individuals at one time.

The implicit relation between diva worship and Catholicism in Cather is manifested through a familiar appendage—the well-turned foot. In "A Gold Slipper" (1920), the soprano Kitty Ayrshire spends a train ride to New York talking to a straitlaced businessman, Marshall McKann, whose carefully calibrated worldview she has disturbed with her performance at his small-town Music Hall. In the course of the train ride, McKann's "natural distrust" of Kitty's "variety" mingles with his obvious desire for her. On waking in his berth he finds "a delicately turned gold slipper" left by "his tormentor," and after trying to throw it away he "decided to keep it as a reminder that absurd things could happen to people of the most clocklike deportment" (*CS* 152). Kitty's "mateless" slipper, likes its unattached former owner, works a "morbid" change in McKann; having locked the slipper "in his vault," he periodically takes it out when alone in his office "and looks at it" (*CS* 152). McKann's intermittent attention to this slipper mimics the recurrent appearances the performer herself makes, the intervals that define her performance. The shoe can fulfill this mimetic function because, in Cather at least, the apparatus and enginery of a performer—how a performer appears—are just as crucial to pleasure, if not more so, than the program itself. Hence during Kitty's performance McKann is indifferent to her singing and spends all his time looking at her body: "She displayed, under his nose, the only kind of figure he considered worth looking at" (*CS* 140). In another opera tale, "A Wagner Matinee," the narrator recollects her first symphony in terms that focus such attention to physical details:

> The clean profiles of the musicians, the gloss of their linens, the dull
> black of their coats, the beloved shapes of the instruments, the patches
> of yellow light on the smooth, varnished bellies of the cellos and the
> bass viols in the rear, the restless, wind-tossed fiddle necks and bows—I
> recalled how, in the first orchestra I ever heard, those long bow-strokes
> seemed to draw the heart out of me, as a conjurer's stick reels out yards
> of paper ribbon from a hat. (193)

What is peculiar about this passage is that in its meticulous, even exaggerated emphasis on the particulars of the orchestra, what matters least is the sound it makes. Instead, the orchestra's outer shapes, its accessories, overtake the narrator's attention. Under her gaze the orchestra's trappings become a sexual body, with "bellies" and "rear" and "restless" "necks" undulating in a display that echoes the corporate eros residing in the Catholic mass. Such moments in Cather depend on a misdirection of aesthetic pleasure from the manifest content of a performance (an aria, a liturgical program) to its most superficial parts.

That shoes and feet, "mateless" "free members," play such an important role in this economy of desire in Cather indicates what I refer to as Cather's hostility to settlement, especially when that settlement is enforced. To the question of what to do with persons who don't fit into the sequences or categories to which their culture assigns them, Cather offers solace in the form of the endless movement that defines both her divas and her Catholics. The repetitions of operatic performance and Catholic mass expose a different sort of narrative structure from the progressive linearity that Cather's Carl Lindstrum despairs of. These repeat performances are circular rather than progressive; they are about nothing but the momentary pleasure they deliver. As with the opera, so with the Church: this delivery is satisfying in itself, independent of the spiritual edifice it presumably shores up. This is why the Indians in *Death Comes for the Archbishop* make such good Catholics; they can appreciate and even revel in the forms of the European religion while keeping their own spiritual beliefs intact. Latour "might make good Catholics among the Indians," or so he is told, "but he would never separate them from their own beliefs" (*DC* 144). In Catholicism, Cather sees the divorce of practice from belief, exterior trappings from innate meanings. The same principle of incongruity also explains why many efforts to reenact the dramatic events of Catholic belief—as the protégé of Padre Martinez, Trinidad Lucero, does when he "has himself tied upon a cross with ropes" (*DC* 162) during Passion Week—turn out to exceed, grotesquely and perversely, whatever proper faith requires. The physical drama that Trinidad undergoes— he is "scourged" with "cactus whips" because "he would bear as many stripes as our Savior"—outstrips the decorum of piety and crosses the line into bodily "extravagance" (154). His is a failed mimesis that hints at a disproportion always lurking in Catholic experience between ceremony and belief.

But such moments of disproportion, of bodies in motion failing to line up with what they are preordained or destined to be, perform a significant office in Cather's fiction. Given how ill-adjusted the typical Cather body is, having at hand a means to make a space of forgiveness and even pleasure for that body's bad worldly fit comes as a relief. If the Catholic Church appears to provide her characters with a way out, we should not assume that this exit strategy belies a necessarily reactionary attitude. Cather's use of anti-Catholic ideology makes her Catholicism so extreme as to void the received understanding of the Church as the repository of sexual conservatism and impossible, inhuman physical purity. As I have been tracing its wayward path through her fiction, Catholicism stands for a very different set of possibilities deriving from a culture of intense commitment to physical objects and corporate desire. More significant, perhaps, is the sense that in both Catholic experience and in operatic performance these commitments to the corporeal surpass, or at least subsume, the spiritual and aesthetic. That one might take pleasure in the singer's voice and nothing else, that forms like shoe lasts and paintings "of almost feminine beauty" can give pleasure irrespective of their symbolic content: such is the state of grace for which Cather's Catholic fictions ultimately pray.

Chapter Six

Merging with the Masses

I

The preceding chapters have put analytic pressure on the historical determinations of modernity's variable concept of desire. I have argued throughout this book that modernists understood desire in large part as the name for the risky and unplanned interpersonal contacts across class and status lines which featured prominently in the daily lives of the new century's inhabitants. In order to make the most out of sexuality as a category of analysis, we must redirect our attention from the heuristic of identity to consider the features of erotic life that work their way into some of the major literary texts of the early twentieth century. Those texts turn out to be relatively indifferent to questions of sexual essence or types and drawn instead to the immense range of ways in which desire comes to be conceptualized after 1900—just as their authors were driven by a powerful need to conceptualize, to describe, and to rewrite the social world in which the desire concept came to prominence.

If desire has been theoretically inexact in this book, this is because the cross-class encounters I have detailed were experienced by and large as insoluble and unresolved, as admitting of no easy explanations. Indeed, they continue to be experienced as such insofar as American society still finds it hard to articulate the idea of class or erotic differences. Class and sexual differences remain, to an astonishing extent, "closeted" phenomena. In this chapter I conclude my analysis with a look at some of the political uses of the desire concept at key moments in the early twentieth century. In bringing together the leftist writers of the 1920s with their reformist forebears in the Progressive era, I seek less to forge a tendentious alliance between different cultural blocs than to demonstrate that the preeminent ideological divide of the modern era (that between market culture and its foes) has always represented itself by way of society's most trenchant superstitions about sexual irregularity and excess. Thus my further aim is to push even more strongly in the wake of queer theory against the leftist critic's belief that sexuality is impertinent to the study of pressing social concerns like class struggle. In practice this belief works its way through the academic left by means of the tacit trivialization of sexual desire, of what sexual desire can contribute to a praxis based on the empowerment and raised consciousness of subaltern classes. Even though their concerns appear to be gaining a privileged hearing in the academy, sexuality studies tend to be marginalized, relegated to a province—or ghetto—of their own. What persons who study sexuality have to teach the rest of "us" is still widely regarded as dubious—at least as far as progressive class politics are concerned.

In drawing attention to this contemporary attitude, I highlight the persistent assumption of an impasse between desire and human agency in modern culture. Far from a presentist concern, this assumption spans and structures the radically different social movements comprising what has been called "the American century." Like the vice reformers whose activism monopolized cultural resources during the Progressive era, twenties leftists considered the impasse between desire and agency a hindrance to political efficacy, since personal desire was seen to undo useful collective action. This field is worth exploring both from the perspective of a genealogy of critical or oppositional cultural studies, then, and for teasing out the complexities of the left's concept of desire, whose evocation then as now concealed a fault line on the terrain of social structures.

As historians of turn-of-the-century American sexuality have documented, one of the most compelling figures situated along this fault line from the 1890s onward was the prostitute, who signified a unilateral anxiety about what kind of subjectivity inhabited the uncharted domain of consumer society. Under the pretext of white slavery, prostitution proved a generous figure for theorizing the problem of agency or will in a social realm where the determinants of community constraint or religious pressures were being superseded by the opportunistic and contractarian amenities of consumer culture. The refiguring of prostitution as a traffic in slavery effectively eliminated the need to imagine the prostitute as a freely contracting individual.[1] And because of its economic nature, prostitution served an even more general purpose as the object of philosophical and social questions around the interaction between commercial society and erotic desire. The antiprostitution discourse of the Progressive era yields a vision of subjectivity in consumerism that equates the exchange of sex for money with the irrevocable displacement of the self into contractual engagements that disable that self's agency. But more important for our purposes, such an equation has a reversible trajectory that equates the refusal to yield to either sex or commerce as the peculiar victory of a progressive worker identity. What makes this victory even more peculiar is that, for leftist modernism, the political identity that resists the depredations of eroticized consumerism is a homosexuality opposed to the irregularities and compromises of heterosexual desire and mass culture alike.

Although by 1920 antiprostitution reformers had helped to legislate the suppression of "red light districts" on a national level by lobbying for the adoption of versions of the Iowa Abatement Act in thirty-one states, they were unconvinced that prostitution had been eradicated.[2] Instead, reformers increasingly focused on the figure of the "occasional prostitute," "the most difficult to cope with of all clandestine prostitutes," according to the Committee of Fifteen.[3] As the reform movement worked to intensify the metaphors of uncontainable female sexuality through recourse to prostitution, it generated the image of the woman whose very "discreetness" could index her "illicit" behavior by virtue of her lack of outward signs of bad behavior. In the view of reformers, simply going on a date turned a woman into a prostitute, whether she wanted to be one or not. "It is of no great moment whether the irregular relation is paid for by a fee, by complete support, by an evening's entertainment," Thomas Galloway's *Sex and Social Health* decreed. "[T]hese distinctions are not vital to the public's morale."[4] The intensive rupture of a "distinction" between "regular" and "irregular" sexuality permitted the model of sexual desire as illicit gain to extend beyond the domain of reform to agendas quite divergent from its own.

One such agenda was the leftist literary culture associated with figures like Mike Gold and Floyd Dell and with journals like *New Masses*. This postwar movement differed from the hedonic cultural radicalism of the teens in numerous ways, although several of its members (including Max Eastman, founding editor of *The Masses*) shared in developing the aims and character of each. As historians of the period have noted, postwar leftism oriented itself almost exclusively around the triumphant bolshevist model, and thus constructed a political model according to a potent Soviet ideology of productivity and purity.[5] The increasingly consumerist vision of American life became a source of deep conflict for the communist left of the twenties, which regarded the ethos of unrestrained consumption as an obstacle to social change. This transfer of attention to the Soviet ideal seemed matched, as Christina Simmons's work on changing sexual attitudes suggests, by a retreat from the sexual liberalism of the teens into the more restrictive sexual model espoused by twenties leftists like Dell and Eastman, whose tolerance of sexual and erotic difference in the earlier period all but vanished under the threat of female empowerment in the twenties. Simmons refers to this group of progressive modernists as "sexual revisionists," whose reworking of myths of sexual repression and liberation concealed "an attack on *women's* control over *men's* sexuality."[6] To the various female types elaborated by this sexual revisionism—the flapper, the career woman—I would add the prostitute as the figure whose blatantly consumerist sexuality impaired the vigorous ethos of productivity that modernist radicalism evolved in its communist guise.

I build on the historical work of Simmons and others by examining the construction of a phallic economy of identity in opposition to the economy of desire in the 1920s. I first isolate the prevalent metaphors of prostitution that permit a commutative relation between illicit sexuality and capitalist desire in the literature of the major leftist journals of the twenties, paying particular attention to the rhetoric of Emma Goldman, Max Eastman, and *New Masses* editor Mike Gold. In the editorial pronouncements of the latter figures a leftist iconography of resistance crystallizes. Gold, Eastman, and their colleagues aim to correct the dissipations that consumerism provoked by reinscribing Whitman as the vehicle for a radical identity of revolt—an identity not at odds with but indeed predicated on Whitman's homosexuality. After situating this vision of agency within the leftist imaginary, I turn to the widely heralded novel of John Dos Passos, *Manhattan Transfer* (1925), which narrates the triumph of identity embedded in left modernism over the anomic and fragmented New York of consumer capitalism. His novel is distinctive in that, although Dos Passos himself was a professed critic of the leftist program of *New Masses* and its adherents, *Manhattan Transfer* is the best articulation of the model of sexual identity and desire made available by that program—a fact not lost on Gold or Eastman. Thus his subscription to the powerful leftist iconography of sexual revolt attested to the strength and universality of the left's vision—and its permanence.

II

"If I were a girl working all day and suffering the imposition of a living wage in a rich country," Max Eastman wrote in a 1913 *Masses* editorial, "I trust I would be either a prostitute or a thief."[7] Eastman's supposition assumes that the fact of wages (and not necessarily their amount) couples them with unlawful desires, an affinity confirmed by the finding of the Committee of Fourteen—the group of vice reformers that succeeded the Committee of Fifteen—that "in fact there is probably more immorality among the higher than the lower paid."[8] According to Eastman, the working girl suffers the "imposition" of desire, which takes the form of a wage "in a rich country." Like his reforming counterparts on the Committee, Eastman envisions an economic world that does not dissociate compensation from sexual satisfaction. For Eastman, the coincidence of prostitution and wage contract is not simply a problem with capitalism. It is also a problem with desire— specifically, heterosexual desire.

The masthead of *The Masses* proclaimed the publication to be "a Free Magazine," adding, "This Magazine is Owned and Operated Cooperatively by its Editors. It has no Dividends to Pay and nobody is trying to make Money out of it." Issuing from the perceived need to be "uninfluenced," as *Masses* editor Art Young put it, this economic freedom was no less predicated on a repudiation of the network of financial and commercial entanglements of a commodified print culture. "We wanted one magazine," Young said, "which we could gallop around in and be free."[9] However directly this "gallop[ing]" freedom emerged from an impassioned disavowal of consumer culture and the commodification of desire, it was equally derived from Progressivism's agitated misgivings about those same conditions, incarnated in the prostitute-citizen. ("The modern prostitute is a citizen," the Committee of Fifteen writes [CF 5].) Progressive reformers tried any number of ways to "save desire" from commodification in wayward lives. Such attempts indicated nothing so much as a nostalgic effort to return to a home-oriented social structure as if, even in the midst of an estranging urban environment, the family or its simulacrum could serve as the one locus where desire was not alienated.[10] On this score, reformers were parallel to Progressive-era labor unionists. In "Women as Bread Winners—the Error of the Age" (1897), Edward O'Donnell claimed that "the growing demand for female labor . . . is an insidious assault upon the home; it is the knife of the assassin aimed at the family circle."[11]

O'Donnell shares Eastman's sense that the "alarming introduction of women into the mechanical industries" leads to "lives of shame" because "wholesale employment" outside the "contented family circle" "gradually unsex[es] them . . . stripping them of that demeanor that lends a charm to their kind" (EO 9). The first taste of wages forms an appetite in the female worker that can never be appeased; she is thus caught in a perpetual cycle of discontent and labor that inexorably drives her to "that deplorable pursuit" (EO 10). Though O'Donnell begins with the protest that the female "breadwinner" threatens the "dignity" of "manhood" (EO 10) with her new economic might, he ends by replacing the independent woman with the greater peril of her loss of agency in her inevitable victimization by a life of "shame." Though AFL leaders and vice reformers were divided on class and political lines, they were united in their sense that female labor was never far removed from prostitution. It seems that women could not work without contaminating the realm of labor with what O'Donnell called "pleasures and vices" (EO 10). For reformers and unionists alike, prostitution was primarily a function of economic contagions. According to the Committee of Fifteen, prostitution derived from "American habits of life" (CF 19), which were intimately bound up in a consumer culture that "thrives . . . upon the disruption, ruin or abolition of the home" (EO 10). Appropriating the chiasmus endemic to the prostitute—who works because she wants, wants because she works, and thus sells as well as buys her pleasures—leftist literary culture argues that the problem of the market economy is the problem of desire already constituted as illicit. Whereas antiprostitution discourse wished to conserve a desire uncontaminated by money, leftist discourse sought a radical disengagement from desire, period, acknowledging the point of no return.

To future *New Masses* editor Mike Gold, a magazine like the *Saturday*

Evening Post was a "filthy lackey rag, so fat, shiny, gorged with advertisements, putrid with prosperity like the bulky, diamonded duenna of a bawdy house."[12] The problem with the *Post,* he said, was that it was both "lackey" and prostitute, only too willing to be swayed by its corporate clientele. In Gold's allegory of the *Post* as prostitute, the advertisements with which the magazine was "gorged" were figured not only as editorializing on behalf of their sponsors in the place of the *Post*'s staff, but as doing so in the guise of a penetration of the magazine's pages that Gold himself termed sexual. Trading "free speech" for the "prosperity" of a "bawdy house," the *Post* believed it was "giving the people what they want."[13] As Gold remarked, however, such fulfillment was fundamentally at odds with the aims of the radical press, which chose to dissociate desire from exchange and, failing that, to dissociate itself from both. The problem Gold found intractable in the *Post* was that magazine's conception of "satisfaction" as a web of capitalist economic entanglements; the *Post* existed solely for its advertisers and consumers. The logic of Gold's polemic makes even clearer the emphatic connection between freedom from commerce and freedom from desire that *The Masses* arrogated to itself in its editorial policy. By refusing (at least in principle) to accept anyone's money, *The Masses*—"whose final Policy is to do as it pleases and Conciliate Nobody, not even its Readers"—was also refusing to accept, much less satisfy, anyone's desire.

By the time Mike Gold helped raise *New Masses* out of the ashes of the celebrated but short-lived *Masses,* prostitution had long been a central topos of cultural debate on the left and right. Indeed, for Emma Goldman writing in 1917, the most scandalous aspect of the crusade against prostitution was that this "institution" "should have been discovered so suddenly."[14] In "The Traffic in Women," the period's most prominent leftist account of prostitution, Goldman pronounces the prostitute as differing from other women not in kind, but only in degree. Since "it is . . . almost inevitable," Goldman argues, that a woman "should pay for her right to exist, to keep her position in whatever line, with sex favors," "it is merely a question of degree whether she sells herself to one man, or to many men" (*TW* 20). While designed to oppose and even to upset the comfortable moralisms of the reform movement, Goldman's proclamation is entirely congruent with that movement's findings, for Goldman sees women as being

> driven into prostitution by American conditions, by the thoroughly
> American custom for excessive display of finery and clothes, which, of
> course, necessitates money—money that cannot be earned in shops or
> factories. (*TW* 28)

Just as all women might be plotted at various points along the graph of prostitution—for Goldman, "it is a conceded fact that woman is being reared as a sex commodity" (*TW*24)—so the defining coordinate of this female spectrum is "money." Thus for Goldman, the more money a woman has, the less apparent is her dependence on prostitution; but the less apparent her dependence, the more hypocritical her situation seems. To "sweep away the attitude of hypocrisy," Goldman writes, "we must rise above our foolish notions of 'better than thou,' and learn to recognize in the prostitute a product of social conditions" (*TW*32). For Goldman, these notions are foolish to the extent that they attempt to detach the virtuous as a class apart from the vicious; we are all prostitutes, according to this argument, so long as we experience the "social conditions" of "industrial slavery" and a consumer economy.

Hence Goldman's sympathy for the prostitute as a victim of the reform movement coincides with her revulsion toward that same figure as a victim of "American conditions" of "excessive display." And however deep this sympathy runs, it is always guided by the assumption that the prostitute and her "procurer" are penalized for openly committing a crime for which "the real perpetrators of social iniquity"—the "owners of department stores and factories"—"enjoyed immunity and respect" (*TW*30–31). What troubles Goldman is not merely that prostitution is legislated against, but that these other "crimes"—forms of procurement—go unpunished. "It is our sham and hypocrisy that create both the prostitute and the cadet [pimp]" (*TW*31), but it is also the "daily routine" (*TW*26) of working life that sets the prostitute on her path. "Girls, mere children, work in crowded, overheated rooms ten to twelve hours daily at a machine, which tends," according to Goldman, "to keep them in a constant overexcited sex state" (*TW*25–26). Prostitution is not only a result of the "imposition of a living wage," as it was for Eastman; it is also intrinsic to the working conditions of urban life, which serve as "the first step toward prostitution" (*TW*26).

Goldman's essay describes the extreme of leftist positions on prostitution. A "thorough eradication of prostitution" is contingent on "the abolition of industrial slavery" (*TW*32), from the factory to the service economy. Goldman's "libertarianism"—her refusal of partisanship and institutional affiliation—ratifies a freedom that opposes itself by definition to both slavery and money. "Free love," the agenda most often ascribed to Goldman by her biographers and critics, becomes the antidote to both marriage (a version of slavery) and prostitution (a version of the money economy). But only in the midst of a consumerist economy that has become hegemonic can political freedom come to mean so distinctly and completely *free of cost,* and sexual liberation—the "sex question" (*TW*21)—come to mean sex outside of payment.

Whereas for Eastman prostitution is the logical outcome of the "imposition" of wages, for Goldman it is the "inevitable" destination of all women living under capitalism. Without enacting its logic, Goldman begins to signal what for leftist modernism would become the necessary ideological move that her reading of prostitution enjoins. If, that is, for Goldman the prostitute is the social index of desire contaminated by commodification and alienation, for leftist modernists like Eastman and Gold, the domain of heterosexual desire indexes the contaminating force of consumer capitalism. If working girls work because working girls want, and moreover perform this wanting in their work habits, as Goldman's factory girls, saleswomen, and waitresses do, they are "willing," as William Thomas puts it, "to adapt themselves to all kinds of work."[15] This adaptability is what compromises working women—no less sexually than economically. Gold and Eastman modify the restricted economy of prostitution—limited in reform discourse to wayward women—and generalize it as the "inevitable" condition of "American life." Thus any acquiescence to desire is equivalent to an illicit exchange, and any commercial transaction is steeped in a desire that compromises the self.

Though almost ten years divide the last issue of *The Masses* from the appearance of the first *New Masses,* between the journals much editorial overlap occurred. One enduring habit was the need to maintain editorial freedom from commercial influence. "To nurse forth something fine and big into life," Mike Gold wrote to Upton Sinclair in 1924, one could not be restrained by economics.[16] Joseph Freeman felt likewise that the magazine "must also be sympathetic to any crudeness which is the expression of something young, vital, and as yet groping and underdeveloped."[17] But if in one way the "fine and big," "vital" aspect of Gold and Freeman's ideal was "underdeveloped," in another way the *New Masses* was not. The magazine's original name was to be *Dynamo.* Its editorial policy was to allow the uninfluenced expression of "crudeness" in its pages because the magazine itself would be unsusceptible to any impact, would generate and contain within itself all its own influences.

For Gold, communism manifests the virtues of a world indifferent to the circulation and hence dissolution of individuals in a pleasure economy. "One feels so normal and strong in Russia," Gold writes in a 1924 letter to Sinclair. "[I]t is the earth and not heaven; the earth in the throes of the birth of a new race of giants."[18] "Giant" is Gold's favorite descriptor of the Soviet republic, frequently invoked: "Hail! red youthful giant.... Our deepest hopes are centered in you, our right arms are yours to command, our life is your life."[19] The identical "fit" here—arm to arm, life to life—signifies an augmentation of potency instead of the dissipation rendered by exchange. This gigantism conduces to an identity that "centers" the subject, rather than atomizes and diminishes him. The fit of arm to arm and life to life instituted by communism is moreover a disavowal of individuation that explicitly denies the kind of influence between separate persons that exchange entails. The communist giants do not require exchange, according to Gold, because they are already satisfied, containing all satisfactions—dynamo-like—within.

Gold finds such a "centered" and total figure of potency not only in "the red giant" but also in Whitman. In the 1921 manifesto "Towards Proletarian Art" (written under the pseudonym Irwin Granich), Gold includes a section titled "Walt Whitman's Spawn," in which he delineates Whitmanian power:

> Walt dwelt among the masses, and from these he drew his strength. From the obscure lives of the masses he absorbed those deep affirmations of the instinct that are his glory. Walt has been called a prophet of individualism, but that is the usual blunder of literature. Walt knew the masses too well to believe that any individual could rise in intrinsic value above them. His individuals were those great, simple farmers and mechanics and ditch-diggers who are to be found everywhere among the masses—those powerful, natural persons whose heroism needs no drug of fame or applause to enable them to continue; those humble, mighty parts of the mass, whose self-sufficiency comes from their sense of *solidarity*, not from any sense of *solitariness*.[20]

In this passage Gold rewrites Whitman as the avatar of a primarily self-incorporating, autoerotic sexuality that stakes its pleasure on the indissoluble "solidarity" of masses conceived as one instinctual body. The passage exemplifies how selective leftist modernism's appreciation of Whitman becomes in the service of a programmatic radicalism. In the *Calamus* section of *Leaves of Grass* and elsewhere, Whitman consistently aligned his notion of omnisexual "adhesiveness" to the rapid urbanization and industrialization of America, developments which he considered instrumental in allowing individuals to come into contact with each other. For Whitman, the "tracks of the railroads of the earth" in "Salut Au Monde!" (line 79) are emblematic of the technologies that serve as transferential nodes of adhesiveness. Yet Gold poses his Whitman against this material culture by erasing its impacts in his poetry.[21] Whitman's masses are "simple farmers and mechanics and ditch-diggers who are to be found everywhere," as though what underlies an industrialized economy, as its repressed antecedent, is an organic world of rustic and unalienated labor. Voiding Whitman's claims as a prophet of egotism (nowhere more emphatic than in "Song of Myself"), Gold insists that Whitman's power resides in his "absorption" of "instinct" from the masses. That no "individual could rise in intrinsic value above them" suggests that none would want such a rise, since the masses need no value—"no drug . . . or applause" to "continue." Division from the masses—"solitariness"—is a dissipation of "instinct," a concession of oneself to the influence of others: "power" is traded for "fame." The masses perpetuate themselves not by any imposition of value, desire for profit, or influence, but by "their sense of solidarity," a term Gold defines here as interchangeable with solidity.

As not merely the inheritors but the "spawn" of Whitman, contemporary workers were ready, says Gold,

> to put forth those striding, outdoor philosophers and horny-handed creators of whom he prophesied. Now their brain and heart, embodied in the revolutionary element among them, are aroused, and they can relieve Walt, and follow him in the massive labors of the earth-built proletarian culture.[22]

It is a stunning creation myth, not least because it depends on a fantasy of "labor" generated by "horny-handed creators" "aroused" to "relieve Walt" in order to bring about "proletarian culture." If the masses are "massive," they are so because they are tumescent in all their parts, and any member of the masses absorbs and actualizes the tumescence of the whole. If this creation myth is a masturbatory fantasy, then it is a fantasy without expense, because nothing is "lost." Instead, all culture is gained. "The method of erecting this proletarian culture," Gold writes, "must be the revolutionary method—from the deepest depths upward."[23] Such a method, that is, entails nothing short of a "revolutionary"—because it is endless and unceasing—erection.

If "the whole monstrous city," as Gold claimed in 1921, "moves down its primrose path, like a courtesan plying her trade," then such a movement can be curtailed only by the arrival of giants: "Send us a man fit to stand up to skyscrapers."[24] Such a man might resemble John Reed, whom Gold eulogized thus in "John Reed and the Real Thing" (1926): "A cowboy out of the west, six foot high, steady eyes, boyish face; a brave, gay, open-handed young giant." The mingling of tender and mannish qualifiers—"high; steady; boyish; brave; gay; open-handed"—would render Reed's "splendid body" ideally homoerotic in Gold's eulogy, except that it is not an ideal. Because Reed "fell in love with the revolution," he "gave it all his generous heart's blood." It is not an ideal, according to Gold, because the homoeroticism of Reed's "splendid," "gifted body" was actual, "the real thing" of Gold's title: "There was no gap between Jack Reed and the workers any more."[25] The same can be said of "Big John Avila," the subject of another Gold eulogy: "How the men loved John and how their eyes followed him as he bustled around the hall."[26]

It is important to stress the "realness" of this adoration, its frankness in leftist discourse, because the ability of the homoerotic affect to distinguish leftist sexuality from corporate culture's prostituted desire lies in the fact that the former is not homosocial.[27] The bond between Reed and the masses, for example, does not repress the erotic in order to separate men into agents of exchange; separation and exchange in any form are conceived as the problem to begin with. Instead, leftist discourse encourages the display of sexualized and tumescent men—"giants"—so that there will be "no gap," no space "between men" from which to mediate an exchange. When Mike Gold fawns over the "splendid body of our comrade," he does so not because he wants it but because he acknowledges he already has it. If there is "no gap" between Reed and the workers, there is also no gap for Gold between himself and Reed. In other words, if leftist discourse dispenses with the homosocial but retains the homosexual, its homosexuality is radically modeled less as a practice of desire than as an assumption of identity.

"We were confident that somewhere in America a new masses existed, if only as a frustrated desire," ran the first editorial for *New Masses*. Because of its freedom from "influence,"

> *New Masses* will blossom profanely on the news-stands in the midst of its respectable contemporaries, the whiz-rags, the success-liturgies, the household aphrodisiacs, the snob-Baedekers, and the department store catalogues.[28]

If the magazine claimed it would satisfy the "frustrated desire" of the masses by differentiating itself "profanely" from "respectable" magazines, its profanity seemed distinctly marked by a refusal to trade in the exchanges that defined the other periodicals, with their "liturgical," "aphrodisiacal," "department store" temptations. In short, *New Masses* stands out more like a virgin than like the fulfillment of desire it claimed to be; rather, its claim to fulfill desire "profanely" rests on its defining such fulfillment as a version of virginal continence. Examples of this continence in *New Masses* embed it in a homosexual potency—a virginity, that is, understood as if it were dynamic.[29]

In a review of a biography of Walt Whitman, for instance, Max Eastman chides Emory Holloway for his need to

> sterilize [Whitman], tame him, bring him into the house and up to the table, take the great rebel heart, the candor and courageous freedom out of his poetry. . . . Holloway makes much of every wavering, every descent of Walt Whitman from the height of himself—the inevitable moments of compromise.[30]

Holloway's fixation on "moments of compromise"—as if these could "fix" the poet's identity as a failure to "marry a good wife and settle down"—results from a "Victorian reticence" on the part of the biographer that refuses "certain honest words." "The fact he fails to state," Eastman contends, "is that Walt Whitman was homosexual, and that at certain moments of his life was strongly in love with himself."[31]

Because Holloway "attempts to judge Whitman with those same little negative moralisms" of "what we might call Christian culture," his refusal to
name Whitman's homosexuality results, according to Eastman, in a de-
tumescence of Whitman "from the height of himself." What Holloway regards as Whitman's failure, Eastman conceives as Whitman's triumph—a
sexual economy without exchange. Because Holloway refuses the homosexual Whitman, regarding him instead as "an impure" failure, "of that peculiar sentimentality which expressed itself in caresses," he refuses also,
according to Eastman, "anything having the remotest similitude to the reality of Walt Whitman." For Eastman, Whitman's homosexuality comprises

> a revolt against the negation and the limitation involved from the very
> beginning in the very fact of civilization itself, a declaration of cosmic
> and animal independence.[32]

Eastman charges Holloway with failing to recognize that Whitman's homosexual identity was not a failure to connect to "a happy home life," but a triumph over connections in toto. In Eastman's estimation, Whitman's
homosexuality made him free from—because he was immune to—"the very
fact of civilization itself." The "solid state" that Holloway locates in "pater-
nity," Eastman locates in a homosexual identity that, "self-sufficient," "independent," and continually tumescent, constitutes "a great poetic life of real
action and free natural experience." It is an identity that does not dissipate
or exchange its desire, but routinely reincorporates it. If for Holloway "perpetual indulgence in loafing on the open road" signifies a failure or diffusion of erotic resource, for Eastman "perpetual indulgence" is precisely the
opposite—a containment and conservation of desire in the homosexual
body, an indulgence that perpetuates itself.[33]

For M. H. Hedges, writing in the first issue of *New Masses,* a containment
and conservation of erotic resource "differentiate him [Hedges] from the
professional prostitutes of the press." The "milieu" that interests Hedges is
decidedly opposed to heterosexual romance: "I do not want to know what
are the sensations of the pale young man as he enters the bed-room of his
mistress," any more than "the sensation of the romantic young parasite who
has seen his illusions destroyed by his class." For Hedges, an exchange of
heterosexual desire is a weakening or sapping of essence conspicuous in the
"pale" or "tired," "parasitic" man. The sensation most engendered by illicit
heterosexuality is that of loss or diminution. "The only hope of the artist,"
Hedges writes, "to bring him back from insanity and ineptitude—is contact
with the masses." This contact precludes mediation by inserting homosexual identification in place of exchange. "In short," Hedges's imagined in-
terlocutor asserts, "you want to exchange gayety for seriousness." To which
Hedges responds: "I shall be gay because I am so dreadfully in earnest."[34]

Hedges invokes a tradition of euphemistic naming of homosexuality that dates back at least to Wilde's *The Importance of Being Earnest,* from which Hedge's self-defining moment here is virtually an exact quote.[35] But the difference between the Wildean euphemism and Hedges's moment of self-definition—"I shall be gay"—is that the latter is not a displacement. In fact, Hedges incorporates the euphemism of "earnestness" into a frank declaration of identity.[36] Just as Eastman regards the "honest word" of Whitman's homosexuality as the source of Whitmanian independence and power, so Hedges's "earnestness" differentiates him from both the "professional prostitutes" and the "pale" and "parasitic" young men who engage them. Hedges and Eastman both invert the conventional typing of homosexuality by attributing degeneration, dissipation, excess, and femininity—long associated in the discourse of inversion with male-homoerotic desire—to the partakers of heterosexual desire. But for leftist literary discourse, the problem is less heterosexual desire than desire in any form; the alternative to desire is not homosexual desire but homosexual identification shorn of desire. This identification incorporates "gayness" as a masculine norm that castigates the "parasitic" "sensations" of pale, thin young men. In Eastman's estimation, Whitman's "natural free experience" is the experience of identity free from desire, in which all the marks of identity obtain, uninfluenced by exchange.

"Writers are queer, variable folk," Mike Gold wrote in a public letter to John Dos Passos, "liable to many accidents of the spirit."[37] What keeps them from variation and "accidents," according to Gold, "as it kept Walt Whitman," is that "they become as little children."[38] But this regression to childhood is less in the service of a return to innocence than to a hallucinatory purity of "revolt"—the "one choice" left to the writer of conscience. "Revolt," according to Gold, "is the organ-bass that softly or harshly throbs through the young literature of America today." It is not far from this throbbing "organ-bass" to the "full, bold, hard consciousness" enabled by such an organ's throbbing "through" the writer.[39] Gold's "consciousness" is contingent on a hardness that is neither aroused from a site outside itself ("revolt" must be self-chosen) nor ever exhausted. It is a hardness independent of influence (variability) but committed to identification (queerness).

III

Although the subject of Gold's letter to Dos Passos is a protest against the "literature of doubt and introspection" (24) that Gold accused Dos Passos of practicing, not a few critics, including Gold, regarded the publication of *Manhattan Transfer* as a thematization of the identity espoused by a journal like *New Masses*.[40] D. H. Lawrence praised the novel for exposing what a lot of financial success has been due to the reckless speeding-up of the sex dynamo. Get hold of the right woman, get absolutely rushed out of yourself loving her up, and you'll be able to rush a success in the city. Only, both to man and woman, the sex must be the stimulant to success; otherwise it stimulates towards suicide, as it does with the one character whom the author loves, and who was "truly male."[41]

If the one "truly male" character is the object of Dos Passos's adoration, according to Lawrence, this adoration is largely chaste, as other critics noted at the time. "His is a fresh virgin mind," Gold wrote of Dos Passos, "and through him one can enjoy a great experience."[42]

For Gold, Dos Passos's virginity is the prerequisite for any "great experience" of him. Dos Passos realizes the "childlike" regression Gold advocates in his call to "revolt": "He has ever loved the visible world with such virgin delight. His senses are so fresh; he smells like a wolf, sees like a child, hears, tastes, and feels with his fingers."[43] Gold was not the sole critic to recognize Dos Passos's virginity and its diffusion through *Manhattan Transfer*. Henry Longan Stuart wrote in *The New York Times Book Review*: "Jimmy Herf . . . is the one sympathetic character in his novel. It may be because childish impressions reach us when the heart is virgin."[44] These critics align "sympathy" and heightened, "fresh," "wolf"-like power with "virginity" to record the distinction *Manhattan Transfer* itself makes between what it valorizes and what it considers sordid. The "much-bruited novel *Manhattan Transfer*," as Paul More stated in a damning critique, "might be described in a phrase as an explosion in a cesspool."[45] If the novel provided its readers with a version of virginity, it provided them not less with a backdrop in which the virginal might be despoiled.

But in fact, as Lawrence's review cannily suggests, the novel allows no such despoliation. Instead, *Manhattan Transfer* generates an antidote to "the reckless speeding-up of the sex dynamo" by shutting it down, or by anatomizing characters unimpeded by its "reckless speeding-up." These characters inhabit a virginity that allows them to dispense with the "cesspool" conditions of desire—a "world caught *en dishabille*," as Stuart observes, "of unmade beds, littered dressing tables and dubious bathrooms"—while preserving a species of sexual identity conceived as an integrity uncompromised by desire. It is this preservation with which I am here concerned.[46]

Desire of "the sex dynamo" sort animates the financial transactions of *Manhattan Transfer* with a version of categorical excess. "Tips," for example, confer an economic superfluity analogous to the erotic superfluity that leftists associated invariably with the service economy. "I always let my friends in on my tips," an investor claims at a dinner in honor of the actress Fifi Waters, recognizing the centrality of "tipping" in the exchange and accumulation of a fortune in "rubber."[47] Likewise, the maitre d' recommends favoring such a patron because "Thisa guy trows money about lika confetti, see. . . . Gives tips, see" (*MT* 26). In waiting, "beaucoup de soing [*sic*]" (*MT* 26)—a kind of attention over and above what is necessary—results in a confetti-like dispersal or excess of payment over and above one's wage: "Waitin's better," Bud Korpenning claims, "they's the tips" (*MT* 43). The stock tip and the service tip are both contingent on an illicit increase of intimacy—the former because it requires secrecy and proximity to effect its disclosure; the latter, because it commits itself to sudden acts of pleasing familiarity, or "beaucoup de soing." "Tips" tip the balance between illicit and licit behavior, as the wages of prostitution are said to differentiate, however equivocally, between conforming and nonconforming conduct.

Whereas the illicitness of the tip, conferred by its nature as surplus, means a gain in excess of regular wages and transmissions of knowledge, it is also their generative medium. According to the novel, the point of cash is to augment itself by a stimulation of exchange that refuses the limits of contract. "Get a good tip and take a chance, that's the only system," the new father Thatcher is told, after avowing that "it's saving that does it" (*MT* 9). The novel not only insists on viewing economics in terms of saving and "gambling" (*MT* 9), care and risk, but also demands that these terms be routinely eroticized, as though competing versions of desire must be linked to economic choices, with risk equivalent to flirtation. When Ed Thatcher hears the "tip" that Viler lets him in on—"It's a sure thing I'm tellin yer" (*MT* 108)—he fantasizes vividly the "pockets full, backaccount full, vaults full of money" (*MT* 110), a fantasy of abundance in which, however, a depletion inheres: "Dollars swarming up like steam, twisting scattering against the stars" (*MT* 111). There is such an expansion of "dollars swarming" that its result is a kind of infinite dissipation of substance. The alignment in Thatcher's fantasy between ejaculation and "spending" also is worth noting. This fantasized excess runs counter to the logic of dynamos by refusing to contain or to regulate the "steam" of the system; in order to circulate in the cash economy devised by the novel, one must also be willfully uncontained.

But if the longing that renders everyone with a job into a prostitute seems to compel a system of unrestrained and mobile desire, the novel is quick to shut down the lengths to which this desire can go. Instead of activating an infinite expansion, desire—especially heterosexual desire—forecloses and paralyzes the agency and autonomy of those who undertake to satisfy it. Contracts designed to liberate exchangeable desire end by contracting around their designers. This foreclosure is most salient in the frequency with which married women become moribund or die in the novel. Herf's mother is redolent of "a wilted smell of cologne and medicines" (*MT* 79), later suffering a fatal stroke (*MT* 96). And Susie Thatcher is never "well enough" with her continual refrain: "I wish I'd die" (*MT* 23). Her daughter Ellen, the novel's central female character, enters the same state of morbidity soon after her elopement to Oglethorpe, repeating her mother's incantation: "I want to die. I want to die" (*MT* 116). The novel's interest in female demise is not misogynistic so much as intent on recording the fatality in any acquiescence to desire, licit or illicit. If Ed Thatcher's fantasy of excessive plenty incorporates a necessary disintegration of that plenty, then the exchange, consolidation, and regulation of desire through marriage and familialism betray a similar disintegration, rather than accumulation, of self and generation. Not of least importance in this self-disintegration is a pervasive stillness or immobilization; to be settled in marriage, according to *Manhattan Transfer,* is to be all but settled in the grave.

Manhattan Transfer advances a crucial antinomy between confinement in systems of exchangeable desire and a freedom or mobility accorded to those who resist desire. This antinomy is ratified at the level of identity. In an important sense, the novel is profoundly heterophobic, construing each instance of desire as a manifestation of illicit heterosexuality. Hence the novel not only reserves its stigmatization for those who desire, but also always constitutes that desire as heterosexual vulnerability. Like Eastman and other leftist modernists, Dos Passos inverts the stigma conventionally leveled against same-sex desire by locating it on the bodies and in the figures of those who yield to any desire at all.

Joe Harland is the exemplary target of this stigmatizing tactic. Described as "the family skeleton" (*MT* 105), Harland at one point relates the saga of his descent from the heights of Wall Street. "For ten years," he says,

> I traded on margins, I bought outright, I covered on stocks I'd never
> even heard the name of and every time I cleaned up. I piled up money. I
> had four banks in the palm of my hand. I began eating my way into
> sugar and gutta percha, but in that I was before my time. . . . But you're
> getting nervous to know my secret, you think you could use it. . . . Well
> you couldn't. . . . It was a blue silk crocheted necktie that my mother
> made for me when I was a little boy. . . . (*MT* 147, ellipses in original)

The elaborate "piling," "covering," and consumption of money Harland describes as conditioned by his "secret" points to a world of plenty that functions solely on the satisfaction of whim—trading "on margins . . . eating my way into sugar and gutta percha"—a litany of gratifications "in the palm of my hand" that literalizes a notion of "playing the market" (*MT* 146). Harland's "secret" as well is uniquely divested of use-value, in that it reiterates "the predominance of luck in human affairs" (*MT* 146); its status is capricious, not a part of the world of labor, but of gaming. But the necktie that is treated as talismanic does figure into a pattern not entirely assimilable to luck: "I began to notice that the times I didn't wear the necktie were the times I lost money" (*MT* 147). Harland's disgrace is precipitated by

> a girl, God damn her and I loved her. I wanted to show her there was nothing in the world I wouldn't do for her so I gave it to her. I pretended it was a joke and laughed it off. . . . She said, Why it's no good, it's all worn out, and she threw it in the fire. . . . (*MT* 148)

Even without the castration allegory that this recounting of financial failure invites, Harland's giving his necktie to the "girl" amounts to a consummation of heterosexual desire in an exchange that, literally incandescent, consumes his livelihood "in the fire."

Because the necktie signifies both a management of "luck" in Harland's affairs (by conferring a sureness to his rhythms of financial loss) and an emblem of his "love" for his "girl," and signifies these two imperatives simultaneously, it acts as an overcharged node, "tying" different domains of social exchange in one vehicle of excessive meaning. The necktie is proper business attire, but "boyish" and, worse, mama's-boyish, at the interface of sober male entitlement and child's play. And so it reproduces the confusion Harland himself exposes between the protocols of business and the enchantment of "playing" the market. (When Jimmy Herf moves in with his relatives, his cousin Billy suggests they "play stock exchange" [*MT* 106], thus affixing the market's interchangeability with the economy of pleasure it exists to exploit.) Harland's sacrifice of the necktie does not just represent a phallic loss. Its being exchanged "for love" in fact extends or realizes the vulnerability that resides in Harland's fortunes and desires all along. The vulnerability originates in an excess of heterosexual desire compounded by a thriving on "play," but its inscription on Harland's body is markedly homosexualized in "the rip in the seat of his trousers" (*MT* 157) that he tries but fails to hide. Yoking the homophobic wisdom of the vulnerable anus to a figure whose pathos is decidedly heterosexual, the novel displaces stigma from homosexual identity squarely onto a heterosexual desire.[48] This displacement allows *Manhattan Transfer* to revise concepts of identity in such a way that heterosexual bodies are always penetrable, while bodies designated homosexual remain intact to the degree that they do not enter into exchange. More important, it is their *not* entering into exchange that renders them homosexual.

"Procreation," Stan Emery claims at one point, "is the admission of an incomplete organism. Procreation is an admission of defeat" (*MT* 210). Prompted by his desire for Ellen, a desire whose consummation in fact results in her pregnancy, Stan's own "defeat" is as much an acknowledgment of incompleteness as a tacit feminization and stigmatization. Almost "drownded" in Ellen's bathtub, Stan is forced to "put on a dress of [hers]"

(*MT* 214). The ensuing drag act—"An indecent sight in this dress"—makes Ellen recoil: "I've never seen anything so disgusting looking" (*MT* 215). But Ellen's recoil elides the fact that desire for *her* is what feminizes *him,* just as impregnating her compromises his completeness, in an exchange of desire amounting to an exchange of identity that the novel treats as irreversible. Even after Stan has "taken off the dress," "her blue padded dressinggown" is "flying out from his thin hairy legs" (*MT* 216).

The antiprostitution discourse that links Progressive reformers to leftist modernists conceives desire as facilitating a relaxation or transgression of the boundaries between individual identities (working girl, clandestine prostitute) and practices (courtship, prostitution, work and play). *Manhattan Transfer* takes the inversion of habitude entailed by the reformer and the leftist's concept of desire to its radical extreme. Influence operates at the level of desire between people to revoke or to reconfigure their personhood. "Funny things get into a man," one of Joe Harland's acquaintances says, to which Joe answers: "There's women and that sort of stuff" (*MT* 208). If women are what happen to a man, according to the novel's key sexual politics, to prevent their "getting into" men requires a withdrawal into a ubiquitously male world, as Ellen's taxi driver plans to do: "I'm gettin an apartment on Twentysecond Avenoo wid another feller an we're goin' to get a pianer an live quiet an lay offen the skoits" (*MT* 168). This foreseen cohabitation coincides with the novel's valuation of detachment and freedom, a "free natural experience" worthy of Gold's or Eastman's Whitman. To enable this withdrawal, the novel must also set into motion a species of homosexual identity divested of influence or longing.

The novel's only "openly" queer character is also the one who feels least comfortable inhabiting his queerness. More than wanting sex with men, Tony Hunter "want[s] to act" (*MT* 234), and these two desires seem to preclude each other: "Whenever I fail to get a part I think it's on account of that. I hate and despise all that kind of men" (*MT* 234). Though he was "horribly oversexed" as a child and is "that way now" (*MT* 233), Tony's appetite seems to represent not a desire for men—"It's not people like that I fall in love with," Tony says (*MT* 234)—but, instead, a *longing for a longing for women.* "That's what's so horrible," he says. "I can't like women. I tried and tried. . . . I'm always fighting to keep it hidden" (*MT* 233). Dos Passos casts Tony's desire for men, and the identity claims that are contingent on such desire ("that way, oversexed"), into a doubly displaced desire for both "acting" (in its theatrical and agential senses) and a normativity inherent in a desire for women. Tony's clandestine "shame" (*MT* 234) could be rectified, according to Herf, "if . . . everybody told everybody else honestly what they did about it, how they lived, how they loved. It's hiding things makes them putrefy" (*MT* 235). For Herf, Tony's problem is not that he is homosexual; it is that he does not want to be. The novel bears out this supposition by pathologizing Tony's dishonesty, as if the desire for desire that he embodies—in the form of wanting to want women—is satisfied at the expense of a wholesale denial of self. Hence Tony's desire to "act," both as agent and artist, is accomplished through an affair with Nevada Jones—who "set out to make a man of [him]" (*MT* 335). Yet this gender performance finally degenerates into a vaudeville routine, "with a dance number see" (*MT* 336), that mockingly exposes the pretense of their arrangement. "You'll pretend to want to pick me up," Nevada says. "I'll be waitin' for a streetcar . . . see . . . and you'll say Hello Girlie an I'll call Officer" (*MT* 336). Trying to be what he is not debases Tony to shtick and rescinds his "will to act" by theatricalizing it. Imagining that will as determined by an exchange of heterosexual desire, Tony ends up a spectacle, reduced to performing *himself* for a circus audience (*MT* 384).

Tony may be "one of God's mistakes" (*MT* 384), but this is a mistake he compounds by misconstruing an affinity between self-mastery and reciprocal heterosexual desire. What Tony wants to be is the opposite of what he is—what he is is "not even in the dictionary" (*MT* 234). But it is this identity outside of dictionary language, detached from the social and from communication and exchange, that the novel most wants its protagonist to embrace. When, at the novel's end, Jimmy Herf finds himself "perhaps" afflicted with "some disease with a long Greek name" (*MT* 403), he embodies the self whose unnamable (and untranslatably "Greek") integrity the novel has proceeded to name and to deploy in various forms throughout. It is a self whose only erotic imperative is to dissociate entirely from desire, to "travel thousands of miles without stopping" (*MT* 81).

The novel's two "beloved" characters, the "truly male" Bud Korpenning and the "virgin-hearted" Jimmy Herf, are tied to each other by a resistance to all desires except the desire to keep moving. In an uneven way, each equates isolation from desire with a refusal to compromise identity, and the novel mediates this unevenness by converting the characters' separate narratives into an isomorphism: Bud's suicide, properly speaking, engenders Herf's adult life (even manhood). Only because Bud and Herf never meet can the novel conceive of their relation as an ideal romance, devoid of exchange. Like Gold and Reed, they do not want each other; they are each other.

Bud is introduced on the novel's first page with "his back turned to the river" (*MT* 3) as he stands on a ferry. He puts a question as to where the boat lands to "a young man in a straw hat wearing a blue and white striped necktie who stood beside him" (*MT* 4). Instead of immediately responding to Bud's question,

The young man's glance moved up from Bud's road-swelled shoes to the red wrist that stuck out from the frayed sleeves of his coat, past the skinny turkey's throat and slid up cockily into the intent eyes under the broken visored cap. (*MT* 4)

"That depends where you want to get to" (*MT* 4), the stranger finally says.

It is not implausible to assert that what proceeds here under the banner of a straightforward inquiry fast converts to another register of solicitation. The ferry setting expedites this change in register by eliciting not only the homophonic "fairy" but also the "something warm and tingling shoot[ing] suddenly through all [Bud's] veins" (*MT* 3), as if perhaps what Bud feels "shoot through" him at this moment has everything to do with fairies. The cruisiness inlaid in the stranger's overture—"That depends on where you want to get to"—derives from the peculiar state of arousal in which the young man finds Bud as he peruses the latter's form with his "cocky" glance, coming to rest on "the intent eyes" (*MT* 4). The muted pace of this visual transfer is in keeping with an implicitness of understanding intrinsic to the phenomenology of cruising; the young man's overture cannot be spoken (it's unspeakable), but its erotic charge and reciprocation depend on its being inferred outside direct speech.[49]

But if it is a pickup—and it appears to be—either Bud understands it as such and rejects it, or he does not understand it and he also rejects it. In any case, the pickup understands him as its object, interpolating him in a meshwork of homoerotic codes. This encoding is what the narrative wants to preserve, while keeping Bud's figure impassable (by not submitting him to passes). This impassability manifests itself in the "back turned to the river," a backside, unlike Joe Harland's, that allows no prospect of trespass; but it also manifests itself in Bud's decline of the transactions that follow the young man's overture. First, to the violinist who serenades him "with crushed eyes like two black pins looking into his," a reiteration of the "cocky glance" that now properly repels him, Bud offers "Nothin" in the way of tipping or being tipped; instead, "he turned away" from the entreaty (*MT* 4). Then, in another exchange soon after landing, Bud is "slip[ped] a bit of advice" that "won't cost nutten" but will somehow make him "more likely to git somethin. It's looks that count in this city" (*MT* 5). The convergence of this other tip, provided by the waiter, with a promise of something for nothing that hangs on "looks" is also rejected by Bud. By not letting the waiter slip this tip to him, Bud is also preventing his own slippage into an economy of pleasure and contract; Bud has already had "looks," both directed at and entreating him, but he has also refused to let himself be circulated by "looks" or by anything else. In a sense, he uses potential exchanges to extricate himself from exchange by repudiating its terms.

Nowhere is this strategy more discernible than in the interaction with his neighbor in the flophouse, "a quiet whisper from the next cot" (*MT* 121) that interrupts his sleep. It is during this scene that Bud relates the secret of his past:

> Bud jumped out of bed and yanked roughly at the man's shoulder. "Come over here to the light, I want to show ye sumpen." Bud's own voice crinkled queerly in his ears. He strode along the snoring lane of cots. The bum, a shambling man with curlyweatherbleached hair and beard and eyes as if hammered into his head, climbed fully dressed out from the blankets and followed him. Under the light Bud unbuttoned the front of his unionsuit and pulled it off his knottymuscled gaunt arms and shoulders. "Look at my back."
>
> "Christ Jesus," whispered the man running a grimy hand with long yellow nails over the mass of white and red deep-gouged scars. "I aint never seen nothin like it." (*MT* 122)

The vulnerability of Bud's unveiled body, which is inscribed in the "mass of white and red deep-gouged scars" on his back, is redeemed by the equal violence with which Bud himself revokes "what the ole man done to me" with a "piece of light chain on my back" (*MT* 122). "I mashed his head in with the grubbinhoe, mashed it in like when you kick a rotten punkin" (*MT* 123).

But Bud's killing is a retaliation as much against engagement with the father's desire as against the violative "scarring" that paternal authority exacts from Bud's body; and the ritualized murder fosters a dissociation or recoil from exchanges both economic (Bud leaves the "roll as big as your head" [*MT* 123] buried on the family farm) and sexual. "Last night I wanted to go with a hooker an she saw it in my eyes an throwed me out" (*MT* 123), Bud tells us, as if the dissociation certified by the murder of his "ole man" were rendered visible in every ensuing encounter. Thus, the dissociation resembles the scars that belie Bud's subjection to a potentially sexualized violence (like the cruise) he has repeatedly to confront and to disown. The hooker throws him out as much because he murdered as because his murdering signifies an unequivocal refusal to exchange desire—he could not do it even if he "wanted to." The novel's central logic forbids Bud from inhabiting the same space as a hooker, and this ejection is corroborated by the "look" in his eyes, a look she cannot tolerate. Instead of "counting," Bud's look abrogates the possibility of circulating himself in any relation, much less a commercial one.

Whereas Bud's scars are the reason he can't go home again, the look in his eyes also signals that he won't contract himself in an arrangement with the bum whose "grimy hand" runs up and down his back. This arrangement turns quickly to the bank roll upstate: "Tomorrer me'n you'll go upstate an

git that roll of bills," the bum says. "Then beat it where they cant ketch us.
We'll split fifty fifty" (*MT* 124). Instead of being "on," though, Bud eludes
the possibility of this deal: "He thought I'd tell him where the ole man's roll
was, the lousy bum. . . . One on him" (*MT* 125). Detaching himself from the
possibility of collusion with the "lousy bum" or any "bum" for that matter—
as explicit a homoerotic possibility as *Manhattan Transfer* is willing to offer—
Bud reverses the presence of the hand on his back by getting the upper hand
"on him." The suicide which follows is the logical trajectory of this reversal,
away from a potential relation, illicit or violative, into a state of pristine dissociation. For Bud to kill himself is for Bud to remain—rather, to revert to—
virgo intacta.

Though Bud's suicide is a sacrifice of the virgin that issues in a kind of renewal for Jimmy Herf, the "paid prostitute of the press" (*MT* 195), it is not
the only sacrifice. Having both cast off all prospects of income and divorced
Ellen, Herf finds himself finally at Bob Hildebrand's party, where Hildebrand asks whether he has "read about the man in Philadelphia who was
killed because he wore his straw hat on the fourteenth of May" (*MT* 401).
"This man," Hildebrand tells him,

> had the temerity to defend his straw hat. Somebody had busted it and
> he started to fight, and in the middle of it one of these steetcorner he-
> roes came up behind him and brained him with a piece of lead pipe.
> They picked him up with a cracked skull and he died in the hospital.
> (*MT* 401)

Bud's "young man" also wears a "straw hat," but this is not the only detail
that ties him to the Philadelphian. Like the young man, Herf's "real hero"
is nameless, "the Unknown soldier" (*MT* 401). The brutality of his death
evokes the sexual breaching that threatens other figures in the novel, an assault "behind him . . . with a piece of lead pipe," but the force of the penetration paradoxically eventuates in a kind of impenetrability for its victim.
Herf renames the "unknown soldier" "Saint Aloysius of Philadelphia, virgin
and martyr, the man who would wear a straw hat out of season" (*MT* 401).
This renaming in its turn recovers the Philadelphian intact, making him
into a virgin because he is a martyr, expressly a martyr for Herf. Early in the
novel Herf asserts, "I've a great mind to join the navy and see the world"
(*MT* 174); and though the unknown soldier is not a sailor, the compound
of military and homoerotic indices he epitomizes for Herf approximates
Herf's ideal of what the "world" should look like. The centrality of an emer-
gent homosexual subculture to the armed forces of the Great War era could
not have been lost on Dos Passos.[50] More interesting here, though, is the
way such a subculture's existence is grafted onto the virginal form of the
man with the straw hat to develop a figure of homosexual chastity that is mil-

itantly pure, an apotheosis of "brotherly love" consonant with his city of origin. What the man in the straw hat most wants to defend, as Herf consecrates him, is his right to have an identity "out of season," an identity that is both irregular and immutable. "Give me liberty," Herf says, transforming the man "who would wear a straw hat out of season" into "Patrick Henry, putting on his straw hat on the first of May, or give me death" (*MT* 402). For Herf, the man in the straw hat organizes the definitive conjunction of an identity irreducible to anyone's influence with a "liberty" grounded on virginity, a conjunction both "sainted" and homoerotic. "If I were a painter," Herf thinks, "I'd do Saint Aloysius of Philadelphia with a straw hat on his head instead of a halo and in his hand the lead pipe, instrument of his martyrdom, and a little me praying at his feet" (*MT* 403). The genuflection to the now tumescently endowed "martyr" here can be imagined only because it will never take place, except in the inviolate solitude of Herf's fantasy. The novel returns Herf to its opening locale, the ferry, but he is the "only passenger" on board, and "he roams round as if he owned it" (*MT* 403). Herf can fantasize about the martyr only because he is alone, and his solitude is what makes for his possessiveness, both of self and "ferry." It would not, I hope, be gratuitous to add that this self-possession is contingent on possession of oneself as a fairy.

If the martyr is also the "unknown soldier," his namelessness is what entrances Herf, who "keeps trying to explain his gayety to himself" (*MT* 403). Herf's "gayety" is lodged beyond explanation or naming, since an identity beyond explaining also cannot be *explained away*.[51] *Manhattan Transfer* takes the debased preterition of homosexual identity—its unspeakability—and turns it into the highest honorific of a self that cannot be compromised by definition. This is what distinguishes Herf finally from Ellen, whose name and identity are as variable as the marriages and affairs she regularly contracts. Ellen is characterized from birth as a slippery figure: "They've oiled her" (*MT* 7) at the hospital, where even then she cannot be "told apart" (*MT* 7) from other babies. Ellen's inborn alterability is the motor that drives her perpetual desire to engage in illicit relations, even with strangers. As a girl she wants to "be able to talk to people on the street" (*MT* 63), and is willing to switch genders to do it: "Oh daddy," she says early on, "I want to be a boy" (*MT* 23). For Ellen, being a boy means getting to circulate. By the same token, circulating at all in an economy of desire dictates the facility with which she assumes new personae; from "Elaine" (*MT* 134) in her marriage to Oglethorpe to "Helena" (*MT* 283) in her marriage to Herf, Ellen is singularly defined by a willingness "to shift things around" (*MT* 260) in order to maximize the distribution of herself. "I don't want to be had by anybody" (*MT* 226), she tells the lawyer George Baldwin at one point, precisely because she wants to be had by everybody.

This distribution of herself fashions Ellen into the novel's version of a prostitute—someone who "sells [or "rents"] her personality" (*MT* 360). To conceive of personality in these terms is to oppose it fundamentally to identity, because personality can be bought and sold (Ellen does it over and over), but identity cannot be influenced, by either money or desire. Since the novel defines economic exchanges as correlates of illicit heterosexual desire, this identity can by no means be heterosexual. It is rather Herf's "gayety" that centers him in an identity outside exchange. Like Whitman "loafing on the open road," Herf ultimately appropriates a homosexuality that frees him from any constraint of desire; his last act in the novel is to get in a truck that will take him "pretty far" (*MT* 405). As counterintuitive as it appears, Herf can assume this sexual identity only so long as it is independent of desire; again, like the homosexuality accorded to Whitman, Herf's is the necessary ground of "a cosmic and animal independence." Homosexuality becomes the means of transmitting a self-integrity that cannot be attained through heterosexual desire, which the novel routinely coordinates with a dispersal or alteration of identity.

IV

For leftist modernists writing in the "nativist decade," homosexuality is the basis of a transmission of cultural identity without an exchange or contract in the economy of desire. Like its nativist counterparts, leftist modernism appears to have been dedicated to a version of cultural identity that could be neither assimilated nor inborn but had to incorporate both technologies—education and biological inheritance—in order to realize a species of cultural purity. But Herf's identity is neither learned nor given; it is epiphanic and "unexplainable." Leftist modernism sanctions an extreme version of nativist self-enclosure by generating an identity both spontaneous and virginally intact. Its nominal aim in figuring this identity is to conceive the self without any influence, a self that is all "will"—"full, bold, hard consciousness"—with a body figured as immune to the desire being exchanged everywhere around it. Leftist modernism views such a body as the necessary condition for any sustained attempt at "revolt." *Manhattan Transfer* announces this necessity quite brutally in the figure of Anna Cohen, the working-class shopgirl whose susceptibility to the desire industry and the temptations it manufactures is fatally incompatible with her revolutionary aspirations, though the two longings—for pleasure and for revolution—blend into a single illicit fantasy:

> If you was your own boss there wouldn't be this fighting about strikers
> and scabs . . . equal opportunity for all. Elmer says that's all applesauce.
> No hope for the workers but in the revolution. Oh I'm juss wild about

> Harree, And Harree's just wild about me . . . Elmer in a telephone cen-
> tral in a dinnercoat, with eartabs, tall as Valentino, strong as Doug. The
> Revolution is declared. The Red Guard is marching up Fifth Avenue. . . .
> And they're dancing the Charleston in all the officebuildings. (*MT* 397–
> 98)

Anna, a former dance hall girl, terminates her "dream" by dancing, "whirl-
ing round fighting with her hands the burning tulle all round her" (*MT*
398), in the dress shop. Her incandescence, like Joe Harland's, stems from
the volatile coexistence in her of desires antithetical to one another. She
wants to dance, but she also want to be "her own boss," but she also wants
"revolution," and these desires become lethally indistinct; she cannot dissociate revolt from the Charleston. Unlike the bohemians who dominated the
leftist literary scene of the teens with a hedonism that linked revolt to an
economy of pleasure, Dos Passos defines hedonism as an impasse to revolt
that will consume those who fall prey to its influence. Instead, he offers a
version of purity that links revolt to a chaste but potent homosexuality, in
the sacramental and Whitmanian figure of Herf.

Though the conclusion to *Manhattan Transfer* bears an uncanny resemblance to the mobility plot in which Henry James inserts Milly Theale and
her friends, we have come a great distance from the perils of groundlessness
with which James was preoccupied in *The Wings of the Dove*. But this is only
to suggest in some ways the longevity of the mobility plot and its liability to
appropriation for unanticipated usages. Given the anxiety that working-class
female sexuality and consumer habits incited among the mostly middle-
class, mostly male writers of the 1920s literary left, the interest in Whitman's
celebration of collectivity and virile homosexuality over James's "minute
description[s]" of female interiority amounted to a political choice of masculine seriousness over feminine frivolity. Dos Passos and his leftist contemporaries understood a figure like James, with his "microscopic" attention to
female psychology and desire, as part of the general problem of perverse society—embodied overwhelmingly for the writers of the teens and twenties
in the figure of the prostitute.[52] From the perspective of the modernist left,
James's Daisy Miller (whose flirtation with Italian men beneath her station
precipitates her "malaria" in James's 1879 story) might be viewed as the prototype of an infectious and indiscriminate heterosexuality to which Whitman offers a prophylactic resistance, as Dos Passos put it in his 1916 screed,
"Against American Literature," by "founding his faith upon himself." In this
model of masculine rectitude (which survives into the present in gay journalist Andrew Sullivan's paeans to testosterone and macho bonding as the
salvation for gay male sexuality), it is almost as though Dos Passos argues
that James cares too much about women to be a good faggot.[53]

In the refusal of both consumption as desire and of sex as labor, the left-ist twenties culture I have been examining in this chapter draws a sharp distinction between desire and identity, consumption and production, in which the former term is inevitably the undoing of the latter. And this distinction has broader implications. Twentieth-century labor historians have often lamented the fact that consumption is a trap for the American working class, preventing it from bearing witness to its exploitation and forming a collective consciousness.[54] By the same token, the relegation of sex to the domain of "leisure," to the space of trivial pursuits, has been (with some notable exceptions) an almost uniform assumption of leftists. Consigned to the realm of play and shopping, sex does not count for much toward social change, whether that change means revolution or multicultural justice. Its commercialization may even prevent change altogether.[55]

How do we extricate ourselves from this compulsory delineation? I submit that we have had something like a language in which to begin such an extrication for a long time, in the realm of modern consumer culture. But like our Progressive-era and modernist forebears, we have been discouraged from engaging it for fear of what using such "market" language might reveal about our own failures of ethics or imagination. I suggest that instead of disowning identity on behalf of desire, or disavowing desire in the constitution of identities, we might finally proceed through an effort to own—and own up to—our desires outright, trading on them as we see fit. The idea of a free market in desire may be naïve, and it may even be reactionary. Or it may be the most radical strategy at our disposal.

Conclusion

The principal authors I have examined here—Henry and William James, Gertrude Stein, Willa Cather, Hart Crane, and John Dos Passos—infused their writing with a simultaneous acknowledgment and evasion of the terminal complexity of modern social relations. Their work both forces and denies a confrontation with the social others who give that work its dynamism, its experimental charge. I argue that much of the modernist enterprise—in particular its ideology of obscurity, its notorious "difficulty"—derives from the impasse to clarity provoked by cross-class encounter. Modernist encounters between disparate or adversarial social groups are a compound of misrecognition and rapport, reciprocity and asymmetry. They are never simple, always highly mediated and opaque. Hart Crane, for instance (arguably the most socially and sexually generous author under consideration here), entered his dealings with soldiers, sailors, and teamsters with a mixture of risk and romance, danger and sentimentality, that overloaded these encounters with utopian erotic possibilities and far more promise than they could ever deliver. None of the writers I scrutinize had an uncomplicated attitude toward social difference. Each conceived of class others as misfits or transgressors of social norms, and each assigned this misfit or transgressive status a different valence.

Yet this is not to deny what I view as the originality of this tradition of writers when assembled for critical inquiry. Beginning with James, these authors were resolved to bring their energy to bear on the question of class difference. Class difference is arguably never a static social reality, but the strain of American modernism I have detailed in this book articulates its mobility and dynamism as the central conceit of class. These writers pursued the wavering class relations of the early twentieth century under the rubric that their socially minded contemporaries also favored—the deviation in sexual norms that may be concisely summarized by the term "cruising." As the name for erotic exchanges that occur off the licit byways of courtship, marriage, and intimacy, "cruising" implies that in American modernism, soliciting the muse becomes virtually inseparable from solicitation in general. Though the term itself flirts with coyness, I have meant in these pages to take the concept of cruising quite seriously, according it a respect and gravity that all the writers I examine felt it was due. Casual, vaguely lewd, and anonymous erotic encounters punctuate the texts I have singled out for exploration—on a subway car in *The Wings of the Dove* or in Crane's *The Bridge,* on the ferry from New Jersey in Dos Passos's *Manhattan Transfer,* in the railway yards to which Melanctha is drawn in *Three Lives.* Public transit and sexual desire seem inescapably reciprocal in these passages; their combination produces the erotic mobility that modernist literary and social thought took as their problem. Even as these moments are foreclosed or deflected, they determine the structure and concerns of American modernist narratives to different degrees. The writers in the preceding chapters "cruise" their culture in the sense that they entertain or enter into unlikely encounters that leave them scarred in ways their writing cannot make caducous. Neither effaced nor assimilated, the marks of the class other appear palimpsest-like on the modernist page. The task of this book has been to raise those marks, putting them into relief without relieving the text of their strenuous affliction.

I began this book as a way to open a conversational path between critics who base their analysis on sexuality and critics who base their analysis on class. To make queer critics and leftist critics more responsive to each other requires reflection on both fronts. For leftist critics, this means acknowledging sexuality as a viable terrain for both critical thought and social change, akin to class, gender, and race relations. For queer critics, this means paying closer attention to historical analysis, or to such historicizing tools as leftist cultural critics have always relied on. To be sure, a compelling model of queer leftist inquiry has been made available through the writing of social historians and critics of sexuality whose work encompasses a dialectical approach to sex and social change. The exemplary authors in this field include Jeffrey Weeks, John D'Emilio, and Gayle Rubin, whose essays and commentaries have incited at least as much important theorizing about sexuality as Foucault's. Yet this is a body of work to which literary critics, attracted to the amenities of discourse analysis and textuality, have by and large paid lip service. Thus in treating literary culture, queer reading continues to follow the prevalent ideology of the text as a formally autonomous construct whose value resides in its fundamental misalignment from the normative or coercive regime of society at large.

As I have tried to convey throughout this book, sexual normativity was scarcely the norm in the early twentieth century. Thus to speak, as some contemporary queer literary critics of the period do, of this or that gay or lesbian figure overturning or subverting sexual norms is historically mistaken. For Progressive-era thinkers, sexuality was widely construed as a flexible and protean set of desires whose proper determination could never be stabilized so much as qualified through ever-shifting balances in a larger economy of desire and opportunity. Just as contamination of the self by the desire concept spans every plane of the social world of modernity, so a strict interpretation of sexual "otherness" should be regarded as a misnomer, if not a fallacy, in the twentieth century. This is not to deny the efficacy of purity movements and other campaigns to purge the social realm of "perverts" and "deviants," but only to acknowledge that perversion itself forms a basic thread of the very pattern of modern society, and cannot be separated out for long without unraveling the social fabric as a whole. In short, there is nothing special about perversion in modern culture, if by "special" we mean rare or oppositional or affecting only a small minority of the populace. If we are accustomed to thinking that we all belong to mass society but that only some of us are queer, early twentieth-century society by contrast declares that to belong to mass society is always to enter the sphere of the illicit, the perverse, the dirty. In short, according to the major thinkers in the Progressive era and beyond, in mass culture everyone is queer.

In threatening to become the latest version of "the endlessly mutating token of non-assimilation,"[1] as Lee Edelman eloquently calls it, queer theory has overlooked a valuable opportunity to demonstrate the intimate connection of sex to how mundane social relations are lived.[2] If the historical dimension of this book has aimed to look past the species model of sexuality by dealing with the more elastic notion of "desire," its theoretical goals have included entertaining the possibility that sex is not really so extraordinary after all. The idea that broad or nonconformist differences in erotic taste, practices, and habits might *not* incite wild rationalizations, defenses, or polemics seems simply beyond our intellectual reach, queer or otherwise. There appears no ordinary language to articulate such a position, to begin "thinking sex" as other than—well, other.[3] Thus has it seemed important to pursue a different tactic in this book from the main line of queer studies of American culture, if only to demonstrate what can be learned from queer analyses when we dilate their purview beyond the painstaking genealogy of sexual identities that has preoccupied critics of the last generation. In my estimation, the most immediate dividend from making sexuality central to our reconstruction of how a culture copes with transformations in both knowledge systems and material relations is a sense of how many more objects of inquiry disclose themselves to a queer-theoretical reckoning. Once we move beyond the evolution of the pervert or the lesbian or the gay man as a species, for example, we discover that scenes of cruising turn out to be more prevalent in modernist texts than mere coincidence would seem to account for. Aside from those occasions of anonymous erotics that I have taken as my starting point in the preceding chapters, I include the cruising scenarios of such disparate writers as T. S. Eliot and F. Scott Fitzgerald.[4] Though beyond the scope of this book, these moments demand dissection, enjoin us to develop a method and a research program whose humble beginnings I have tried to limn in these pages.

It is my more immodest hope that this book has contributed to our sense of what queer studies can do in the broad scheme of cultural and literary history when enlisted in reading against the grain of knowledge about the past. Both sexuality and class analyses have been understood in the larger academic universe as coterie pursuits—one the province of gay men and lesbians, the other the territory of a beleaguered Marxist clique. These assumptions have tacitly dominated a critical hegemony that, in its commitment to business as usual, has deemed sexuality and class as "motivated" or special-interest or "politicized" concerns. As such, sexuality and class may be of significance to those who care about them, but clearly do not matter very much to the rest of "us." Yet sex is not a "minority interest"—a fraught notion if there ever was one—any more than class difference is. Nor does one category map readily onto the other. Instead, their complicated overlap in the discourses of early twentieth-century social and literary thought suggests a rich perplex that will reward critics of whatever persuasion who mine it with all the resources—queer or otherwise—that an informed scholarship can muster.

Notes

INTRODUCTION

1. On the relation between classes of persons and classification as an epistemological category, see Mary Poovey, "The Social Constitution of Class: Toward a History of Classificatory Thinking," in *Rethinking Class: Literary Studies and Social Formation,* ed. Wai Chee Dimock and Michael Gilmore (New York: Columbia University Press, 1994), 15–56; Dimock's "Class, Gender, and a History of Metonymy," in the same volume, 57–104; and Geoffrey Bowker and Susan Leigh Star, *Sorting Things Out: Classification and Its Consequences* (Cambridge: MIT Press, 1999).

2. See Martin J. Burke, *The Conundrum of Class: Public Discourse on the Social Order in America* (Chicago: University of Chicago Press, 1995). Burke notes that by the late nineteenth century the "growth of an apparently permanent laboring or working class" (133) threatened the traditional "ideology of class harmony" (134) that held dominion prior to the incorporation of America.

3. "Producer culture" has become shorthand for historians describing the general economic shape of American life before 1900. See American Social History Project, *Who Built America? Working People and the Nation's Economy, Politics, and Society,* vol. 2, *From The Gilded Age to the Present* (New York: Pantheon, 1989); Roy Rosenzweig, *Eight Hours for What We Will: Workers and Leisure in an Industrial City* (New York: Cambridge University Press, 1983); Lewis A. Erenberg, *Steppin' Out: New York Nightlife and the Transformation of American Culture: 1890–1930* (Chicago: University of Chicago Press, 1981).

4. Lester Ward, *Applied Sociology* (Boston: Ginn, 1906), 44, 46.

5. Simon Patten, *The New Basis of Civilization* (1907; reprint, Cambridge, Mass.: Belknap Press, 1968), 23.

6. Robert Park, "The City: Suggestions for the Investigation of Human Behavior in the City Environment," *American Journal of Sociology* 20 (March 1915): 609.

7. Park, "The City," 611.

8. "It was because men were grouped, and thought of themselves in the form of groups, that in their ideas they grouped other things." See Emile Durkheim and Marcel Mauss, *Primitive Classification,* trans. Rodney Needham (London: Cohen and West, 1963), 82.

9. William Graham Sumner, one of the earliest of academic-professional American sociologists, confirmed the class-ratifying function of social science in his 1883 book, *What Social Classes Owe to Each Other* (reprint, Caldwell, Idaho: Caxton, 1954). For studies representing the increased interest in class instability in the next generation, see Josiah Flynt, *Tramping with Tramps* (New York: Century Co., 1899), and Nels Anderson, *The Hobo: The Sociology of the Homeless Man* (1923; reprint, Chicago: University of Chicago Press, 1961).

10. Robert Park, "The Mind of the Hobo: Reflections upon the Relation between Mentality and Locomotion," in *The City,* ed. Robert E. Park, Ernest W. Burgess, and Roderick D. McKenzie (Chicago: University of Chicago Press, 1925), 158.

11. In the introduction to a 1923 anthology of social theory, editor James Ford wrote: "The lines between the Social Sciences are not sharply drawn. Sociology is often defined to include Social Ethics. . . . [I]t is important that a group of specialists should work at the synthesis of the findings of all antecedent and special Social Sciences in order to determine how their accu-

mulated knowledge may be coordinated and applied for the general welfare." See James Ford, ed., *Social Problems and Social Policy* (Boston: Ginn, 1923).

12. For the most compelling analysis of "identitarian" modernism, see Walter Benn Michaels, *Our America: Nativism, Modernism, and Pluralism* (Durham: Duke University Press, 1995). For a persuasive history of the period's racialist discourses and their impact on modernism, see Werner Sollors, *Beyond Ethnicity: Consent and Descent in American Life* (New York: Oxford University Press, 1986). For excellent cultural studies of rationality in American life around 1900, see Martha Banta, *Taylored Lives: Narrative Production in the Age of Taylor, Veblen, and Ford* (Chicago: University of Chicago Press, 1993), and Mark Seltzer, *Bodies and Machines* (New York: Routledge, 1992).

13. On the embattled affinity between social science and literature around 1900, see Wolf Lepenies, *Between Literature and Science: The Rise of Sociology*, trans. R. J. Hollingdale (New York: Cambridge University Press, 1988). For an excellent treatment of literature and social science from a period slightly earlier than (but overlapping with) the one I consider here, see Susan Mizruchi, *The Science of Sacrifice: American Literature and Modern Social Theory* (Princeton: Princeton University Press, 1998).

14. Andre Siegrid, "Race Consciousness and Eugenics," in *The Sex Problem in Modern Society*, ed. Francis McDermott (New York: Modern Library, 1930), 234.

15. Siegrid, "Race Consciousness," 236.

16. Henry James, *The American Scene*, ed. Leon Edel (Bloomington: Indiana University Press, 1968), 119.

17. Willa Cather, *O Pioneers!* (1913; reprint, Lincoln: University of Nebraska Press, 1992), 247.

18. Henry James, *The Wings of the Dove* (New York: Charles Scribner's Sons, 1909), 1:4. All references to the novel are to this edition (vols. 19 and 20 of the New York edition); hereafter cited in text as *WD*.

19. James was no stranger to the social theory of his day, as Ross Posnock has demonstrated in *The Trial of Curiosity: Henry James, William James, and the Challenge of Modernity* (New York: Oxford University Press, 1991).

20. The literature on risk relations within contemporary social theory is too lengthy to cite exhaustively. No account of risk could omit Niklas Luhmann, *Trust and Power* (Chichester: Wiley, 1979), which has incited useful and provocative commentary in Adam Seligman, *The Problem of Trust* (Princeton: Princeton University Press, 1997); Anthony Giddens, *Modernity and Self-Identity: Self and Society in the Late Modern Age* (Stanford: Stanford University Press, 1991); and Barbara Misztal, *Trust in Modern Societies: The Search for the Bases of Social Order* (Cambridge, U.K.: Polity Press, 1996).

21. Willa Cather, *Alexander's Bridge* (1912; reprint, New York: Oxford University Press, 1997), 11. Hereafter cited in text as *AB*.

22. Edward Alsworth Ross, *Social Psychology: An Outline and Source Book* (New York: Macmillan, 1919), 362.

23. Carleton Parker, *The Casual Laborer and Other Essays* (New York: Harcourt, Brace and Howe, 1920), 153. Hereafter cited in text as *CL*.

24. Frankwood Williams, *The Sex Problem in Modern Society*, 66. I discuss this anthology at length in chapter 1.

25. Ross, *Social Psychology*, 126.

26. Marco Orru usefully traces the vexed semantic descent of this term from antiquity to modernity in *Anomie: History and Meanings* (London: Allen & Unwin, 1987).

27. Hence the sociologist Grove Samuel Dow claimed in 1920 that "the immigrant . . . brings with him ideas of sexual morality that differ from the American point of view." See *Society and Its Problems* (New York: Thomas Crowell, 1920). And in "How to Read" (1929) Ezra Pound disdainfully notes that an author's "unrewarded gropings, hopes, passions, laundry bills, or erotic experiences" are widely "considered germane to the subject" of "literary instruction in our 'institutions of learning.' " See *Literary Essays of Ezra Pound*, ed. T. S. Eliot (New York: New Directions, 1968), 15.

28. See Paula Rabinowitz, *Labor and Desire: Women's Revolutionary Fiction in Depression Amer-*

ica (Chapel Hill: University of North Carolina Press, 1991); Michael Denning, *The Cultural Front: The Laboring of American Culture* (London: Verso, 1997); Cary Nelson, *Repression and Recovery: Modern American Poetry and the Politics of Cultural Memory, 1910–1945* (Madison: University of Wisconsin Press, 1989).

29. See Colleen Lamos, *Deviant Modernism* (Cambridge: Cambridge University Press, 1998); Joseph A. Boone, *Libidinal Currents: Sexuality and the Shaping of Modernism* (Chicago: University of Chicago Press, 1998).

30. Some exceptions to this general lack of communication between sex- and class-based modernist criticism include Michael Tratner, *Deficits and Desires: Economics and Sexuality in Twentieth-Century Literature* (Stanford: Stanford University Press, 2001); Michael Moon, *A Small Boy and Others: Imitation and Initiation in American Culture from Henry James to Andy Warhol* (Durham: Duke University Press, 1998).

31. On class as the great American taboo, see Benjamin Mott, *The Imperial Middle: Why Americans Can't Think Straight about Class* (New Haven: Yale University Press, 1990), and Benita Eisler, *Class Act: America's Last Dirty Secret* (New York: F. Watts, 1983). Americans have as much trouble thinking class as they do "thinking sex," to borrow the title of Gayle Rubin's groundbreaking essay on the inarticulateness of American public discourse on sex. See "Thinking Sex: Notes for a Radical Theory of the Politics of Sexuality," *The Lesbian and Gay Studies Reader,* ed. Henry Abelove, Michele Barale, and David Halperin (New York: Routledge, 1993).

32. Richard L. Bushman, *The Refinement of America: Persons, Houses, Cities* (New York: Vintage, 1993), 446.

33. The locus classicus of this dynamic is Nella Larsen, *Passing* (New York: Knopf, 1929).

CHAPTER ONE: PERVERT MODERNISM

1. James Roscoe Day, *My Neighbor the Working Man* (New York: Abingdon Press, 1920), 12–13.

2. Hence in *The Casual Laborer* (introduction n. 23), economist Carleton Parker pays his respect to Sigmund Freud for giving him "a scientific approach which might lead to the discovery of important fundamentals for a study of unrest and violence" (28); and in *The Social Philosophy of Instinct* (New York: Charles Scribner's Sons, 1922), the sociologist Charles Conant Josey cites Havelock Ellis's *Studies in the Psychology of Sex* as a primary influence on his own thought (76).

3. On the conceptual transformation precipitated by this crisis, see Henry May, *The End of American Innocence: A Study of the First Years of Our Own Time, 1912–1917* (Chicago: Quadrangle, 1959). The "instinct of sex," May maintains, had "a specially powerful place" (157) in the new psychology that influenced a whole range of social sciences.

4. Day, *My Neighbor,* 29.

5. Walter Lippmann, *Drift and Mastery* (1914; reprint, Madison: University of Wisconsin Press, 1985), 91, 92. Hereafter cited in text as *DM.*

6. Day, *My Neighbor,* 125.

7. Lester Ward, *The Psychic Factors of Civilization* (Boston: Ginn, 1893), 53.

8. Ibid., 54.

9. Carleton Parker, *The Casual Laborer* (introduction note 23), 30. Hereafter cited in text as *CL.*

10. "Within the emerging idiom of American liberalism," Martin Burke writes, " 'classes' signified occupational groups and vertical distinctions of wealth, but these classes were not fixed, nor were they necessarily collective actors in social and political life." See *The Conundrum of Class* (introduction note 2), 162.

11. Lewis Mumford, "The City," in *Civilization in the United States,* ed. Harold Stearns (New York: Harcourt Brace, 1922), 7.

12. Ibid., 8.

13. Ibid., 13.

14. Edith Wharton, "Terminus," in *American Poetry: The Twentieth Century,* 2 vols., ed. John Hollander (New York: Library of America, 2000), 1:19–20. Though he does not consider this particular Wharton poem, Mark Seltzer offers a compelling rubric for it when he writes of "how

the uncertain status of the principle of locomotion precipitates the melodramas of uncertain agency and also what amounts to an erotics of uncertain agency." See *Bodies and Machines* (New York: Routledge, 1992), 17.

15. Emile Durkheim, *The Division of Labor in Society,* trans. W. D. Halls (New York: Free Press, 1984), xxxiii.

16. Ibid., lii, liv. Christopher Herbert writes of Durkheim's "fable of modern desire" in terms that have been useful to my thinking about the relation between anomie, perversity, and social theory. See *Culture and Anomie* (Chicago: University of Chicago Press, 1991), 68–89.

17. Frederick Winslow Taylor, *The Principles of Scientific Management* (1911; reprint, New York: Norton, 1967), 5.

18. Ibid., 142–44.

19. Robert and Helen Merrell Lind, *Middletown: A Study in Modern American Culture* (New York: Harcourt Brace, 1929), 109.

20. Lothrop Stoddard, *The Rising Tide of Color against White World-Supremacy* (New York: Charles Scribner's Sons, 1920), 11, 145. Hereafter cited in text as *RT.*

21. In Walter Benn Michaels's analysis, the paranoia Stoddard directed at the "rising tide of color" placed him squarely, if paradoxically, in the "anti-imperialist" camp among American thinkers of the twenties. See *Our America* (introduction note 12), 23.

22. Lothrop Stoddard, *The Revolt against Civilization* (New York: Charles Scribner's Sons, 1922), 166. Hereafter cited in text as *RC.*

23. Prescott Hall, *Immigration and Its Effects upon the United States* (New York: Henry Holt, 1913), 110.

24. Will Durant, "The Breakdown of Marriage," in *The Sex Problem in Modern Society,* ed. John Francis McDermott (New York: Modern Library, 1930), 150. Hereafter cited in text as *SP.*

25. Herbert Croly, *The Promise of American Life,* ed. Arthur M. Schlesinger Jr. (Cambridge, Mass.: Belknap, 1965), 132.

26. Robert Park and Herbert Miller, *Old World Traits Transplanted* (1921; reprint, New York: Arno, 1969), 27.

27. Rexford Tugwell, "The Gypsy Strain," *Pacific Monthly Review* 3 (1920): 177.

28. Ibid., 176.

29. Charles Ellwood, *Cultural Evolution: A Study of Social Origins and Development* (New York: Century Co., 1927), 16.

30. Ibid., 18.

31. Ibid., 200.

32. Samuel Schmalhausen, *Why We Misbehave* (New York: Macauley, 1928), 45. Schmalhausen was a psychologist who coedited, with V. F. Calverton, an anthology similar to McDermott's called *Sex in Civilization* (London: Allen & Unwin, 1929).

33. Josey, *Social Philosophy,* 260.

34. Ibid., 171.

35. Ibid., 213.

36. Ernest Groves, *Personality and Social Adjustment* (New York: Longmans, 1923), 123.

37. Dr. Moses Schotz, *Sex Problems of Man in Health and Disease: A Popular Study in Sex Knowledge* (Cincinnati: Stewart and Kidd Co., 1916), 22.

38. Ibid., 28.

39. Olive Schreiner, *Woman and Labor* (New York: Frederick Stokes, 1911), 34. Hereafter cited in text as *WL.*

40. Michel Foucault, *The History of Sexuality,* vol. 1, *An Introduction,* trans. Robert Hurley (New York: Vintage, 1980), 71.

41. Observers at the time could be quite explicit about the connection between casual sex and casual people. In an essay in the McDermott anthology, "The New View of Sex," George John Nathan assesses the role of sex "as a much more casual and unimportant thing than it is customarily assumed to be" (*SP* 26) by emphasizing how working-class immigrants figure into this transposition of values. The trivialization of sex—its loss of tragic gravitas and hence of serious meaning—becomes linked to a democratization of social life that likewise verges on the anarchistic.

42. Edmond Kelly, *The Elimination of the Tramp* (New York: G. P. Putnam's Sons, 1908), 13.

43. Ibid., 14.

44. Whiting Williams, *What's on the Worker's Mind* (New York: Charles Scribner's, 1920), 303.

45. Sigmund Freud, "Observations on Transference-Love," *The Standard Edition of the Complete Psychological Works of Sigmund Freud*, 24 vols., ed. and trans. James Strachey et al. (London: Hogarth, 1955–74), 12:159.

46. Iwan Bloch, *The Sexual Life of Our Time in Its Relations to Modern Civilization*, trans. M. Eden Paul (New York: Allied Book Co., 1928), 4.

47. Ibid., 46.

48. Ibid.

49. Havelock Ellis, *Studies in the Psychology of Sex*, vol. 2, *Sexual Inversion*, 3d ed. (Philadelphia: F.A. Davis, 1921), 91. Hereafter cited in text as *SI*.

50. August Forel, *The Sexual Question: A Scientific, Psychological, Hygienic, and Sociological Study*, trans. C. F. Marshall (1906; reprint, New York: Physicians and Surgeons Book Co., 1924), 73. Hereafter cited in text as *SQ*.

51. On the class dimensions of early twentieth-century gay male identity, see George Chauncey, *Gay New York: Gender, Urban Culture, and the Making of the Gay Male World, 1890–1940* (New York: Basic Books, 1994); for an early twentieth-century account of the class dimensions of male homoeroticism, see Earl Lind, *Autobiography of an Androgyne* (1909; reprint, New York: Arno, 1975).

52. William James, *The Principles of Psychology* (Cambridge: Harvard University Press, 1983), 1054. James also shares the contemporary sexological assumption that "the sexual instinct is particularly liable to be checked and modified by slight differences in the individual stimulus, by the inward condition of the agent himself, by habits once acquired" (1053)—in other words, that "the sexual impulses" (1053) are shaped by environment as much as by physiology.

53. Otto Weininger, *Sex and Character* (New York: G.P. Putnam's Sons, 1906), 54.

54. Ibid., 55.

55. In an essay in the McDermott anthology called "Heredity and Sex," the geneticist Edward East maintained a similar dynamism with regard to sex traits: "What we must hold fast," he claims, "is that the two sexual states, maleness and femaleness, are not mutually exclusive" (*SP* 220). The point here is that even hereditarian thinkers acceded to the dynamic model of sexual difference to be found throughout the era.

56. Beatrice Hinkle, "Women and the New Morality," in *Our Changing Morality: A Symposium*, ed. Freda Kirchwey (New York: A.C. Boni, 1924), 34.

57. If "the increasing structural complexity of society led to dissentious descriptions, to truth wars, to humanistic skepticism," Luhmann writes of the early modern period, then the solution to this "dissolution of order" was more of the same—"a plurality of forms of rationality." See *Observations on Modernity*, trans. William Whobrey (Stanford: Stanford University Press, 1998), 24–25.

58. Foucault, *History*, 47.

59. Ibid., 48.

60. Zygmunt Bauman writes that what defines modernity is ambivalence, "the possibility of assigning an object or an event to more than one category." See *Modernity and Ambivalence* (London: Polity, 1991), 1. For an instructive revisionist account of modernity, see Scott Lash, *Another Modernity, a Different Rationality* (London: Blackwell, 1999).

61. Elsie Clews Parsons, *Social Freedom: A Study of the Conflicts between Social Classifications and Personality* (New York: G.P. Putnam's Sons, 1915), 7. Hereafter cited in text as *SF*.

62. Michel Foucault, "Two Lectures," *Power/Knowledge: Selected Interviews and Other Writings, 1972–1977*, ed. Colin Gordon (New York: Pantheon, 1980), 106.

63. Anthony Giddens, *The Consequences of Modernity* (Stanford: Stanford University Press, 1990), 39.

64. Niklas Luhmann, *Observations on Modernity*, trans. William Whobrey (Stanford: Stanford University Press, 1998), 25.

65. See Niklas Luhmann, *Love as Passion: The Codification of Intimacy*, trans. Jeremy Gaines

and Doris L. Jones (Stanford: Stanford University Press, 1998). In *The Transformation of Intimacy* (Stanford: Stanford University Press, 1992), Giddens brings his ideas about "reflexive modernization" to bear on the structure of interpersonal desire. For Giddens's definition of reflexivity, see *Modernity and Self-Identity* (Stanford: Stanford University Press, 1991), 19–21.

66. Peter Taylor, *Modernities: A Geohistorical Interpretation* (Minneapolis: University of Minnesota Press, 1999), 8.

67. H. Stuart Hughes, *Consciousness and Society: The Reconstruction of European Social Thought 1890–1930* (New York: Vintage, 1958), 66.

68. James Livingston, *Pragmatism and the Political Economy of Cultural Revolution, 1850–1940* (Chapel Hill: University of North Carolina Press, 1994), 176.

69. Ibid., 78.

70. William James, *Talks to Teachers on Psychology and to Students on Some of Life's Ideals* (1899; reprint, Cambridge: Harvard University Press, 1983), 165.

71. Ibid., 297.

72. See Max Weber, *The Protestant Ethic and the Spirit of Capitalism,* trans. Talcott Parsons (1905; reprint, New York: Scribner, 1952).

73. Livingston, *Pragmatism,* 167.

74. Ibid.

75. Simon Patten, *The New Basis of Civilization* (Cambridge, Mass.: Belknap Press, 1968), 8. Hereafter cited in text as *NB.*

76. William Miller Collier, *The Trusts: What Can We Do with Them? What Can They Do for Us?* (New York: Baker and Taylor, 1900), 158.

77. Ibid., 156.

78. Livingston, *Pragmatism,* 176.

79. Don D. Lescohier, *The Labor Market* (New York: Macmillan, 1919), 13.

80. Ibid.

81. Lewis A. Erenberg, *Steppin' Out: New York Nightlife and the Transformation of American Culture: 1890–1930* (Chicago: University of Chicago Press, 1981), 62, 79, 84.

82. Ethel Mumford, *Harper's Monthly,* January 1912, 12.

CHAPTER TWO: CHANCE, CHOICE, AND *THE WINGS OF THE DOVE*

1. Henry James, *The American Essays of Henry James,* ed. Leon Edel (Princeton: Princeton University Press, 1989), 200.

2. Henry James, *The Wings of the Dove* (New York: Charles Scribner's Sons, 1909), 1:53–54. All references to the novel are to this edition (vols. 19 and 20 of the New York edition); hereafter cited in text as *WD.*

3. Recent critical accounts have taken much interest in James's thoughts on trains. See Kenneth Warren, *Black and White Strangers: Race and American Literary Realism* (Chicago: University of Chicago Press, 1993), and Sara Blair, *Henry James and the Writing of Race and Nation* (New York: Cambridge University Press, 1996).

4. Eve Kosofsky Sedgwick, "Is the Rectum Straight? Identification and Identity in *The Wings of the Dove,*" *Tendencies* (Durham: Duke University Press, 1993), 75.

5. Thus according to Jean-Christophe Agnew, the "hotel civilization" (190) that James ostensibly disdains "was the same medium through which he had just become acquainted with midcentury Europe" (193). See "The Consuming Vision of Henry James," in *The Culture of Consumption: Critical Essays in American History 1880–1980,* ed. T. J. Jackson Lears and Richard Wrightman (New York: Pantheon, 1983). James was clearly wed to the more ideologically retrograde notions of his class and time. Yet I wish to qualify Agnew's detective work into James's biases by suggesting that James doesn't deny his complicity with normative culture so much as he has qualms—which it is the task of his novels to unfold and to shape—about what counts as normative to begin with, given the transient or unsettled nature of "hotel civilization" itself.

6. Or to borrow Mark Seltzer's insight, culled from his suggestive reading of *The American Scene:* "It is the pathology of desire that James pursues. . . . Deviation from the normal state constitutes narrative for James." See *Henry James and the Art of Power* (Ithaca: Cornell University Press, 1984), 137.

7. Henry James, *Hawthorne* (New York: Harper and Brothers, 1879), 1. Hereafter cited in text as *H*.

8. *Congressional Record*, 67th Congress, 1st session, 1921, 61, part 1:917.

9. On the phenomenon of "birds of passage," see Maxine Seller, *To Seek America: A History of Ethnic Life in the United States* (New York: Jerome Ozer, 1977), and Walter Nugent, *Crossings: The Great Transatlantic Migrations, 1870–1914* (Bloomington: Indiana University Press, 1992).

10. John Higham documents the rise of nativism in *Strangers in the Land: Patterns of American Nativism, 1860–1924* (New Brunswick, N.J.: Rutgers University Press, 1988).

11. Lawrence Friedman, *The Republic of Choice: Law, Authority, Culture* (Cambridge: Harvard University Press, 1990), 25.

12. Cornelius Castoriadus, *The World in Fragments: Writings on Politics, Society, Psychoanalysis, and the Imagination*, ed. David Ames Curtis (Stanford: Stanford University Press, 1997), 185.

13. Gary S. Becker, *The Economic Approach to Human Behavior* (Chicago: University of Chicago Press, 1976), 8, 7.

14. Elizabeth Deeds Ermath, *Realism and Consensus in the English Novel* (Princeton: Princeton University Press, 1983), 41, 5.

15. Henry James, *The Portrait of a Lady* (1881; reprint, New York: Charles Scribner's Sons, 1909), 1:228. All references to the novel are to this edition (volumes 3 and 4 of the New York edition); hereafter cited in text as *PL*.

16. William James, *The Will to Believe and Other Essays on Popular Philosophy* (Cambridge: Harvard University Press, 1979), 19. Hereafter cited in text as *WB*.

17. William James, *Pragmatism and the Meaning of Truth* (1907; reprint, Cambridge: Harvard University Press, 1975), 111. Hereafter cited in text as *PMT*.

18. William James, *A Pluralistic Universe* (Cambridge: Harvard University Press, 1977), 651. Hereafter cited in text as *PU*.

19. William James, *Essays in Radical Empiricism* (Cambridge: Harvard University Press, 1976), 32.

20. Richard Rorty, "Feminism and Pragmatism," in *Pragmatism: A Contemporary Reader*, ed. Russell Goodman (New York: Routledge, 1985): 128, 125–48.

21. James Livingston, *Pragmatism and the Political Economy of Cultural Revolution, 1850–1940* (Chapel Hill: University of North Carolina Press, 1994), 100.

22. Luhmann, *Trust and Power*, 68, 69.

23. See Leo Bersani, *A Future for Astyanax: Character and Desire in Literature* (Boston: Little, Brown, 1976), chap. 4.

24. I feel guilty of partaking of the tradition of interpretation that locates "self-negation" at the heart of the concerns of James's novel. Marcia Ian makes the case that such readings, extending from the most philosophically attuned to the most ethically preoccupied critiques of *Wings*, have overlooked what she calls the "elaborate coherence" of the self in the novel. Yet I am less concerned with the achievement or negation of self-integrity in the novel than with an aspect of the self neither Ian nor any other critic has taken up: the way the self presented in *Wings* is not so much absent or present as relentlessly *anticipatory*. See "The Elaboration of Privacy in *The Wings of the Dove*," *English Literary History* 51 (1984): 107–36.

25. Henry James, *The American Scene*, ed. Leon Edel (Bloomington: Indiana University Press, 1968), 116. Hereafter cited in text as *AS*.

26. Francis Walker, "Our Foreign Population, II: What They Are Doing," *The [Chicago] Advance* (10 December 1874): 261.

27. E. L. Godkin, "The Rationale of Immigration," *The Nation* 19 (August 1874): 117.

28. Edward Steiner, *On the Trail of the Immigrant* (1906; reprint, New York: Arno, 1969), 263.

29. Ibid., 304.

30. Henry James, *Italian Hours*, ed. John Auchard (University Park: Pennsylvania State University Press, 1992), 33. Hereafter cited in text as *IH*.

31. William Shakespeare, *The Merchant of Venice*, ed. Ivor Brown (London: Arden, 1955), 2.1.15–16, 2.9.20. In the preface to *Portrait of a Lady*, James singles out *The Merchant of Venice*

for its ability to make Portia "matter to *us*" both despite and by virtue of being a "mere young thing" (10).

32. Katharine Anthony, "The Family," *Civilization in the United States*, ed. Harold Stearns (New York: Harcourt Brace, 1921), 333.

33. If, as Sharon Cameron argues, *The American Scene* is a book in which there are virtually no people or in which persons have been shunted offstage so that James or his chosen surrogates (houses, buildings, and so on) can do the talking, this may have as much to do with James's domineering consciousness as with the book's routine suspicion that everyone has left town, that all the places James visits are in a constant state of abandonment. The grotesque scale of the Newport mansions is far less "disturbing" (219) to James than the fact that no one actually inhabits them. On James's "de-peopling" *The American Scene* in order to let his own voice have unlimited sovereignty, see Sharon Cameron, *Thinking in Henry James* (Chicago: University of Chicago Press, 1988), 1–18.

34. *Congressional Record*, 67th Congress, 1st session 1921, 61, part 1:511.

35. A. Mitchell Palmer, "The Case against the 'Reds,'" *The Forum* 63 (February 1920): 185.

36. "Thinking about death," Cameron argues, "is the test case for what thinking can do," because "death is the one subject about which there is nothing *to* think. . . . Death is just what you cannot think about." Cameron, *Thinking*, 158.

37. Henry James, "Is There a Life after Death?" In William Dean Howells et al., *In After Days: Thoughts on the Future Life?* (New York: Harper & Brothers, 1910), 147.

38. Ibid., 206.

39. Ibid., 206.

CHAPTER THREE: MAKING DO WITH GERTRUDE STEIN

1. Gertrude Stein, "Pissez Mon Chien," n.d., box 86, folder 1640, Gertrude Stein and Alice B. Toklas Papers, Yale Collection of American Literature, Beinecke Rare Book and Manuscript Library. The translation is my own. Here is the original:

Pissez mon chien.
Pissez mon chien.
Pissez sur le longue des maisons
Si J'etais un concierge je vous flanquerais un coup de pied.
Pissez mon chien.

Pissez mon chien.
Pissez mon chien.
Si je pissais sur le mur de botre [*sic*] maison vous me tuerez avec un coup de fusil.
Pissez mon chien.

Pissex [*sic*] mon chien.
Pissez sur la reverbere
Un pauvre chiminot serait forcer de la nettoyer.
Pissez mon chien.
Pissez mon chien

2. Gertrude Stein, *Ida*, in *Writings and Lectures 1911–1945*, ed. Patricia Meyerowitz (London: Peter Owen, 1967), 318, 332.

3. "If I Told Him. A Completed Portrait of Picasso," in *A Stein Reader*, ed. Ulla Dydo (Evanston, Ill.: Northwestern University Press, 1993), 464. Hereafter cited in text as *SR*.

4. John Watson and William MacDougall, *The Battle of Behaviorism: An Exposition and an Exposure* (London: Kegan Paul, 1928), 28. Hereafter cited in text as *BB*. Watson's portion of this book reworks some material in his 1924 textbook *Behaviorism*.

5. For the history of behavioral psychology, see John O'Donnell, *The Origins of Behaviorism: American Psychology, 1870–1920* (New York: New York University Press, 1985); John A. Mills, *Control: A History of Behavioral Psychology* (New York: New York University Press, 1998); and G. E. Zuriff, *Behaviorism: A Conceptual Reconstruction* (New York: Columbia University Press, 1998).

6. E. L. Thorndike, *Animal Intelligence* (New York: Macmillan, 1911), 2, 3. Hereafter cited in text as *AI*.

7. Thorndike's opinion of the general stupidity of animals was echoed by his colleague W. T. Shepherd, who concluded that dogs lacked "adaptive intelligence" in comparison with primates. See "Tests on Adaptive Intelligence in Dogs and Cats, Compared with Adaptive Intelligence in Rhesus Monkeys," *The American Journal of Psychology* 26 (1915): 211–16.

8. For the arrival of vivisection laboratories at Johns Hopkins Medical School under the direction of Harvey Cushing, see A. McGehee Harvey et al., *A Model of Its Kind* (Baltimore: Johns Hopkins University Press, 1989), 1:76.

9. Ivan Pavlov, *Conditioned Reflexes: An Investigation of the Physiological Activity of the Cerebral Cortex*, trans. G. V. Arnep (New York: Dover, 1960), 42.

10. In *The Casual Laborer* (introduction n. 23), economist Carleton Parker claims that the study of economics is merely "a descriptive sub-science" (28) compared with which "the training of a bird dog is full of infinitely more human attentions" (29).

11. The word actually splices together two French terms, *cheminot* and *chemineau*, the first of which means "railway worker" and the second of which means "tramp." This splicing seems intended on Stein's part, since she was well versed in the American custom of aligning tramps with railways.

12. Gertrude Stein, *Three Lives* (1909; reprint, Harmondsworth: Penguin, 1980), 21. Hereafter cited in text as *TL*.

13. Stein, *Ida*, 331.

14. Josiah Flynt, *Tramping with Tramps* (New York: Century Co., 1899), 32–33.

15. The widespread dissemination of talking-dog stories can be glimpsed in a 1903 review of London's *Call of the Wild*, in which the anonymous critic observes that "Canine fiction already shows symptoms of differentiation into the romantic and the realistic schools, and once the main principle of cleavage is established we may expect to see a variety of subdivisions appearing on either hand, according as show dogs, pet dogs, sporting dogs, fighting dogs, or mongrels are selected for treatment." See *The Spectator* (1903); reprint, in *The Critical Response to Jack London*, ed. Susan Nuernberg (Westport, Ct.: Greenwood, 1995), 62.

16. This proximity of dog and underclass denizen was something of a reflex in diverse canine discourses around the turn of the century. According to antivivisection rhetoric, dogs are too much like persons to be subjected to the very medical research that likewise equates their resemblance to persons with their exceptional suitability for experimentation. On the antivivisection movement, see Susan Lederer, *Subjected to Science: Human Experimentation in America before the Second World War* (Baltimore: Johns Hopkins University Press, 1995).

17. Jack London, *The Call of the Wild, White Fang, and Other Stories*, ed. Andrew Sinclair (1907; reprint, Harmondsworth: Penguin, 1981), 258. Hereafter cited in text as *JL*.

18. John Galsworthy, *Memories* (New York: Charles Scribner's Sons, 1912), 23. Hereafter cited in text as *JG*.

19. In a metaphor that will become almost eerily apt in our reading of Stein, Galsworthy's dog is likened to "a man, naturally polygamous, married to one loved woman" (*JG* 46) in his having surrendered "the satisfaction of his primitive wild yearnings" to the "love for us we had so carefully implanted" (*JG* 45).

20. William James, *The Principles of Psychology* (1890; reprint, Cambridge: Harvard University Press, 1981), 279. Hereafter cited in text as *PP*.

21. In A. P. Terhune's *Lad: A Dog* (New York: E.P. Dutton, 1919), Lad attacks a "trespasser" in the night who turns out to be "a negro" (45). Terhune's novel makes recourse to a widely available antinomy that incorporates the antisocial, disobedient, or criminal underclass figure—in this as in other cases marked as racially different from the dog's master.

22. G. Stanley Hall, *Adolescence: Its Psychology and Its Relation to Physiology, Anthropology, Sociology, Sex, Crime, Religion and Education*, 2 vols. (New York: Appleton, 1904), 2:572.

23. Mark Twain, *A Dog's Tale* (New York: Harper and Brothers, 1904), 1.

24. Rudyard Kipling, "The Dog Hervey," in *Collected Dog Stories* (London: Macmillan, 1934), 90.

25. Cary Nelson, *Repression and Recovery* (introduction n. 28), 278.

26. For an adept reading of Stein that approaches her style through its absorption of

James's psychology and Whitehead's mathematics, see Jennifer Ashton, "Gertrude Stein for Anyone," *ELH* 64.1 (1997): 289–331.

27. The idea of animal language has invited speculation from the philosophically rigorous to the fanciful and cute. By far the most interesting account is found in the work of Vicki Hearne, who uses Wittgenstein to promote a view of canine-human relations as modeled on language games in *Adam's Task: Calling Animals by Name* (New York: Knopf, 1986). The phrase "talking dog" appears, appropriately enough, as the title of a 1912 article on animal communication. See H. M. Johnson, "The Talking Dog," *Science* 35 (1912).

28. Gertrude Stein, "Lesson I," n.d., box 86, folder 1630, Gertrude Stein and Alice B. Toklas Papers, Yale Collection of American Literature. Beinecke Rare Book and Manuscript Library.

29. Edward Alsworth Ross, *Sin and Society: An Analysis of Latter-Day Iniquity* (1907; reprint, Gloucester, Mass.: Peter Smith, 1965), 21.

30. Gertrude Stein, *Lectures in America* (1935; reprint, Boston: Beacon Press, 1985), 93. Hereafter cited in text as *LA*.

31. Gertrude Stein, *Geography and Plays* (Boston: Four Seas Co., 1922), 217. Hereafter cited in text as *GP*.

32. Gertrude Stein, *The Autobiography of Alice B. Toklas* (1933; reprint, New York: Vintage, 1990), 164–65. Hereafter cited in text as *AA*.

33. Gertrude Stein, *Paris France* (London: Batsford, 1940), 132.

34. The classic account of this doctrine is Ernst Kantorowicz, *The King's Two Bodies: A Study in Mediaeval Political Theology* (Princeton: Princeton University Press, 1957).

35. Charles Darwin, *The Expression of the Emotions in Man and Animals* (London: J. Murray, 1872), 54.

36. Habitus is Pierre Bourdieu's name for the small and unremarkable ways a culture makes a body obey its social calling: "One could endlessly enumerate the values given body, *made* body, by the hidden persuasion of an implicit pedagogy which can instill a whole cosmology, through injunctions as insignificant as 'sit up straight' or 'don't hold your knife in your left hand.'" See *The Logic of Practice*, trans. Richard Nice (Stanford: Stanford University Press, 1990), 69.

37. *Behaviorism* (1924; reprint, New York: Transaction, 1998), 42, 72.

38. Harriet Chessman also singles out the first sentence of "Melanctha," glossing its "story of maternal resistance" as a "parable about the dangers of maternal creation and authorship." See *The Public Is Invited to Dance: Representation, the Body, and Dialogue in Gertrude Stein* (Stanford: Stanford University Press, 1989), 19.

39. O'Donnell's *The Origins of Behaviorism* (see note 5) traces the evolution of animal research from a theory of education based on the "stamping-in of learned responses" in Thorndike (167) to a full-blown theory of psychology in Watson (185). Both Watson and Thorndike first came to animal experimentation in the interests of pedagogic theory; Thorndike spent the large part of his career in a post at New York's Teachers College and Watson's 1903 dissertation was entitled "Animal Education."

40. Harriet Ritvo, *The Animal Estate: The English and Other Creatures in the Victorian Age* (Cambridge: Harvard University Press, 1987).

41. Andre Siegrid, "Race Consciousness and Eugenics," in *The Sex Problem in Modern Society* (see chap. 1, n. 15), 241.

42. Sterling Brown, *The Negro in American Fiction* (1937; reprint, New York: Arno Press, 1969), 12.

CHAPTER FOUR: HART CRANE'S EPIC OF ANONYMITY

1. Hart Crane, "Episode of Hands," *The Poems of Hart Crane,* ed. Marc Simon (New York: Liveright, 1986), 173. All citations of Crane's poems are to pages numbers in this edition; hereafter cited in text as *P*.

2. John Unterecker, *Voyager: A Life of Hart Crane* (1969; reprint, New York: Liveright, 1987), 166.

3. Hart Crane, *O My Land My Friends: Selected Letters of Hart Crane,* eds. Langdon Hammer and Brom Weber (New York: Four Walls Eight Windows, 1997), 99. Hereafter cited in text as *SL.*

4. On Hemingway's insistent integrity, see Michael Szalay, "Inviolate Modernism: Hemingway, Stein, Tzara," *Modern Language Quarterly* (1996): 457–85.

5. On boxing as an only quasi-legal pastime in the early twentieth century, see Jeffrey T. Sammons, *Beyond the Ring: The Role of Boxing in American Society* (Urbana: University of Illinois Press, 1988). Boxing was not only working-class sport but also working-class play, and so as an occupation it straddled a line between labor and leisure that seemed to Crane and his culture increasingly slender and in need of clarifying.

6. Marianna Torgovnick has analyzed the role of primitivism in modernist contexts in *Gone Primitive: Savage Intellects, Modern Lives* (Chicago: University of Chicago Press, 1990); Michael North looks at the vogue for "primitive" African art among modernists in *The Dialect of Modernism: Race, Language, and Twentieth-Century Literature* (New York: Oxford University Press, 1994). On Crane as religious visionary, mystic, or prophet, see R. W. B. Lewis, who assigns Crane "the role of the religious poet par excellence in his generation" (x) and who argues that "from 1922 onward Crane never approached a subject in anything but a religious mood" (11) in *The Poetry of Hart Crane* (Princeton: Princeton University Press, 1967); and Harold Bloom, who is "concerned here with Crane's 'religion' *as a poet*" (199) in *Agon: Toward a Theory of Revisionism* (New York: Oxford University Press, 1982).

7. When sex becomes an object of analysis in Crane studies, critics resort to a psychoanalytic formalism that appraises Crane's erotic composition by way of the oedipal triangle, the castrating mother, the unconscious, and so on. The violence that emerges in a poem like "Episode of Hands" is understood as a primal violence, a matter of deep or unconscious structure. It has everything to do with introspection. Thus Tim Dean suggests that the violence in Crane's poems reproduces "an experiential intensity that affects the reader with a sense of his or her own privacy" (89). See "Hart Crane's Poetics of Privacy," *American Literary History* 8.1 (spring 1996): 83–109.

8. Thus Eric Sundquist writes: "Crane plays obsessively on an autobiographical stage" (378). See "Bringing Home the Word: On Magic, Lies, and Silence in Hart Crane," *English Literary History* 44 (summer 1977): 376–99. And Alan Trachtenberg writes: "Crane demands to be taken *personally,* in the double sense of a speaker uttering poems from the immediacy of experience and a reader receiving a new personal experience by that very act" (3). See "Introduction: Hart Crane's Legend" in Alan Trachtenberg, ed., *Hart Crane: A Collection of Critical Essays* (Englewood Cliffs, N.J.: Prentice-Hall, 1982).

9. Langdon Hammer, *Hart Crane and Allen Tate: Janus-Faced Modernism* (Princeton: Princeton University Press, 1993), 130.

10. Robert K. Martin, *The Homosexual Tradition in American Poetry* (1979; expanded ed., Iowa City: University of Iowa Press, 1998), 115.

11. Thomas Yingling, *Hart Crane and the Homosexual Text: New Thresholds, New Anatomies* (Chicago: University of Chicago Press, 1990), 34.

12. I want to draw a distinction that I think is crucial when thinking about the seeming reticence or bashfulness of sexually active gay men and lesbians in the historical past—and of Crane in particular. In an important sense, the terminology of the closet fails to capture this reticence and its rich social meanings. Such terminology tends not to know what to do with the strategic caution that sexually gay men and lesbians manifested repeatedly in the narratives of the pre-Stonewall era—a caution that readily blended into the risk calculus of sexual experience in general, thus making risk-taking itself erotically pleasurable. What I am calling a risk calculus—the elaborate dress codes, linguistic nuances, and passwords of gay and lesbian life before 1969—formed a central dimension of that life's sexual excitement (a claim whose validity one might entertain without, I hope, the assumption that I am romanticizing the closet).

13. Hart Crane, "Modern Poetry," *The Complete Poems and Selected Letters and Prose,* ed. Brom Weber (New York: Doubleday, 1966), 143.

14. Hammer, *Hart Crane and Allen Tate,* 130.

15. This line originally appeared in a poem called "Poster," published in *Secession* 4 (January 1923): 20.

16. Sherwood Anderson, *Winesburg, Ohio* (1919; reprint, New York: Norton, 1996), 12–13.

17. On the compounding of these categories, see Leo Bersani, "Pedagogy and Pederasty," *Raritan* 5.1 (summer 1985): 14–21.

18. Edmond Kelly, *The Elimination of the Tramp* (New York: G. P. Putnam's Sons, 1908), 15.

19. Ibid., 14.

20. Mrs. John [Bessie] Van Vorst and Marie Van Vorst, *The Woman Who Toils: Being the Experience of Two Ladies as Factory Girls* (New York: Doubleday Page, 1903), 69.

21. John Guillory, *Cultural Capital: The Problem of Literary Canon Formation* (Chicago: University of Chicago Press, 1993), 175.

22. Hammer notes that Crane worked for the J. Walter Thompson agency briefly as a writer, but gave up the job in despair because, as Hammer aptly puts it, writing copy seemed to call for the same kind of "sacrifice" or "extinction of personality" that Eliot deemed necessary for the writing of poetry. See Hammer, *Hart Crane and Allen Tate*, 22–23.

23. The year before composing "Episode of Hands," Crane enthusiastically reviewed *Winesburg, Ohio* for its "significant material." See Hart Crane, "Sherwood Anderson," *The Pagan* 4 (September 1919): 61. As one of the earliest readers of "Episode of Hands," Anderson was instrumental in Crane's repression of the poem from publication. "The owner's son and all that is a bit patronizing," Anderson wrote to Crane. "Doubt laborer's caring much for it" (cited in Unterecker, *Voyager*, 168).

24. Sherwood Anderson, *Poor White* (New York: B. W. Huebsch, 1920), 148–49. Crane's underlining appears on pages 148 and 149. Crane's copy of *Poor White* is housed in the Columbia Rare Book Library, Columbia University.

25. Ibid., 159.

26. Ibid., 160.

27. Hart Crane, "Bathsheba's Bath," 1922, box 4, folder 130, Hart Crane Collection, Yale Collection of American Literature, Beinecke Rare Book and Manuscript Library.

28. Hart Crane, "Bathing by the Kalendar," 1922, box 4, folder 129, Hart Crane Collection, Yale Collection of American Literature, Beinecke Rare Book and Manuscript Library.

29. For a detailed account of the Y's place in the history of modern sexuality, see John Donald Gustav-Wrathall, *Take the Young Stranger by the Hand* (Chicago: University of Chicago Press, 1998), in particular chapter 7, "Cruising."

30. Sherwood Anderson, *Memoirs* (New York: Harcourt, Brace, 1942), 202.

31. Guillory, *Cultural Capital*, 154.

32. T. S. Eliot, *The Sacred Wood: Essays on Poetry and Criticism* (1920; reprint, London: Methuen, 1960), 53. Hereafter cited in text as *SW*.

33. On the rise of "personality" as the determinant feature of the "bureaucratic ethic" see Warren Susman, *Culture as History: The Transformation of American Society in the Twentieth Century* (New York: Pantheon, 1984), 274–84.

34. Jean-Pierre Vernant calls Hesiod's *Theogony* a "drama" that explains the birth of *eris* (glossed variously as "strife" or "toil") as the definitive component of human existence. "There is no way for mortal man to escape *eris*, which completely bounds his life. There is only the choice of the good over the bad. It is not by idling away the hours talking in the agora, meddling in disputes, and avoiding agricultural labor that [man] can hope to manage his affairs. If he is to have the means to live . . . he must devote himself to the task—water the furrows with his sweat, and compete with others in the work." See Vernant, "At Man's Table," in *The Cuisine of Sacrifice among the Greeks*, ed. Marcel Detienne et al., trans. Paula Wissing (Chicago: University of Chicago Press, 1989), 34.

35. Dante, *Inferno*, trans. Robert Pinsky (New York: Farrar Straus and Giroux, 1994), 125.

36. For a subtle analysis of this canto's centrality to Pound, Eliot, and Joyce, see Blake Leland, "'Siete Voi Qui, Ser Brunetto?' Dante's *Inferno 15* as a Modernist Topic Place," *ELH* 59 (1992): 965–86.

37. Dante, *Inferno*, 125.

38. Van Vorst and Van Vorst, *Woman Who Toils*, 71, 82, 83.

39. Carleton Parker, *The Casual Laborer and Other Essays* (New York: Harcourt, Brace and Howe, 1920), 54, 49.

40. Ibid., 73.

41. Ibid., 40.

42. Van Vorst and Van Vorst, *Woman Who Toils*, 92.

43. The epithet was so common, in fact, that Roger Bruns used it as the title for his important study of hoboes in the early twentieth century. See *Knights of the Road: A Hobo History* (New York: Methuen, 1980).

44. Nels Anderson, *The Hobo: The Sociology of the Homeless Man* (1923; reprint, Chicago: University of Chicago Press, 1961), 141, 144. Hereafter cited in text as *H*.

45. Josiah Flynt, *Tramping with Tramps*, 56.

46. Ibid., 58.

47. In *The Fall of the House of Labor: The Workplace, the State, and the American Labor Union 1865–1925* (New York: Cambridge University Press, 1987), David Montgomery refers the absence of this type of laborer from the historical record to a distinctly American urge to disown or to erase the material past, especially when that material past was constructed with the aid of indigent bodies. "Consider the name American society has given those who carried out its most spectacular feats of engineering—the railroads, dams, subway tunnels, and sewer systems. . . . These men had no name, except perhaps the colloquial ditchdigger. What does this lack of a suitable name tell us about the place of such laborers in America? It reminds us that wherever they worked, they were strangers" (65). This namelessness is close to the anonymity that Crane's poem dramatizes.

48. Yingling, *Hart Crane*, 204, 223, 203, 202.

49. Eric Sundquist speculates on this code at work in "Bringing Home the Word," 377.

50. Montgomery, *Fall of the House of Labor*, 89.

51. See Eli Ginzberg and Hyman Berman, *The American Worker in the Twentieth Century: A History through Autobiographies* (New York: Free Press, 1963), 47.

52. "Many [single men] care little how they live so long as they live cheaply," the observer cited in the previous note writes. "While this program is an economical one, it by no means furnishes to this group of homeless foreigners a normal life. . . . . . As in all barracks life, drunkenness and immorality are common." Ibid., 47.

53. Montgomery (see note 47) writes: "Whether by choice or necessity, most laborers . . . moved incessantly from one job to another" (87).

54. Robert Park, "The Mind of the Hobo," in *The City*, ed. Robert E. Park et al. (Chicago: University of Chicago Press, 1925), 160.

55. Michael Warner suggests how Irving's "bachelor" fiction might be seen as a way of "imagining the development of intimate cultures outside the family" within patriarchal nineteenth-century culture. "Irving's writings," Warner argues, "show how reproductive narrative exerts itself, often successfully, against a lot of half-articulate discontent. But it also shows that some half-articulate discontent has been audible for a long time" (794). See "Irving's Posterity," *ELH* 67.3 (2000): 773–99.

56. Parker, *Casual Laborer*, 86.

57. Mary Simkhovitch, *The City Worker's World in America* (New York: Macmillan, 1917), 110–12.

58. Ibid., 124.

59. Dr. Anna Shaw, in *Moving Picture World*, 12 March 1910; cited in Eileen Bowser, *The Transformation of Cinema, 1907 to 1915*, vol. 2 of *History of the American Cinema* (New York: Scribner, 1990), 38.

60. "Since these places are the breeding places of a moral plague far worse than any physical ills," *The Catholic Messenger* asked in 1910, "why hesitate to close them?" Cited in Roy Rosenzweig, *Eight Hours for What We Will: Workers and Leisure in an Industrial Society* (New York: Cambridge University Press, 1983), 206.

61. A reform body called the Worcester Public Education Association took note of this acute problem, observing that in nickelodeons "audiences [are] under no *supervision* or *surveillance* as to age or character" (cited in Rosenzweig, *Eight Hours*, 207).

62. Paul Giles, *Hart Crane: The Contexts of the Bridge* (New York: Cambridge, 1986), 228.

63. Ibid., 228. Interpreting Crane's "panoramic sleights" in light of Plato's allegory of the

cave has become a hallowed critical custom originating with Joseph Arpad, "Hart Crane's Platonic Myth: The Brooklyn Bridge," *American Literature* 39 (1967): 82.

64. Steven Kern, in *Culture of Time and Space, 1880–1918* (Cambridge: Harvard University Press, 1983), writes in general of equivocal matter in the period under discussion: "The general theory of relativity demolished the conventional sense of stability of the entire material universe" (185). Michael Baxandall, in *Patterns of Intention: On the Historical Explanation of Pictures* (New Haven: Yale University Press, 1985), 12–36, writes in particular of the equivocal matter of bridges in turn-of-the-century culture. Both writers are interested in how the perception of matter's lack of solidity contributed to modernist pictorial representations.

65. Alan Trachtenberg, *Brooklyn Bridge: Fact and Symbol* (New York: Oxford University Press, 1965), 167. Trachtenberg criticizes Crane for what he takes as the poet's commitment to his myth "while condemning the actuality of his culture. . . . The purity was essential; the bridge could harbor no ambiguities" (165). By looking precisely at such "ambiguities," I suggest that Trachtenberg's reading of the relation between "fact" and "symbol" in Crane may be short-sighted.

66. Sundquist argues that *The Bridge* chronicles a series of "ritual repetitions which appear as a series of Orphic descents into historical memory" in "Bringing Home the Word": 378–79.

67. Giles, *Hart Crane: Contexts*, 134.

68. Trachtenberg, *Brooklyn Bridge*, 157.

CHAPTER FIVE: WILLA CATHER'S CATECHISM

1. Willa Cather, *The Professor's House* (1925; reprint, New York: Vintage, 1990), 96. Hereafter cited in text as *PH*.

2. These phrases appear in Cather's essay on literary craft, "The Novel Demeuble," in her collection *Not Under Forty* (1922; reprint, Lincoln: University of Nebraska Press, 1936), 50.

3. Douglas's line appears in "Two Loves," in *The Chameleon* (1890). On the tendency to assimilate Cather to this strategic misdirection of sexual identity, see Sharon O'Brien, "'The Thing Not Named': Willa Cather as a Lesbian Writer," *Signs* 9.4 (summer 1984): 576–99. Current Cather scholarship takes for granted that she was a lesbian; disagreements among her readers focus thus on to what extent she and her work acknowledge or deny this. Eve Sedgwick's "Across Gender, across Sexuality: Willa Cather and Others," *South Atlantic Quarterly* 88.1 (1989): 53–72, has opened a space for many critics to recuperate a positive view of Cather's sexuality by focusing on her stories of men and boys just barely encrypted as gay—figures with whom Cather is understood to perform an authorial cross-identification. For work influenced by Sedgwick, see Jonathan Goldberg, *Willa Cather and Others* (Durham: Duke University Press, 2000); Christopher Nealon, "Affect-Genealogy: Feeling and Affiliation in Willa Cather," *American Literature* 69.1 (March 1997): 5–37; and Judith Butler, "'Dangerous Crossing': Willa Cather's Masculine Names," in *Bodies that Matter: On the Discursive Limits of "Sex"* (New York: Routledge, 1993). On a somewhat different wavelength though sharing the concern with how comfortable Cather was with her sexual identity, Sharon O'Brien, in *Willa Cather: The Emerging Voice* (Oxford: Oxford University Press, 1987), positions Cather as a woman-identified woman in a female literary tradition. While slightly displaced by the trend toward "queering" Cather, O'Brien's model of an identity-based tradition-making still has currency in Cather studies. See, for example, Marilee Lindemann, *Willa Cather: Queering America* (New York: Columbia University Press, 1999), and John P. Anders, *Willa Cather's Sexual Aesthetics and the Male Homosexual Literary Tradition* (Lincoln: University of Nebraska Press, 1999). I do not dissent from the opinion that Cather's closest erotic ties were with other women; this much Cather herself repeatedly if only tacitly implied. But other dimensions of her work are worth pursuing from the angle of a critical reading grounded in the analysis of desire, and recognition of Cather's nonnormative—even eccentric—sexual orientation is the point of departure, rather than arrival, for our consideration of her work.

4. Joan Acocella, *Willa Cather and the Politics of Criticism* (Lincoln: University of Nebraska Press, 1999).

5. Linda Dowling, *Hellenism and Homosexuality in Victorian Oxford* (Ithaca: Cornell Univer-

sity Press, 1993), offers an ingenious account of how homophile writers like Wilde, Symonds, and Pater borrowed Attic glory to legitimate male-male sexuality.

6. Eve Kosofsky Sedgwick, *Epistemology of the Closet* (Berkeley: University of California Press, 1990), 26. Sedgwick brilliantly summarizes the appropriation of Catholicism's perverse traits thus: "Catholicism in particular is famous for giving countless gay and proto-gay children the shock of the possibility of adults who don't marry, of men in dresses, of passionate theater, of introspective investment, of lives filled with what could, ideally without diminution, be called the work of the fetish" (140).

7. Isaac Lansing, *Romanism and the Republic: A Discussion of the Purposes, Principles, and Methods of the Roman Catholic Hierarchy* (Boston: Arnold, 1890), 154, 176, 177, 180.

8. Ibid., 150.

9. Ibid.

10. Winfred Ernest Garrison, *Catholicism and the American Mind* (Chicago: Willett, Clark, and Colby, 1928).

11. Lansing, *Romanism*, 175.

12. Justin Fulton, D.D., *Washington in the Lap of Rome* (Boston: W. Kellaway, 1888), 248.

13. On the tendency of alleged ex-priests to draw audiences by spicing their lectures with lewd details about "the secrets of the confessional," see Donald Kinzer, *An Episode in Anti-Catholicism: The American Protective Association* (Seattle: University of Washington Press, 1964), 82.

14. "Sin may have been deadly and guilt may have been intense," Jay Dolan notes, "but the 'waters of grace' washed it all away and restored the sinner to virtue and life." See *The American Catholic Experience: A History from Colonial Times to the Present* (1985; reprint, Notre Dame: University of Notre Dame Press, 1992), 229.

15. Harold Fredric, *The Damnation of Theron Ware* (1896; reprint, Harmondsworth: Penguin, 1986), 76.

16. William James, *The Varieties of Religious Experience* (Cambridge: Harvard University Press, 1985), 432. Anti-Catholics were particularly exercised over the concept of "plenary indulgence," whereby a supplicant could buy his own or a dead loved one's way out of punishment. An authority on Church teachings defined this practice in 1935 as follows: "An indulgence is the remission, in God's tribunal, of the temporal penalty due to sins whose guilt has been forgiven." See Henry Davis, S.J., *Moral and Pastoral Theology in Four Volumes* (1935; 2d ed., London: Sheed and Ward, 1936) 3:415.

17. Willa Cather, *Shadows on the Rock* (New York: Alfred A. Knopf, 1931), 37. Hereafter cited in text as *SR*.

18. "Nebraska is particularly blessed with legislation that restricts personal liberty," Cather said in a 1921 interview that sought her opinion on school board standardization; cited in *Willa Cather in Person: Interviews, Speeches, and Letters*, ed. L. Brent Bohlke (Lincoln: University of Nebraska Press, 1986), 149.

19. On the disastrous effects of this anti-McKinley campaign on the APA's survival, see Kinzer, *An Episode in Anti-Catholicism* (see note 13), 214–18, and Humphrey Desmond, *The APA Movement: A Sketch* (Washington, D.C.: New Century Press, 1912), 78–86. On the APA's strategy of recruitment through local Republican parties, Kinzer writes: "The APA operated within the Republican party. Active members were frequently lifelong Republicans, and the similarities between APA and Republican party heroes were remarkably close" (140).

20. Fredric, *Damnation*, 48.

21. On Charles Cather's Republican politics and his daughter's having imbibed them, see *The World and the Parish: Willa Cather's Articles and Reviews, 1893–1902*, ed. William Curtin (Lincoln: University of Nebraska Press, 1970), 98. Charles Cather joined a local committee called the Big Eight, established to clean up corruption in state and local Republican Party politics.

22. Lansing, *Romanism*, 175.

23. Dolan (see note 14) observes that confession, a relatively rare practice prior to 1860 (with most parishioners confessing once a year), became increasingly common in American Catholicism between the Civil War and the 1920s: "[C]rowds of people would line up in church on Saturday afternoons and evenings in order to go to confession" (226).

24. Fulton, *Washington*, 174. This confessional debauchery was understood to be so preva-

lent that the Church invented a name for it: solicitation, which means "inducement by a confessor of a penitent to sin grievously against the sixth commandment." In that meticulous detail with which the Catholic Church outlines its regulatory codes, we see the numerous variants of this sin: "Solicitation can take place during actual confession, or immediately before or after confession, or on the occasion of confession (that is, when a penitent is on the point of confessing even if no confession follows), or on the pretext of hearing confession even if no confession follows, and finally, if, having no immediate connection with confession, it takes place in the confessional or any other place serving as, or chosen for, confession, provided that there is some appearance of a priest acting as confessor." See Henry Davis, S.J., *A Summary of Moral and Pastoral Theology* (New York: Sheed and Ward, 1952), 321.

25. Willa Cather, *Collected Stories* (New York: Vintage, 1992), 66. Hereafter cited in text as *CS.*

26. Willa Cather, *O Pioneers!*, ed. Susan Rosowski and Charles W. Mignon with Kathleen Danker (Lincoln: University of Nebraska Press, 1992), 139. Hereafter cited in text as *OP.*

27. The many examples in the novel include Cecile's cup, which Jacques loves to "trace with his fingertips" and considers "almost sacredly hers" (*SR* 87).

28. Willa Cather, *Death Comes for the Archbishop* ed. Charles W. Mignon (Lincoln: University of Nebraska Press, 1999), 53. hereafter cited in text as *DC.*

29. F. Marion Crawford, *The Novel: What It Is* (New York: Macmillan, 1893), 10, 8.

30. Willa Cather, "Selling Out: F. Marion Crawford," in *The World and the Parish: Willa Cather's Articles and Reviews, 1893–1902* (Lincoln: University of Nebraska Press, 1970), 1:261.

31. F. Marion Crawford, *The Primadonna* (New York: Macmillan, 1908), 3.

32. Willa Cather, *My Mortal Enemy* (New York: Alfred A. Knopf, 1926), 112.

CHAPTER SIX: MERGING WITH THE MASSES

1. Though it may have been a sociologically negligible phenomenon, forced prostitution ("white slavery") formed the basis of the reform movement's ideology precisely because the prostitute threatened to reveal the opposite of sexual coercion by exercising some agency or control over the exchange of her body. As Timothy Gilfoyle has pointed out, prostitution was a tolerated if not encouraged form of economic gain in working-class communities around 1900. See *City of Eros: New York City, Prostitution, and the Commercialization of Sex, 1790–1920* (New York: Norton, 1992). The debate over whether prostitutes are simply degraded and exploited or in some measure empowered by their labor may never be resolved to anyone's satisfaction. The example of organized sex-workers in Western Europe and in small pockets of the United States indicates to what extent prostitutes understand themselves as economic agents entitled to just compensation, protection, and benefits.

2. For the history of prostitution in the early twentieth century, see Ruth Rosen, *The Lost Sisterhood: Prostitution in America, 1900–1918* (Baltimore: Johns Hopkins University Press, 1982); Mark Connelly, *The Response to Prostitution in the Progressive Era* (Chapel Hill: University of North Carolina Press, 1980); and Barbara Meil Hobson, *Uneasy Virtue: The Politics of Prostitution and the American Reform Tradition* (New York: Basic Books, 1987).

3. Committee of Fifteen, *The Social Evil: With Special Reference to the City of New York*, ed. Edward Speligman (2d ed., New York: Putnam, 1912), 121. Hereafter cited in text as *CF.*

4. Thomas Galloway, *Sex and Social Health: A Manual for the Study of Social Hygiene* (New York: American Social Hygiene Association, 1924), 74.

5. On the history of leftist modernism, see Daniel Aaron, *Writers on the Left: Episodes in American Literary Communism* (1961; reprint, New York: Octagon, 1979); Cary Nelson, *Repression and Recovery: Poetry and the Politics of Cultural Memory, 1910–1945* (Madison: University of Wisconsin Press, 1989); Michael Denning, *The Cultural Front: The Laboring of American Culture* (London: Verso, 1997).

6. Christina Simmons, "Modern Sexuality and the Myth of Victorian Repression," in *Passion and Power: The Meaning of Sexuality in History*, ed. Kathy Peiss, Christina Simmons, and Robert Padgug (Philadelphia: Temple University Press, 1989), 169, 170.

7. Max Eastman, "Investigating Vice," *The Masses*, May 1913, 5.

8. Cited in Max Eastman, "Knowledge and Revolution," *The Masses,* April 1915, 5.

9. Young is cited in Rebecca Zurier, *Art for the Masses (1911–1917): A Radical Magazine and Its Graphics* (New Haven: Yale University Art Gallery, 1985), 18.

10. For the transformative impact of urbanization on working-class sexuality, see Kathy Peiss, *Cheap Amusements: Working Women and Leisure in Turn-of-the-Century New York* (Philadelphia: Temple University Press, 1986); Sharon Ullman, *Sex Seen: The Emergence of Modern Sexuality in America* (Berkeley: University of California Press, 1997); George Chauncey, *Gay New York: Gender, Urban Culture, and the Making of the Gay World, 1890–1940* (New York: Basic Books, 1994).

11. Edward O'Donnell, "Women as Bread Winners—the Error of the Age," *American Federationist* 4.8 (October 1897): 8. Hereafter cited in text as EO.

12. Mike Gold, "Thoughts of a Great Thinker," *The Liberator,* April 1922, 22.

13. Ibid.

14. Emma Goldman, *The Traffic in Women and Other Essays on Feminism* (Albion, Calif.: Times Change Press, 1970), 19. Hereafter cited in text as TW.

15. William Thomas, *The Unadjusted Girl: With Cases and Standpoint for Behavior Analysis* (1923; reprint, Montclair, N.J.: Patterson Smith, 1969), 15. In *The Lost Sisterhood,* Rosen notes: "Many occupations (dance-hall hostess, waitress, department-store clerk, factory worker, domestic) made the difference between 'pleasing' male customers or employers and occasional prostitution seem rather arbitrary" (151).

16. Gold's letter is cited in Aaron, *Writers on the Left,* 97.

17. Cited in Aaron, *Writers on the Left,* 101.

18. Cited in Aaron, *Writers on the Left,* 144.

19. Mike Gold, "Let It Be Really New," *New Masses,* June 1926, 4.

20. Irwin Granich [Mike Gold], "Towards Proletarian Art," *The Liberator,* February 1921, 7.

21. All citations for Whitman are from Walt Whitman, *Leaves of Grass,* ed. Sculley Bradley (New York: Norton, 1973).

22. Gold, "Towards Proletarian Art," 7.

23. Ibid.

24. Mike Gold, "America Needs a Critic," *Mike Gold: A Literary Anthology,* ed. Michael Folsom (New York: International Publishers, 1972), 129.

25. Mike Gold, "John Reed and the Real Thing," *New Masses,* November 1926, 7.

26. Gold, "Thoughts," 23.

27. In *Between Men: English Literature and Male Homosocial Desire* (New York: Columbia University Press, 1985), Eve Kosofsky Sedgwick defines "male homosocial desire" as the "prohibitive structure" on the continuum of "men-promoting-the-interests-of-men" (5) that both constitutes what is conceived as actively sexual desire between men and represses such desire in the service of mediating other social bonds—particularly those that secure and transmit male privilege and entitlement.

28. Editorial, *New Masses,* May 1926, 2.

29. It seems no accident that leftist discourse resorts to Henry Adams's terminology throughout its elaboration of a sexual identity. As Mark Seltzer notes, Adams's "treatment of the virgin and the dynamo" is "certainly the most familiar American naturalist treatment of the relations between thermodynamics and sexual production." See *Bodies and Machines* (New York: Routledge, 1992), 30. Whereas Seltzer locates the stress of naturalist concerns with thermodynamics in an economy of male reproduction, I suggest that leftist modernism adopts Adams's terms in the service of a similarly male fascination with imagining a sexual identity without desire for—or exchange of—women.

30. Max Eastman, "Menshevizing Walt Whitman," *New Masses,* December 1926, 12.

31. Ibid.

32. Ibid.

33. Ibid.

34. M. H. Hedges, "The War of Cultures," *New Masses,* May 1926, 12.

35. For the best reading of this euphemistic strategy in Wilde, see Christopher Craft, "Alias Bunbury: Desire and Termination in *The Importance of Being Earnest,*" *Representations* 31 (1990):

19–46. One of the meanings embedded in the name "Ernest," according to Craft, is "a pun-buried and coded allusion (and here two tongues, German and English, mingle) to a specifically homosexual thematics, to the practices and discourses of the 'Urning' and of 'Uranian love' " (42).

36. For a similar usage of Wilde as a figure for the queering of leftist solidarity, see the poem by Joseph Freeman titled "De Profundis," *The Liberator,* April 1922, 20. The poem concerns the speaker's belated realization of his love for a dead addressee whose "ways were darker than the night," "written in an ancient tongue." This paramour is a barely veiled figure for Wilde, who composed his own "De Profundis," a long letter-essay to his estranged lover Alfred Douglas, while imprisoned in Reading Gaol. With its longed-for attachment to Wilde, the regnant icon of gay male aesthetics, Freeman's poem complements Gold's adulation of Whitman; in both cases, the venerated male poet-lover is both possessed and radically distanced by virtue of the grave.

37. Mike Gold, "Let It Be Really New," *New Masses,* June 1926, 20–26.

38. Ibid., 24.

39. Ibid., 20.

40. Ibid., 24.

41. D. H. Lawrence, review of *Manhattan Transfer,* in *Dos Passos: The Critical Heritage,* ed. Barry Maine (New York: Routledge, 1988), 74–76.

42. Review of *Manhattan Transfer, New Masses,* August 1926, 25.

43. Ibid.

44. Henry Longan Stuart, review of *Manhattan Transfer, New York Times Book Review,* November 29, 1925, 5.

45. Paul Elmer More, *The Demon of the Absolute* (Princeton: Princeton University Press, 1928), 63.

46. Stuart, "Review," 10.

47. John Dos Passos, *Manhattan Transfer* (Boston: Houghton Mifflin, 1925), 33. Hereafter cited in text as *MT.*

48. For an account of this homophobic wisdom that details its recurrence in contemporary AIDS panic, see Leo Bersani, "Is the Rectum a Grave?" *October* 43 (1987): 197–222.

49. The erotics of this scene are amplified by the lengths to which Dos Passos goes to emulate the first scene of the century's most conspicuous homoerotic intertext: Thomas Mann's "Death in Venice." In that story's opening pages, Aschenbach too encounters a figure whose "broad, straight-brimmed hat . . . made him look distinctly exotic" and whose "appearance," including an "Adam's apple" that "looked very bald in the lean neck rising from the loose shirt," "gave his thoughts a fresh turn" (4): "he felt the most surprising consciousness as of a widening of inward barriers, a kind of vaulting unrest, a youthfully ardent thirst for distant scenes" (5). See Thomas Mann, *Death in Venice and Seven Other Stories,* trans. H. T. Lowe-Porter (New York: Vintage, 1954).

50. On the history of the male-male sexual relations in the armed forces of World War I, see George Chauncey, "Christian Brotherhood of Sexual Perversion? Homosexual Identities and the Construction of Sexual Boundaries in the World War I Era," *Hidden From History: Reclaiming the Gay and Lesbian Past,* ed. Chauncey, Martin Duberman, and Martha Vicinus (New York: New American Library, 1989), 294–317.

51. Nothing has surpassed Lord Alfred Douglas's notorious articulation of this unnamable self: "I am the love that dare not speak its name." See "Two Loves," *The Chameleon* (n.p.; 1894): 28.

52. These writers antedate Maxwell Geismar's *Henry James and the Jacobites* (Boston: Houghton Mifflin, 1963) by half a century. Geismar's leftist attack on the elitism and aloofness of James and his adoring critics also took aim at James's obsessive interest in female psychology and desire.

53. For a representative sampling of Sullivan's encomia to machismo, log on to www.andrewsullivan.com.

54. For a prominent example of such lamenting in American labor history, see Stanley Aronowitz, *False Promises: The Shaping of Working Class Consciousness* (New York: McGraw-Hill, 1973); for an unsurpassed defense of the indispensability of idleness or leisure in a progressive

class politics, see Sebastian de Grazia, *Of Time, Work, and Leisure* (New York: The Twentieth Century Fund, 1962).

55. Thus in "Sexual Taboos and the Law Today" (1963), Theodor Adorno discredits the notion that proscriptions of sex have been relaxed, declaring this respite a "mere illusion" perpetrated by "an unfree society": "[S]exuality is disarmed as sex," he writes, "as though it were a kind of sport" (73). What Adorno means here is that sex has not been emancipated; it has just gone public, subjected to and deceived by the rationality of market culture and the "monopolistic sex industry" (72). Viewing surface gratification as a diminution of the self, Adorno's essay is in keeping with the tenacious depth-model of enclosed identity that steers the leftist vision of sexual potency. See *Critical Models: Interventions and Catchwords,* trans. Henry Pickford (New York: Columbia University Press, 1998): 71–88.

CONCLUSION

1. Lee Edelman, *Homographesis: Essays in Gay Literary and Cultural Theory* (New York: Routledge, 1994), 133.

2. Some of the most important exceptions to this generalization include Michael Warner, *The Trouble with Normal: Sex, Politics, and the Ethics of Queer Life* (New York: Free Press, 1999), and his introduction to Warner, ed., *Fear of a Queer Planet* (Minneapolis: University of Minnesota Press, 1993); Henry Abelove, Michele Barale, and David Halperin, eds., *The Lesbian and Gay Studies Reader* (New York: Routledge, 1992); George Chauncey, *Gay New York* (New York: Basic Books, 1994); and Michael Moon, *A Small Boy and Others: Imitation and Initiation in American Culture from Henry James to Andy Warhol* (Durham: Duke University Press, 1998). With these and other exceptions, the newest and "queerest" cultural criticism has remained somewhat indifferent to the supposed empiricism of such authors as D'Emilio, Rubin, and Weeks in favor of the more amenable textualities of deconstruction and linguistic psychoanalysis. See the constructive interview between Judith Butler and Gayle Rubin, "Sexual Traffic," *differences: A Journal of Feminist Cultural Studies* 6.2–3 (1994): 70–92, in which Rubin complains of the social-theoretical aporia among queer theorists (89).

3. The phrase "thinking sex" of course provides the title to Gayle Rubin's seminal essay on the subject. Though current queer theory has given us rapt and even heroic rhetorical accounts of pleasure and desire, it has been less successful at paving the way toward what Rubin calls an account of "benign sexual variation" (6). See "Thinking Sex: Notes for a Radical Theory of the Politics of Sexuality," ed. Abelove et al., *Lesbian and Gay Studies Reader,* 3–44.

4. Eliot's "The Wasteland," for instance, is populated by numerous figures of illicit erotic opportunism (who give added weight to the sense of loss, disjunction, and anomie in the poem), just as F. Scott Fitzgerald's first novel, *This Side of Paradise,* features numerous scenes of potential same-sex and cross-class solicitation that its sexually compromised hero, the fey Blaine Amory, must fend off. These are just two examples of the scenes of nonnormative erotics, too numerous to name, in the work of both writers.

Index

MICHAEL TRASK teaches English at Yale University.